FLOWERS THAT HEAL

FLOWERS THAT HEAL

Indian Flower Remedies

Cure self with Flower Energies in Holistic Way

Dr. Malti Khaitan

AITBS PUBLISHERS, INDIA

First Edition : 2010
Second Edition : 2023

ISBN: 978-93-7473-463-6

Published by:
Virender Kumar Arya for
AITBS Publishers, India
MEDICAL PUBLISHERS
J-5/6, Krishan Nagar, Delhi 110051 (INDIA)
Phone: 011-40167052, 49067602; Fax: 011-22009074
E-mail: aitbsindia@gmail.com & aitbsindia@hotmail.com

Printed by AITBS, Delhi

PREFACE

It is with great pleasure that we present the second edition of the book **"Flowers That Heal".** Since publication of the first edition I had great experiences in treating all kinds of patients with various ailments/diseases and also was able to extend my research by adding 18 new flower remedies in this second edition. The book describes 81 flower remedies — one for each of the most negative states of mind or moods that affect people.

I am very confident that readers will definitely take benefit by using more and more of these natural God given remedies to treat themselves and their family members and friends to make life healthier without any side effects.

Compiling this book has given me immense pleasure, and it is the result of years of tireless striving.

Sharing my knowledge of Bach flower remedies (spanning more than twenty years on this subject) has been my main aim, and I would like to help people with my experiences, obstacles and trials.

Awareness of alternative medicine is fast spreading the world over, and flower remedies provide one such method of healing. Flower remedies have no side effect sand are holistic, therefore they enlighten, comfort and console in totality.

Dr. Menon, a father figure, has encouraged me and showed me the way to this path. I will always be indebted to him.

My husband, Shri Dinesh Khaitan, has been a pillar of strength and the inspiration behind all my efforts and without his support, I could not have achieved this.

Dr. Saxena provided me information willingly.

Mukta Kumar has been by my side as a right hand.

My daughter-in-law Radhika has worked long hours on the computer and my daughter Shreerupa, an all-rounder, has solved my problems relentlessly and has been nicknamed 'puzzle-solving lady' affectionately!

Last, but not the least, my grand-daughter Riddhi, a source of constant joy, has contributed her budding talent for the front cover.

My grand sons Akshat and Vishrut has helped me with photographs.

I must thank my sister in law (Shuchi Aggarwal) who helped me in making the repertory.

Raksha Walia has edited the book, hearty thanks to her.

I thank each one of them from the bottom of my heart.

I earnestly wish that all those who read and study this manual will benefit from it, in cleansing their **mind, body and soul.**

I extend my sincere and whole-heartly thanks to *Virender Kumar Arya,* the publisher of AITBS Publishers, India for his motivating guidance and cheerful co-operation of his staff members during preparation of this book.

– Author

CONTENTS

INTRODUCTION

Have you ever felt happier by surrounding yourself with fresh flowers, been especially attracted to certain kinds of blooms or found solace strolling among fields or gardens filled with flowering plants? If so, you have already experienced the therapeutic power of flowers.

Symbolizing love and friendship, flowers have always been a source of pleasure and happiness – of healing in its quintessential form. From the sensuous rose to the humble daisy, the delicate blooms adorning gardens, fields, hedgerows, mountainsides, woodlands and jungles throughout the world possess special qualities that can ease emotional stress, boost self-confidence, lift energy levels, increase resilience to all kinds of illness and even enrich our relationships. Most importantly, they offer the perfect antidote to stress in its many different guises.

Since the dawn of time we have instinctively known that flowers lift our spirits and make us feel well again. Flowers and their remedies feature in the traditional healing practices of many cultures around the world. They play an important role in restoring or evoking a sense of harmony of the mind, body and spirit. This concept of wholeness is a recurring theme in many ancient philosophies, and we are now rediscovering its relevance to us. True well-being is something that lies beyond this limited concept, encompassing contentment and security, peace of mind and an abundance of vitality that is essential if our lives are to be enjoyable and fulfilling.

Our existence is becoming increasingly artificial. Cocooned in towns and cities, it is easy to feel isolated from the natural environment. We no longer rely on the flowering of different plants to tell us what time of year it is as our distant ancestors once did. In severing the bond with nature, we risk losing our sense of wholeness. When this happens we become increasingly vulnerable to stress.

The state of the world has altered dramatically in the last 50 years. Many new sources of stress have arrived on the scene. Horrific events such as wars, famines, tragic accidents, violent incidents and natural disasters, though we may not think about them, but still they often shake us to the core.

Over-population in many areas creates competition for vital resources and work, leading to widespread greed and insecurity. Meanwhile the breakdown of close-knit communities has left many people feeling lonely and isolated.

It not only plays havoc with our nervous system, but also weakens our immunity.

Stress is recognized as a major source of unhappiness and ill-health. Too many people feel completely at its mercy, powerless either to avoid or conquer its disruptive effects.

Orthodox medicine offers little by way of resolving stress-induced turbulence. Drugs such as tranquillizers may ease the discomfort by dulling our perceptions and reactions, but they do not really help us to stay afloat in this sea of turmoil. This is where flower remedies come to our rescue.

A HOLISTIC APPROACH TO TREATMENT

Revolutionary discoveries in medical science have given us an understanding of how the body works and how intricately it is linked with the mind. But a new breed of spiritual scientists has begun to explore this link between the body and the mind and the spiritual nature of human beings. Our physical bodies are controlled by many biochemical cellular systems, which are, in turn, finely tuned by subtle energy systems. Quantum physicists have begun to awaken to the concept that the subatomic particles that make up the entire universe, including people, are actually patterns of frozen energy and light.

Vibration medicine is the evolving field of healing research that focuses on these links between body and mind. Although the principles behind vibration medicine are quite ancient, the development of modern technologies which can visualize and quantify the energetic nature of the links between body and mind is very new.

The new field of vibrational medicine is actually a fusion of science and spirituality, which has defined the energy network linking the physical body and its energetic substrates to the more rarefied world of the spirit.

The aim of these remedies is to raise our vibrations and open up our channels for the reception of the spiritual self; to flood our nature with the particular virtue we need, and wash out from us the fault that is causing the harm. They are able to raise our very nature and bring us closer to our soul and by that very act, bring peace and relieve our sufferings. They cure, not by attacking the disease, but by flooding our bodies with the beautiful vibrations of our higher nature, in the presence of which, disease melts away as snow in the sunshine.

Being part of the great plan of creation, every human being has an immortal soul, which is aware of the particular mission a person has; and which endeavors, with the aid of the higher self and through the flesh and blood personality, to make this mission a concrete reality. The qualities of the higher self include gentleness, firmness, courage, constancy, wisdom, joyfulness and purposefulness. But human beings also have a negative side which possesses such defects as pride, cruelty, hatred, self-love, ignorance and greed. These defects, as Edward Bach tells us, are the true causes of disease. Every person has the unconscious desire to live in harmony. Nature may be considered as a huge energy field which is always endeavoring to produce the most effective energy state. As long as the soul and personality are in harmony, all is joy and peace, happiness and health. It is when our personalities are led astray from the path laid down by the soul, either by our own worldly desires or by the persuasion of others, that the conflict arises. This conflict is the root cause of disease and unhappiness.

Wherever the personality is not connected harmoniously to the great cosmic energy field by its soul, there is disruption, congestion, friction, distortion, disharmony, and loss of energy. These conditions are first present in a subtle, non-material form, but then progress to the material level, manifesting in the form of negative moods, and physical illness. The function of physical illness is that of a final corrective.

Many ancient and native cultures believe that everything in nature is infused with a vital energy, the spark of life. Wise men living several thousands of years ago proposed that when mind, body and spirit are perfectly integrated, this life-force abounds, bringing with it a real sense of health and happiness. The way to attain such inner harmony, they claimed, is to respect nature and her ways.

Each individual is like a chariot with two wheels [MIND+SOUL]. When these two wheels do not move at the same speed, or do not synchronize, the chariot does not move smoothly, and the body does not function properly. If a person is under extreme tension, the nerves will be pressured with work and the mind will be thinking constantly with no rest. Without rest, the person becomes susceptible to ailments like migraine, excessive eye strain, high blood pressure, etc. A sudden shock may cause an aversion to food. Old people often react to stressful situations by frequent urination or diarrhea. Such physical reactions in turn increase stress levels. Thus, physical symptoms and mental states are closely interlinked and form a vicious circle.

Physical and psychological symptoms are a warning, indicating that something has to be done immediately, otherwise total breakdown will follow sooner or later. It is better to attend to these symptoms in the nascent stage in order to avoid complete disruption of the body system. Every true healing process is an affirmation of our wholeness, indeed our holiness. The remedy re-establishes contact and harmony with our wholeness, the true source of our energy.

Flowers are nature's most beautiful gift, with their colorful petals of different shapes and sizes and varied scents. The five elements which nature provides for every living thing to grow are: Air, Light, Water, Earth and Ether.

Flowers are used on all occasions – birth, death, joy, sorrow, marriage or illness. They are cherished for their beauty and fragrance. They also have incredible healing powers. Flowers help to establish a balance between the energies of the mind and body.

Flowers have traditionally been valued for their captivating scents. Perfumes made from the essence of flowers are used for their refreshing and soothing qualities. Hence it should come as no surprise that they have amazing healing properties too.

Modern medicine has become rigid and locked into a mechanistic model of the body, and the model does not explain how subtle life energies can affect the cellular system. It is only when one takes into account the larger picture of human beings from a newly evolving multidimensional perspective, that flower essences as a healing modality begin to make sense. Flowers possess a very subtle yet very deep power and influence. They work invisibly within the body, alleviating stress, negative energies and the symptoms of disease. Flower therapists base their diagnoses on the mood and temperament of a patient, because these have a definite relationship with physical disorders.

Flower essences do not work like drugs. Instead they work by influencing the subtle energy of the body/mind. The essences of flowers have been used in healing for hundreds (and possibly thousands) of years. Dr. Bach was one of the modern pioneers of healing with flower essences.

The influence of nature on the mind and spirit is well known. When we meditate, we try to imagine soothing scenes like a flower-filled meadow or a sunny beach. In the same way the intake of flower remedies can also help treat physical ailments.

If you suffer from stiffness in joint or a limb, you can be equally certain that there is stiffness in your mind; that you are rigidly holding on to some idea, some principle, some convention may be, which you should not have. If you suffer from asthma, or have difficulty in breathing perhaps you are in some way stifling another personality, or you lack the courage to do the right thing.

How the Remedy Works

Flower essences are not like other medicines. They do not contain active chemicals nor possess pharmaceutical properties. They are best described as a sort of liquid energy, a vibrating medicine that brings about benefits by influencing each person's own life-force. Taking these remedies can be likened to surrounding yourself with exquisite flowers which never fade or die.

Flower remedies are needed now more than ever. Responding to this cry for help, certain people have set out to research and rediscover the therapeutic properties of indigenous flowers growing in countries all over the world. The new flower essences are made from an extraordinarily diverse variety of flora, ranging from the modest hedgerow and alpine flowers to romantic roses, exotic orchids and the blossoms of fruits like the banana and avocado. Some flowers, especially those from the Australian Bush and Himalayan mountains, have a long tradition of being used in natural healing. The beneficial properties of others are only just being discovered.

While some flower essences free us from negative moods and emotions, others go further, helping us to recognize and let go of behavior patterns that generate negative feelings.

When we feel confused about a situation or relationship in our lives, flower essences help to us to see things from an entirely different perspective – just as escaping to a place of stunning natural beauty leaves you feeling that your problems and worries back home are less daunting than you had imagined.

Some essences act at the physical level, strengthening and re-balancing various areas of the body such as the immune system. Others offer protection against new sources of environmental stress. Many aspire to more spiritual realms, helping us to find our true direction and purpose in life.

Although I have been a professional flower remedy practitioner for more than 20 years, I actually grew up with this form of healing. As a child I would watch my father with herbs. I have always been amazed by the profound ways of treatment. I have witnessed the emergence of the newer flower essences and steadily added them to my own repertoire of remedies. Using specially chosen combinations of essences from around the world, I have treated infertility, pre-menstrual tension, hay fever, arthritis and nervous exhaustion. I firmly believe that what sets remedies and therapies apart is their ability to address physical, mental, emotional and spiritual aspects of ourselves simultaneously, to bring about complete healing.

The beauty of flower remedies is that they are relatively inexpensive, easy to use and totally free from any unpleasant side-effects. Furthermore, you can prescribe them for yourself.

THE LANGUAGE OF FLOWERS

With the birth of modern medicine, belief in the healing power of flowers appeared to die out. But this was not so. It simply became channeled into the popular notion that certain qualities or virtues are associated with flowers. Roses, for example, typically signify love and romance, which is why lovers give each other red roses on St. Valentine's Day.

To the Egyptians, flowers also represented certain thoughts and feelings. Just as we might send telegram or cards to wish someone good health during an illness or to show or affection or love, they would send an appropriate flower.

Flowers had their own language and meaning to the ancient Greeks and Romans as well. It should come as no surprise that the Rose is associated with Aphrodite/Venus, the goddess of love.

The Rose is by no means the only flower linked to love. Others include the Iris, which is named after the goddess of the rainbow, who guided the souls of women to their final resting place.

Carnations also express pure love and constancy, while the Tulip denotes a declaration of love.

Many of the classical gods, goddesses and nymphs such as Hyacinthus and Narcissus are remembered today because they gave their name to flowers. Narcissus owes its name to the young man who, it was prophesied, would have a long and happy life unless he caught sight of his reflection and fell in love with his own beauty. To his cost he did indeed become enraptured by himself. Thus in most books about the language of flowers the Narcissus represents egotism. In the Middle East, however, it is traditionally linked with love, the beginning of new relationships and the enhancement of existing ones.

Flower symbolism occurs throughout the world. In India flowers are associated with various deities and ceremonies, pujas, prayers and certain festive occasions. A sprig of the magical Mimosa is often suspended above the bed to ward off ill-fortune. Its yellow flowers give a sweet aroma which is also said to evoke psychic dreams. To the Chinese, Jasmine represents feminine sweetness, while in India it is considered sacred. The flower of sensuousness and physical attraction, the Jasmine is believed to enhance self-esteem and is always used in traditional bridal wreaths.

Flowers often have religious significance. The Lotus flower is recognized as a symbol of spirituality all over the world. It is sacred not only to the ancient Egyptians, but also throughout Asia and the Far East, where it is associated with Buddhism and the state of enlightenment. The figure of Buddha is often depicted sitting on a Lotus flower.

Good fortune, protection and strength have also traditionally been associated with flowers. For this reason they have often been adopted by kings and leaders. The Sunflower became the symbol of Atahualpa; King God of the Incas, for it was believed to hold great magical properties. Like the sun itself it has a strong life-force, encouraging action and strengthening will-power.

The English Plantagenet derived their name from planta genista (Latin of Broom) after Geoffrey Count or Anjou wore it as an emblem on his helmet when he went into battle in 1140. The sweet scent of its fresh flowers is said to purify thoughts and feelings. Inhaling the aroma also instills a sense of peace and tranquility.

The people of Shakespeare's day were well acquainted with the ancient meaning associated with plants and flowers. 'There's rosemary, that's for remembrance,' cries Ophelia in Hamlet. It was not until 300 years later that the language of flowers really took shape, however. In 1817 the first real flower dictionary, Le Language des Fleurs by Madame Charlotte de la Tour, was published in Paris. It proved so popular and sparked off such great interest that other versions followed.

With the help of these flower dictionaries, shy Victorians found ways to express what they would not say in words. They sent each other bouquets in which every blossom, leaf and stem was fraught with significance. The language of flowers flourished, and was even given the special name fluorography.

Folklore tells us that if we wish to see the fairy kingdom we should make a concoction of Rose-water, Marigold water and wild Thyme. After leaving this lotion in the sun of three days, apply it to the eyes and the windows of the fairy world will magically open.

THE POWER OF FLOWER REMEDIES

Here are flowers and benedictions!
Here is the smile of divine Love!
It is without preferences and without repulsion
It streams out towards all in a generous flow and
Never takes back its marvelous gifts.

(The Mother)

"Even the part of the body affected indicates the nature of fault. The hand, failure or wrongful action; the foot, failure to assist others; the brain, lack of control; the heart; deficiency or excess or wrongdoing in the aspect of love; the eye, failure to see right and comprehend that truth when placed before you."

The following phrases demonstrate the intimate connection between the body and states of mind:

Chills going up one's spine
Butterflies in one's stomach
Being heartbroken
Something hard to swallow
The load on one's shoulders

According to Dr. Bach, suffering originates when a person is not in tune with his or her higher Self. It is a state that changes virtues into negative images.

Courage and faith into fears
Self-esteem and cheerfulness
into inferiority complexes
Humility into arrogance
Forgiveness into blame
Hope into hopelessness and despair
Belief into disbelief and pessimism

We all have different needs, and the flowers that may benefit one person will differ from those that can help another. As you begin to use the flower essences, you will embark on a journey of self-discovery. You will become aware of your strengths and weaknesses as well as the stress patterns you have acquired over the years. These are reactions and responses to situations and people that, if left unchecked, gradually undermine your health and happiness.

Flower remedies give you the strength and support you need to cope with change in your life. There is no doubt that anything that calls for a shift in our lives and thinking generates stress. The more we resist the challenges and transitions we have to face, the more painful the change tends to be. Flower essences can help us to go with the flow; to be more flexible, and enable us to respond appropriately to the increasing demands made upon us. In these testing times let flower essences play an increasingly important role in helping you regain control of your life and destiny, to find the vitality you need to pursue your dreams and goals and, above all, to rediscover the true joy of living.

The Smile of the Divine
Express the Beauty
Love for the Divine
Aspire for the Light (the Lord,
a medium for transmitting power)
Connect for Mind and Soul
Positive thinking
Flows Energies in Bodies

FLOWERS AND HEALTH

What can one do about obsession when there is very intense suffering?

Look at a flower, which is beautiful, soothing, smiling and satisfying.

But, when one is in very great suffering even a beautiful flower is boring.

Inhale the intense smell; it clears your mind when confused.

What if the disease is not cured with this?

Take the essence, this will synchronize the mind and soul and you will be cheerful from inside. Energy spreads equally in the body, fights with the negativity, and you will feel better and become a healthier human being.

Flower Essence Intake

You become like two little girls,
Playing in the bushes, climbing hills,
Dancing, jumping and singing as the flowers
Have arisen them from sleep.
The dove let cooed drowsily in protest at the disturbance
But smiled and mused,
"Better I bear with them the sweet little things".

Mind and Soul

Now, I have harmonized to
Beauty of the soul
Beauty of the sentiments
Beauty of the thoughts
Beauty of the actions
Beauty of the work
With the Divine help

"Maa" Thanks

O, "Maa" I thank you for
Introducing me to these
flower energies, curing me
from this disease, making
me feel happy, full of life.
And to think positive
which connects me to
You.

REDISCOVERING THE HEALING POWER OF FLOWERS

In the 1930s healing with flowers was rediscovered by Dr. Edward Bach. He was born near Birmingham in England in 1886. From his early age he was fascinated by nature and loved going for walks in the countryside.

He pursued a career in medicine specializing in pathology and bacteriology. In 1920 he established a successful practice in Harley Street, London. During his work Bach noticed that his patients tended to fall into distinct personality types, and that those in a particular group frequently responded to the same treatment. Ahead of his time, he also recognized the link between stress, emotions and illness.

In the course of my extensive research, **the remedies have been developed for different personality types. Each flower remedy featured in the book is suitable for certain people with**

specific personality traits and patterns of behavior. Hence the primary focus of each remedy is on the psychological make-up of the personality. Most physical ailments are merely bodily expressions of states of mind. Once the state of mind has been healed, the physical symptoms also disappear.

My remedies treat both physical symptoms and mental states of mind. For example, when an accident takes place, the viewer also gets affected by the sight and may display signs of trauma such as crying, vomiting, fainting, rushes to the toilet, trembling and numbness. The same sight may elicit different reactions from different witnesses. Louise L. Hay, in her book **Heal Your Body,** points out that this is because each individual's mental make-up is unique. Similarly, it is well known that prolonged fear or worry depletes an individual's vitality in the long run. It causes the person to feel out of sorts all the time, and the body loses its natural resistance to disease. The remedies in this book may be used with beneficial effects for such harmful or negative states of mind.

The remedies are all prepared from the flowers of plants, bushes and trees, except for the section on home remedies, which contains remedies made from other parts of the plant such as roots and leaves. None of the flower remedies are harmful or habit forming. It is entirely up to the practitioner how to use it. However, it is recommended that flower extracts be obtained from qualified practitioners, since their efficacy depends on the careful blending of ingredients in the right proportions. Besides, identification and proper treatment of a particular flower requires the expertise of a person knowledgeable in this field.

ADVANTAGES OF THESE REMEDIES

- They are dilute, harmless, natural and gentle.
- You can treat the disease when it is at the energy level rather than when it reaches the pathological stage.

- The flower remedies have a great role to play in the more psychosomatic type of illness. These remedies can do no harm.
- The flower remedies are good in cases of chronic illness, but can also be used in acute cases. They usually work best over a period of time, although you can get very dramatic results too.
- You can start using these remedies at any time and stop when you like, because they have no side effects. There is no such thing as taking a pill and being cured. Curing is a lifelong process.
- To understand how the remedies work, it must be kept in mind that if the mental attitudes are treated, the physical problems, if they are in the early stages, will be reversed.
- Flower remedies have particular value in terms of prevention. If you have anxieties and fears that could eventually lead to an ulcer, these can be treated quite easily.
- The thoughts or attitudes which create illness may be present in the subconscious for 20 or 30 years before they show up as physical disease. Even then they can be treated. However, one should not wait until the problem has manifested itself in physical symptoms, and then try to change attitudes overnight.
- Dr. Bach was the inventor of these remedies. He writes that illness, disharmony and imbalance are often the result of a gap between the inner state and the 'face' that a person puts on daily for those around him. The closer the two faces, 'inner and outer' are, the better.
- A primary characteristic of degenerative disease is the difference between the way a person appears and the way he really feels.

METHODOLOGY IN USING FLOWER REMEDIES

There are certain physical manifestations of psychological states of mind which are mentioned with the remedial flower essences.

It must be understood that similar physical ailments can occur with different emotional conditions.

It is very important and essential to take into account the emotional state of mind of the patient and these essences can be prescribed according to those symptoms.

The resulting physical ailments will automatically be taken care of.

Always keep in mind that the key word is the "emotional state of mind".

The therapeutic uses must also be correlated with the state of mind.

When the essence is selected according to the physical problem of the patient, the patient's nature has to be considered before giving the essence.

The concentrate can be diluted as per the requirement of the patient. Put four drops in a glass of water and sip at regular intervals, or put 4 drops in half glass of water and have four times a day.

GLOSSARY

The information on each flower is presented in an easy-to-read format under the following subheads:

Name of the flower

(Personality name)

Botanical name

Family name

English name

Hindi name

Group: This identifies the category of emotional problems treated by the flower. The types of emotional problems have been broadly classified into seven categories.

Plant: This gives a concise description of the flowering plant.

Keywords: This refers to the key symptoms that can be treated by the particular flower. The keywords help in instant diagnosis of the problem.

Emotional symptoms due to energy block : This enumerates the mental signs exhibited by people belonging to a particular category and comprises an exhaustive list of physical ailments that confirm the diagnosis.

Physical symptoms due to emotional block: These are the physical manifestations which appear, as a result of emotional blocks.

Practice: Speaks about the precautions a practitioner must take before giving a remedy.

Therapeutic uses: This is a compilation of the numerous beneficial effects of the essence derived from this particular flower.

Positive qualities: This describes the positive changes in character and personality that occur as a result of the remedy.

Transformation: This describes the transformation which takes place as a change in character and personality occurs as a result of taking flower remedies.

GROUPS

This book deals with 63 flower remedies, one for each of the most common negative states of mind, or moods that afflict people. These negative states have been classified into seven groups based on the predominant emotions or characteristics that identify each group.

Loner: Some people prefer to live alone or are left alone on account of their reclusive nature. The hostility and resentment they feel on this account is suppressed. The goal of treatment in this case is to engender love.

Social influence: Certain people are easily influenced by others or by their social environment. Such people have a constant need for attention and love. The goal of treatment is to instill a sense of service.

Fear: People belonging to this category are scared of known or unknown things. Such people are constantly in a state of anxiety. They fear rejection and are full of an inner uncertainty. The goal of treatment is to achieve wisdom.

Absent from present life: There is a class of people who may be physically living in the present but mentally they are preoccupied or dreaming or living in another world. Such people exhibit signs of personal carelessness and ignorance. Treatment with flower essence gives such people intellectual knowledge.

Indecisive: People belonging to this group find it difficult to decide on the solution to any problem. Their personality type is characterized by instability, conflict and emotional maladjustment. Flower therapy helps these people achieve a balance in their lives.

Exhaustion: This is a group of people, whose predominant trait is that they get easily exhausted physically or mentally on account of over-ambitiousness. The aim of treatment in such cases is to give them a sense of strength.

Unhappy: People in this category are not happy with their present life and constantly find cause for complaint. They tend to be mentally obsessive, with a strong perfectionist streak. The aim of treatment in such cases is to focus on spiritual perfection rather than perfection in the material world.

The groups broadly outlined in the previous section may manifest themselves in different ways. Some of the personality characteristics and emotions that are typical of each group and the flower remedies suitable for them are listed below:

FLOWER REMEDY GROUPS BASED ON STATE OF MIND

LONER

1. Cosmos : Happy when alone
2. Lotus : Meditation
3. Marjoram : Feel lonely
4. Rangoon creeper : Wanderer can't decide his place
5. Periwinkle : Impatient
6. Tamarind : Selfish

SOCIAL INFLUENCE

1. California poppy : Smile in public
2. Champa : Subservient
3. Corn : Not happy with a change
4. Mulberry : Hate
5. Onion : Domestic disturbances
6. White rose : Uncultured
7. Yarrow : Disturbance in life

INDECISIVE

1. Chamomile : Changeable
2. Curry leaf : Tension
3. Drum stick : Negative thinking
4. Goose berry : Insecure for the new happening
5. Holly hock : Lack of trust
6. Lemon : Mental haziness
7. Peppermint : Mental lethargy

8. Sweet pea : Difficulty in finding his path

FEAR

1. Amaltas : Dreading of terror and anger
2. Balsam : Deep emotion
3. Bottle brush : Anxiety
4. lendula : Anger and harsh words
5. Fever few : Hysteria
6. Garlic : General fear
7. Pansy : Fear of viral or epidemic
8. Peepal : Anticipatory fear
9. Petunia : Mischievous

ABSENT FROM PRESENT LIFE

1. Ashwagandha : Faint feeling
2. Canna : Mind is always busy with thoughts
3. French marigold : Inactive mind
4. Jasmine : No complain in life
5. Kachanar : Assimilation of inflamed thought
6. Morning glory : Active body and mind at night
7. Mustard : Blank mind, unknown black clouds
8. Neem : No concentration
9. Ox eye daisy : Vision in life
10. Poppy red : Mind is making castles in air

EXHAUSTION (DUE TO VARIOUS CAUSE)

1. Aloe Vera : Workaholic
2. Basil : Have no energy
3. Eucalyptus : Oxygen

4. Harshringar : Un changeable
5. Him water : Too rigid
6. Nasturtium : Strong person get exhausted
7. Rose red : Lack of love
8. Snapdragon : Mentally determined
9. Sunflower : Egoistic
10. Tuberose : Tonic for rich people
11. Walnut : Delinker

UNHAPPY

1. Ashoka : Depression
2. Bougainvillea : Inferiority complex
3. Geranium : Unhappy with life
4. Ginger : Shock
5. Hibiscus : Trauma
6. Pine : Guilt feeling
7. Pomegranate : Insecure women
8. Radish : Unable to cope
9. Salvia : Unclean
10. Watermelon : Fertility
11. Willow : Self pity "poor me"
12. Zinnia : Feel over burden life is too serious

'I rescue' : Any emergency

1

ALOE VERA
(The Flower of Regeneration)

Botanical Name	:	*Aloe barbadensis*
Family Name	:	*Asphodelaceae*
English Name	:	Indian aloe
Hindi Name	:	Gwarpatha

GROUP

Exhaustion due to over work.

PLANT

Throughout the tropical parts of the country, aloe can be cultivated indoor or in green houses where the plant can be exposed to southern, southern eastern, or eastern sun. They thrive best in light, well drained soil and do not require frequent watering. A healthy plant potted in a wide, shallow pot continuously sends up offshoots, which can be potted separately, when they are only one to two inches tall. Aloes are resistant to drought, taking in water very easily and losing moisture very slowly.

This succulent perennial of the lily family is indigenous to east and southern Africa. Flowers are yellow with red stripes in colour.

KEY WORD

→ Workaholic.

EMOTIONAL SYMPTOMS DUE TO ENERGY BLOCK

- ❖ Aloe Vera people **think they are right** and have **firm principles.**
- ❖ They are over enthusiastic and **intensely involved in work.**
- ❖ They plan ahead and want to keep themselves busy all the time, that is the reason they are hyperactive and mind is not at rest at any time of the day.
- ❖ They suffer from **stress** and they stretch themselves so much that they are on the verge of breaking down and they enjoy that situation, because they are occupied.
- ❖ They are difficult people as far as relaxation is concern.
- ❖ They do injustice to themselves while over working and become fanatic and also, when they fall sick the ailment is the hindrance in their work, due to the illness they get irritated because it is hampering their work.
- ❖ Typical of the Aloe Vera type are **"workaholics"** whose drive is so intense that they neglect their emotional and physical needs, often sacrificing rest, food, and social contact in order to accomplish their goals.
- ❖ Aloe particularly suits those who have a **creative constitution**, who are suffering from lethargy or exhaustion due to a burn out effect.
- ❖ They may be driven by **self-criticism** and have **strong willpower**, but eventually **deplete their inner energy.**

- Aloe Vera **pours 'water' on excess 'fire'.**
- An Aloe Vera person tends to feel angry at himself, and feels dissatisfied and **ill humored particularly on cloudy days.**
- Such an attitude cripples the ability to experience life in a heart-felt way, and drains the body of vital energy.
- While will power can carry such persons quite far, eventually they reach a point of exhaustion, **burnout, or breakdown.**
- For those **who get dreams at night.**
- For hyperactive and stressed children.
- Executives on the road to burn out.
- Those people who are unable to stop and enjoy the fruits of their labour, believe life should be an effort.

PHYSICAL SYMPTOMS DUE TO EMOTIONAL BLOCK

- It is for **hot fiery** people, who are prone to **inflammatory problems** and to feelings of **anger, irritability** and self-criticism.
- Aloe Vera also has an affinity with the **digestive tract**, the liver and reproductive system.
- Their physical symptoms are characterized by **heat and congestion**, and internal complaints are often expressed through inflammatory skin problems.
- They are generally **worse in hot conditions**, worse if constipated, and **feel better in cool conditions** or with cool applications and they long for juicy things.
- There can be a feeling of **fullness in the liver area, burning and irritating hemorrhoids,** which may be so bad as to resemble a bunch of grapes.
- These type of people have **painful periods** or **labour-like pains** in the groin, which are worse on standing.

- ❖ Generally have an upset stomach and **indigestion.**
- ❖ Aloe Vera essence stimulates the nervous system.

Practice

The circulatory flow is increased, particularly when it is rubbed over the skin. If rubbed on the feet, it improves the effects of reflexology. Upset stomachs and indigestion are relieved also.

Aloe leaf has hundreds of uses, the most popular being its ability to alleviate the pain of burns and hasten healing. It is the best remedy for sunburn, often preventing later peeling.

They suffer from stress or nervousness and all related physical ailments.

Find it difficult to relax an incensed by injustice, they can become fanatical.

Note

In Sanskrit aloe's name is Kumari, which means a young girl or virgin, because the plant apparently imparts the energy of youth and **brings about the renewal of female energy.** The theme of renewal of energy and rejuvenation continues through aloe's use as a flower essence.

Therapeutic Uses

Aloe Vera is a powerful laxative (but it may be combined with ginger to stop gripping pain) **and cleanser for liver, kidney, spleen, piles, cough, allergy, gasses, liver pain, intestine, bacteria, uterus problems.**

It is an astringent, and an excellent blood cleanser.

Aloe Vera alleviates mucus from the body and gives relief from gasses, rashes, burns, and ulcers.

Aloe Vera works on the **thyroid**, the pituitary gland and the ovaries.

It acts as a bitter tonic to the liver and the whole digestive tract.

It enhances the secretion of digestive enzymes, balances acid in the stomach, aids digestion and regulates sugar and fat metabolism.

It can be used to treat colitis, peptic ulcers and irritable bowel syndrome.

Use as a mouthwash for sore gums.

Aloe Vera essence can be taken internally for candidacies (thrush).

Juice with salt and turmeric is good for dysentery, liver and kidney problems.

Note

For treating cancer, take flower essence and juice internally and use the oil to massage over the body. It is effective for many skin conditions, especially burns and laceration. It can be added to essential oils. Put a few drops of the essence on your hands and rub that over the body. Then apply the oil that you use. This is how it enhances from the oil into the body.

Externally the gel can be applied for **breast cancer,** skin disease, eye sight.

The sticky fresh juice of aloe leaves serves as an emollient (skin-softening) ingredient in many skin lotions and creams, salves, and shampoos.

POSITIVE QUALITIES

For restoring inner balance, helps in a state of exhaustion, replenishes life energies, while letting things be as they are and allowing others their opinion.

TRANSFORMATION

When the soul learns to balance the forces, a tremendous outpouring of positive creativity and spirituality gets realized.

TO MAKE OIL

Slice the leaves of the plant and place them in a glass jar.

Cover the leaves with any vegetable oil or olive oil. Any oil can be used as the base. Allow the mixture to soak for 60 days, then strain. Keep the oil in a dark glass container. Label the container, as the scent is subtle, and will not be easy to identify. The oil will keep indefinitely.

ALOE GEL

Wash the leaves. Cut into 2 in. (5 cm.) lengths. Slice each piece in half, to expose the largest amount of gel. Wrap each piece in plastic wrap and date.

TO USE

Remove plastic and apply the gel side of the leaf to the skin. Smear over the affected area, or hold in place with a bandage.

2

AMALTAS
(The Flower that Energizes)

Botanical Name : *Cassia fistula*
Family Name : *Fabaceae*
English Name : Indian Laburnum
Hindi Name : Amaltas

GROUP

Social influence.

PLANT

Grows at a height of 1220 meters. A medium size tree, large compound leaves with 4 to 8 pairs of leaflets, flowers, golden yellow on racemes, fruits long cylindrical legumes. Taste is sweet. It grows in Africa, South America and the West Indies. In the ancient time it was named Golden Shower because of the colour and density of its flowers.

KEY WORD

- Dreading for terror and anger.

EMOTIONAL SYMPTOMS DUE TO ENERGY BLOCK

- These people are **unable to make a decision** and get swayed by the thought of **onslaught of terror and anger** upon themselves.
- They are **escaping from the situation**, because they do not have the guts to face the realities of life, that's why when ever any difficult situation arises they want to run away.
- **Wishy-washy** people, are very insincere in their commitments and generally they do not mean to do what they say. Their life is full of superficiality. Their resistance power is very low. So they become **unstable in their work.**
- With their own **negative thinking,** these people feel victimized by the impending situation and get the feeling of **self pity.**
- Inability to speak up for themselves, so they go on **swallowing their anger,** and as a result, they develop chronic **bitterness** and **resentment.**
- They feel as if they **do not get love** and affection from any source and that is the reason they develop chronic bitterness and resentment.
- Because of being unable to express themselves, and not finding any outlet of anger, their **creativity gets stifled.**
- Such people also **refuse to change.**
- These type of people are soft spoken and **mild by nature.**
- Want to be in the lime light and are self centered.

PHYSICAL SYMPTOMS DUE TO EMOTIONAL BLOCK

Any sort of **twitching** may give the sign of this remedy

PRACTICE

It is helpful for children, T.B patients, having low vitality, severe skin problem and soft hearted people.

THERAPEUTIC USES

Amaltas essence helps in curing ringworms, is effective for **facial paralysis** (taken internally and massaged on face).

It also acts as an analgesic, good for rheumatism and inflammation.

Effective for mouth problems like pyorrhea, and for irritated throat as an expectorant (can be gargled and taken directly).

It has cooling properties for stomach, indigestion and can help in constipation, acting as a laxative.

Good for fever, heart problems, gasses, itching, blood circulations, body stiffness, low resistance, and lower part of the body.

POSITIVE

Essence helps to overcome the blockage and get the strength to face the situation.

TRANSFORMATION

They face the situation bravely without anger and their decisions are correct and perfect for them.

3

ASHOKA
(The Flower of Fertility)

Botanical Name	:	*Saraca indica*
Family Name	:	*Caesalpinioideae*
English Name	:	Jonesia Ashoka
Hindi Name	:	Sita Ashok

GROUP

Unhappy.

PLANT

Ashoka is one of the most legendary and sacred trees of India. It is a medium sized evergreen tree, reaching to a height of 8-10 mtrs. It has an erect trunk covered with smooth dark brown bark, with deep green foliage and very fragrant bright orange yellow flowers, which later turn red. The flowering season is around April and May. It is found in central and eastern Himalayas as well as the west coast of

Bombay. They arise in numerous clusters in various sizes, mainly from older branches and some from the trunk. In India it is considered as a sacred tree. The bark of the tree is bitter.

Note

Ashoka is a Sanskrit word meaning "without grief" or that which gives no grief; of course the tree has many other names, in local languages as well, as one such name means the tree of love blossoms. The Hindus regard it as sacred, being dedicated to Kama deva, God of love. The tree is a symbol of love. Its beautiful delicately perfumed flowers are used in temple decoration. There are also festivals associated with flowers. Lord Buddha was born under the Ashoka tree, so it is planted in Buddhist monasteries.

The tree is found in abundance, a false Asoka known as "Polyalthia longifolia" which is just an ornamental tree, has no use for therapy.

KEY WORD

- Trauma, disease, or failure.

EMOTIONAL SYMPTOMS DUE TO ENERGY BLOCK

- The essence is for those women who want to be fertile. There is a saying **"weeping women, weeping womb".** It is the emotional state that affects her reproductive organs.
- For those who have gone through a **trauma** such as a **bereavement**, disease or **failure** and are suffering from deep seated sorrow, sadness, grief, isolation and **disharmony.**
- Those who are suffering from an incurable disease or **a prolonged illness.**
- The people who are upset due to the **death** of a loved one or an accident.
- Who have been cheated by people and **lost their business.**

- Indeed it is for those who have gone through great trauma and suffering.
- It works very gently, in that it changes one's perception of the sorrow.
- When a person gets disheartened due to any event in life.
- For those who have failed in life in business, lost money or have been cheated by people.
- For those who prefer to be alone due to an **inferiority complex.**

Physical Symptoms Due to Emotional Block

- Ashoka is also seen as a remedy for women, allowing them to be feminine. The tree is regarded as a guardian of female chastity.
- The Vriksha Devatas the Gods of trees who represent fertility—are known to dance around the tree, and are worshipped by childless women.

Practice

Now in modern society every human being goes through stress. Ashoka can be given in general to relax the mind.

Note

In Indian mythology Sita stayed under the Ashoka tree when Ravana had taken her to Srilanka. The place was called Ashoka Vatika.

Therapeutic Uses

It is for fertility, womb, irregular menstrual periods, excessive bleeding.

It acts directly on the muscular fibers of the uterus and has stimulating effect on the ovarian tissues. So, it is used in the treatment of hemorrhage and allied diseases. It is useful for uterine infections especially during menses.

Good for high blood pressure, and dizziness; healing wounds, blood dysentery cooling, gasses, indigestion, and leucorrhoea.

Menorrhagia, uterine affections, disuria, leucoderma, calculi, cardiac stimulant, anti-bacterial, anti-fungal, anti-tumor, anti-cancer, improves complexion, colic, dysentery, piles, ulcers, flowers are used in blood dysentery.

This essence has a tranquillizing effect on the nerves and is used in painful disorders.

Because of its astringent, and anathematic and anti-dyspeptic properties, it is used in diarrhea and dysentery.

Because of its blood purifying qualities, it is used for diseases of the blood and edema. Flowers are used in internal bleeding.

It has diuretic properties.

POSITIVE QUALITIES

Brings colour and spice into your life, lifting depression and negativity. Instills deep and abiding faith, equanimity and optimism

TRANSFORMATION

Develops attachments and promotes a sense of well being through communication with others.

Brings a profound inner state of joy, harmony and well-being.

Note

It is one of the five remedies in rescue remedy.

4

ASHWAGANDHA
(The Flower of Strength)

Botanical Name	:	*Withania somnifera*
Family Name	:	*Solanaceae*
English Name	:	Winter cherry
Hindi Name	:	Ashwagandha

Group

Absent from present life.

Plant

A small hairy under shrub, about 3-4 feet high, branches are zigzag and clothed with satellite hairs, stout, roots flashy. Leaves simple, cineaste, narrow at base and clothed with satellite hairs. Flowers in clusters, is yellowish green and in axils. Fruits are berry enclosed with persistent calyx. It is locally named "Asgandh" as it smells like a horse. It is found extensively in the northern region of Punjab,

Himachal Pradesh, Gujarat, Maharashtra and Uttar Pradesh. It is known as Indian ginseng. It is cultivated in China. For a nameless disease Ashwagandha is the medicine.

Note

Two varieties:

1. Cultivated and used for internal.
2. Wild and used externally.

KEY WORD

- Giddiness Fainting.

EMOTIONAL SYMPTOMS DUE TO ENERGY BLOCK

- These types of people are **nervous** by nature.
- They **get tense** with little things.
- Due to their nervous or tense behaviour, they find it **difficult to sleep at night.**
- They have a tendency to faint. Nature goes for **giddiness.**
- This type of people feel **mentally imbalanced** due to tension and feel exhausted.

PHYSICAL SYMPTOMS DUE TO EMOTIONAL BLOCK

- It acts like a tonic to balance the mind.
- For women who have **itching, uterus swelling, inflammation, leucorrhoea.**
- For women who have loss of appetite and **weakness after delivery.**
- For women with **heavy bleeding** during menstruation.
- To boost the energy levels of **weak and under weight children.**

- Actions of body humours—the air and phlegm humours of the body get decreased.
- It is soothing and **calms the brain.** It is therefore a good brain tonic and cures ailments connected with the brain including insomnia.
- Being naturally diuretic it is very useful for the malady of diminished urination.

PRACTICE

As a special use it raises the **lowered blood pressure** to normal level. Good for those who have low hemoglobin.

The essence is the treasure of our inherent herbs, and has the capacity to rejuvenate and revive the overall health of an individual. It restores the energy **levels of an infirm person and delays the process of ageing.**

THERAPEUTIC USES

It helps in fever, painful swellings, ulcer, carbuncles, neurological disorder, respiratory system, cardiovascular system, gastric activity, leucoderma, bronchitis, asthma, abdominal pain, constipation, worms, tuberculosis, rickets, immunity, vitality, blood purifier, sperms count increase.

Removes water retention, cough and swelling.

Gasses and mucus in the body are reduced.

Good brain tonic, digestive system, blood circulation, rheumatoid, osteo-arthritis, gout, back pain, low body weight and weakness, nerve tonic, painful joints and boils, poisoning. Good for liver and kidney, mental health, old age and diabetes, skin disease and blisters. It is a good rejuvenator.

It helps in the nervous system and acts as a sedative, helps in relieving faint feeling, giddiness and insomnia.

Circulatory system – Effect on the heart, purifies the blood, reduces edema, weakness of heart, decoction is used in rheumatic arthritis.

Respiratory system – As an expectorant it has anti-asthma properties.

POSITIVE

Bring a feeling of "I am safe," I trust the process of life to bring only good to me. It balances the mind to tackle any sort of emotional problems.

TRANSFORMATION

After taking this essence the immunity system improves and the person can stand on his own feet, face the problems of life and solve them easily.

1. Aloe vera

2. Amaltas

3. Ashoka

4. Ashwagandha

5. Balsam

6. Basil

7. Bottle brush

8. Bougainvillea

5

BALSAM
(The Flower of Concern)

Botanical Name : *Impatiens balsamina*
Family Name : *Balsaminaceae*
English Name : Balsam
Hindi Name : Gulmehndi

Group

Fear.

Plant

It is an annual shrub, grows in summer, flowers are pink in colour.

Key words

- Deep emotions.

EMOTIONAL SYMPTOMS DUE TO ENERGY BLOCK

- **Worry over other's** troubles, over concern for problems of the world; fear that a small complaint from another will become a serious problem.
- For deep **emotionalism concerning family,** nation and race.
- **Upset** when the link is broken for example: If they go to a hostel or if they lose a loved one etc.
- Their over concern introduces a negativity in their love.
- **Apprehensive** when children are away from home for the first time or partner is travelling a long distance, will be afraid that some disaster will occur, that their children will catch pneumonia if they are not kept warm, or that their partner will be involved in an accident and they will not rest until their loved ones are safely home again. They tend to project anxiety.
- These people do not worry about themselves; their only concern is for the safety and health for their family. **Self-sacrificing.**
- Constantly warn children to be careful. Always imagine the **worst, mentally congested.**
- Children may have been given a great deal of responsibility at an early age, perhaps caring for a new baby, or they could be a reflection of the attitude of a partner or guardian.
- People who worry about the welfare of parents, that they may get a **threatening disease.** If they are travelling then **afraid** of an accident or any negative thought which aggravates anxiety.

PHYSICAL SYMPTOMS DUE TO EMOTIONAL BLOCK

- With too much of emotions one can have a problem of blood pressure or nerve exhaustion.

- ❖ Used as a tonic for congestion of the liver and to prevent or cure scurvy.

PRACTICE

Balsam has also proved helpful during weaning. It may be combined with Canna. Can help in alleviating anxiety for loved ones or when one is not able to support ones family. These people are nervous by nature, over sensitive to noise, strife and controversy, sapped by others, sometimes talkative.

THERAPEUTIC USES

Good for anxiety, insomnia, nerve problem, goose fleshes, stomach cramps, gastric, duodenal ulcers, stuttering, breathlessness, physical pain.

It is helpful for glandular disease, venereal disease, anemia and disorders of the blood and diarrhea.

POSITIVE

The ability to send out thoughts of safety, health and courage to those in need, in danger or in an illness. Helps those who are afraid of something happening to their loved ones. It is good to keep calm in times of emergency.

TRANSFORMATION

The Balsam helps these people to put their fears into perspective, so that they can love and care for their family without losing sight of rational thoughts or the reality of the situation. People who frequently need Balsam find it easy to tune into other peoples situations and are able to project strongly. From the energy point of view, they are great transmitters, people for whom they feel concerned, relatives, friends know all about it.

6

BASIL

(The Flower of Vishnu)

Botanical Name	:	*Ocimum Basilicum*
Family Name	:	*Lamiaceae*
English Name	:	Sweet Basil
Hindi Name	:	Tulsi

GROUP

Exhaustion.

PLANT

There are many different varieties of Basil. The Indian variety is also known as Basil Krishna, because it is said that Krishna wore garlands of this herb around His neck to increase His detachment and His faith. This practice was continued. Basil is believed to be a protector in life and after death.

Ocimum basilicum—Rama Tulsi

Ausimum american—Black Tulsi

Ausimum greticum—Ban Tulsi

Ausimum veridi—Krishna or Shyama Tulsi

The Greeks considered Basil to be a regal plant. It is also valued and widely used in traditional Chinese and Indian Ayurvedic medicine. French Basil is the most commonly used in aromatherapy. This uplifting and refreshing oil has a strong spicy-sweet smell that is often most appealing in a blend with other oils.

Note

In Italy basil signified love, in Greece it meant hate and in Jewish lore, basil was said to bring strength during long fasting.

KEY WORD

- Tendency to polarize sexuality and spirituality.

EMOTIONAL SYMPTOMS DUE TO ENERGY BLOCK

- For people who have **lack of concentration** and **lazy memory.**
- It is for people who lack **clarity of mind** and sharpness of memory.
- Beneficial for emotional people who get easily **fearful** and sad.
- For those who feel **unable to integrate their sexual** and spiritual lives. Sex is often seen as secret or wrong, impure in relation to the purity of the spirit. It helps to resolve conflicts in relationships, which arise because of polarization.
- This affliction is most evident in relationships, where there is a **compulsive need to seek sexual** liaisons outside the main partnership.

- Quite **often sexual** activity is associated with that which is secret or sinful.
- There is also a very strong attraction to **pornography** and other forms of illicit or illegal sexuality
- In the unconscious struggle to reconcile these forces, the soul often capitulates to or becomes enmeshed in debasing and dehumanizing sexual activity.
- Once these polarities are brought together as a conscious unity, the soul no longer feels compelled to separate them into opposing and destructive activities.
- They are fearful of their sexuality, or disgusted by it and want to hide it but are often drawn to illicit or illegal sexual activities.
- For critical people, high achievers who feel they are not good enough.
- Helps those who need to put aside what was useful before, but is now hindering life's purpose.

PHYSICAL SYMPTOMS DUE TO EMOTIONAL BLOCK

- Basil is a stimulating and **antidepressant** flower essence, which relieves mental fatigue, clears the mind, and improves concentration.
- It is reputed to be one of the best **nerve tonics.**
- Encourages self-nurturing habits.
- Helps purify the blood.

PRACTICE

Down to the present day, herbalists have recommended tea made from the leaves of the basil plant for nausea, gas pains, and dysentery. **Imbibed by the nursing mothers, it is a safe, gentle tonic that helps expel gas in the infant and increase lactation in the**

mother. Basil's effectiveness as a carminative (a substance that relieves gas) has been established, and researches show that extracts of the plant inhibit organisms that can cause dysentery. Tea made with basil and peppercorns is an old remedy reputed to reduce fever. A popular culinary herb, basil is easy to grow, and to dry for storing. It fills the heart with joy.

Note

Basil has also been associated with the need for courage in times of great difficulty. The Greeks carried it on journeys for safety, and it was thought to aid the journey of the soul after death

In Tudor England it was customary to present departing guests with a pot of miniature basil to help them on their journey.

In India basil is grown in domestic courtyards for three months and then worshipped with offerings of rice, flowers and lighted lamps.

In Crete bush basil is a symbol of 'love washed with tears'. In Italy it was worn by courting peasants in remote areas as an emblem of love and fidelity.

Basil is often planted on window ledges to purify the air. In India wherever it is planted is a place of peace, piety and virtue.

It has been used since ancient times as a tranquilizer and an aid to digestion.

Therapeutic Uses

Traditionally classified as a warming and moistening herb, basil is regarded as slightly antiseptic, a mild nerve tonic, cures for menstrual problems, imbibed as an infusion by nursing mothers, basil is considered a safe, gentle tonic that helps.

Basil acts as a diaphoretic, a febrifuge (a fever reducer). Basil is antibacterial and antifungal. Basil stimulates the immune system by increasing the production of antibodies.

It relieves fainting, disorganization, mental fatigue, nervous exhaustion, P.M.S., engorged breasts, painful or scanty menses.

It is also good for stomach, neuralgia, rheumatism, stress-related problems such as indigestion, back pain, migraine, kidney, blood ailments, nervous disorder, obstruction of the internal organs.

It is an expectorant and antiseptic, used for all types of chest infections, also good for congested sinuses, chronic colds, feeling cold in the head, and whooping cough.

The antispasmodic and carminative properties of basil help to relieve abdominal pains, vomiting and nausea.

Basil can provide relief for asthma, arthritis, fevers, insomnia.

For sinus try Basil pure ganga gel mother tincture in each nostril.

Basil is bitter, warm for the body, good for heart, skin problem, bad breath, digestive, for burning and acidity, appetizer, kills fever germs, specially malaria, leprosy, impure blood, rib pain, chronic cough, gasses, hiccups, poison in body, liver, hysteria, eye problem, vitality, energy, impotency, erection of the penis.

Basil **has immense energy to fight T.B germs.**

It is used to treat mild nervous disorders, and in stopping vomiting and nausea.

Positive Qualities

Basil is revered for its ability to open the heart and mind to engender devotion, and to **strengthen faith,** compassion and clarity.

Transformation

Able to integrate sexuality and spirituality into a sacred wholeness Basil flower essence helps the soul to experience the world and integrate sexuality as a natural part of life.

7

BOTTLE BRUSH
(The Flower of Transitional Period)

Botanical Name : *Callistemon phoeniceus*

Family Name : *Myrtaceae*

English Name : Bottlebrush

Hindi Name : Cheel

GROUP

Fear.

PLANT

This evergreen tree, which is native to Australia, is now common in Florida and California. The red flowers are densely packed in terminal, cylindrical spikes resembling a bottlebrush in size and shape. In India the flowering time is February to May.

KEY WORD

- Anxiety.

EMOTIONAL SYMPTOMS DUE TO ENERGY BLOCK

- They are panicky by nature, having a deep fear about what will happen.
- Because of their panicky nature they can form an addiction to drugs.
- Sometimes anxiety might lead to tics or nervous **body shaking.**
- Experience feelings of **helplessness, terror, blind panic.**
- At night they get anxious and upset even in their dreams.
- Bottlebrush is for those who are **overwhelmed** by major **life changes** such as puberty or pregnancy.
- Holding on to the past and **old habits** when approaching the end of a phase in life.
- Good for pregnant women and new mothers who feel inadequate.
- Assists bonding between mother and child.

PHYSICAL SYMPTOMS DUE TO EMOTIONAL BLOCK

- They suffer sometimes from nocturnal attacks of suffocation as if something is **compressing their throat.**
- They are hyper about every thing, also good for someone trying to give up smoking.
- Children walking and screaming from the **nightmare,** or **numbness** when the individual can neither speak nor move, as though **paralyzed by fear.**
- Physical symptoms can appear such as paralysis, sudden loss of hearing, or speech, feelings of being ice cold, loss of control, feelings of helplessness.

- Bottlebrush helps when there is insufficient clearing of **toxic waste** products giving rise to toxemia.
- This essence can be used for treating the **muscular tissue** when there is physical exhaustion.
- It is good for athletes specifically because it eliminates lactic acid, which develops during strenuous exercise.
- It also strengthens the kidneys, and is a good tonic for the nerves.
- It can be used when there is a deterioration of muscular tissue because toxemia is not being eliminated from the cellular tissue of the muscular structure.
- It is helpful for removing drug addiction, for heatstroke and sunstroke.

PRACTICE

- Bottlebrush augments the ethereal fluid in the cellular walls to better eliminate waste products. In doing this, it also aids in the general assimilation of various nutrients into the system. "If an individual experienced a general sense of **anxiety,** that would be a clue to using this essence."

THERAPEUTIC USES

It is good for removing addiction, arteriosclerosis, thoracic region, blood disorders, breasts related problems, cellulite, colitis, constipation, cramps, muscle cystitis, elbow, Epstein-Barr virus, foot problems, hemorrhoids, jet lag, menopause, smoking, difficulty in quitting, skin problem, swelling general and strengthens the kidney.

Flower essence as a gargle will help to relieve **sore mouth ulcers.**

Skin problems such as **acne, eczema, and varicose veins** are relieved with lotion application

POSITIVE QUALITIES

It brings about a state of mind where there is complete forgetfulness of self.

TRANSFORMATION

Objective caring and concern, inner peace, trust in the unfolding of life. The goal is personal courage.

Note

One of the essences in Indian rescue remedies.

8

BOUGAINVILLEA
(The Flower of Pity)

Botanical Name	:	*Bougainvillea*
Family Name	:	*Nyctaginaceae*
English Name	:	Bougainvillea
Hindi Name	:	Booganbel

Group

Unhappy.

Plant

It is a popular ornamental plant in Indian gardens and is grown both as a shrub and a climber. The genus is known to owe its origin to tropical and Central America. Bougainvillea flowers in a group of trees. The colour is red. It flowers throughout the year.

Key word

- ✈ Low self-image.

EMOTIONAL SYMPTOMS DUE TO ENERGY BLOCK

- For those people who have **anxiety and stress** due to financial problems.
- For **guilt,** not being able to meditate, and fear.
- Despondency due to loss and failure in business.
- When a person is **upset in life** due to financial conditions and gets an inferiority complex.
- Feels **unhappy** in family life.
- Has a low opinion of himself in social circles.
- For **grinding oneself down.**
- When a person is upset and cannot control his mind and uses **abusive language** or hurts any body.
- The **fear that they may want to take revenge, leave them guilty.**
- For a person who has been **manipulative.**
- Feels guilty for not controlling his mind.
- For **accepting blame** from others for no fault of theirs.
- For **biting off more than one can chew.** Can't decide the path of life.
- When **anxiety, fear or mediocrity swamps us. Low self image.**

PHYSICAL SYMPTOMS DUE TO EMOTIONAL BLOCK

- Due to this emotional nature one can develop body stiffness, pains and aches, breathing problems.

PRACTICE

Bougainvillea gives Physical protection, helps in abdominal pain, lumbar pain, or headache originating from the neck.

THERAPEUTICS USES

Eases local aches and rheumatic pain.

Eases breathing difficulty, cervical, spine, body stiffness.

Cold, catarrh, hay fever, sore throat, sinus, diabetes and excessive perspiration.

POSITIVE QUALITIES

While spreading the joy of life, bringing spiritual abundance and uplifting feelings to those following their path in life, it promotes universal love and compassion for others.

TRANSFORMATION

This person changes to self-acceptance, self-forgiveness, ability to let go of the past and rekindles enthusiasm, interest and emotional well being, promoting one's sense of the sacred in life, for mystical and higher inspiration, enthusiasm.

9

CALENDULA
(The Flower of the Sun)

Botanical Name	:	*Calendula officinalis*
Family Name	:	*Asteraceae*
English Name	:	Pot Marigold
Hindi Name	:	Zergul

GROUP

Unhappy.

PLANT

One of the most versatile herbs, it is called "Flower of Sun" or garden flower. It is used in cosmetic and culinary recipes, as a dry plant, and for its healing properties. It is a handy annual plant, blooms from December to February. The colour is golden yellow and orange. Plants grow up to the height (30-45 cms.). Persian and Greeks garnished and flavoured food with its golden petals.

Note

Calendula is also known as Marigold. It should not be confused with the African marigold, "tagets" which is toxic.

Do not use Indian Marigold that is called gainda in Hindi.

KEYWORD

- Tendency to use cutting or sharp words.

EMOTIONAL SYMPTOMS DUE TO ENERGY BLOCK

- For those who lack receptivity in communication with others and are intolerance.
- It is particularly recommended for people who **lack warmth.**
- Who tend to use sharp words and **cutting words,** which may lead to argument or miss- understanding.
- For those who **listen only superficially** and who are often hurtful in what they say.
- They have **non-attachment** in personal relationship.
- They are touchy about what is said to them yet insensitive in what they say to others.
- Find it difficult to tolerate others and be friendly and **always complaining.**
- If they get very angry they can harm themselves and others, so they are scared of their own anger, and will not admit their mistake and will try to justify.
- **Conflict, destructive, discontented, unhappy, dislike routine.**
- **Impatience in intimacy** and listening to the message.
- Children are **irritable,** needing constant attention; when older, easily **bored.**

- Calendula is associated with **pain** and **grief.** (It is because the flower daily mourns the departure of the sun, when its petals are forced to close.)

PHYSICAL SYMPTOMS DUE TO EMOTIONAL BLOCK

- These type of people can be thin, with dark hair, and long legs, sensitive cuts, scalds, perennial tears, bleeding after tooth extraction, mouth ulcers.

PRACTICE

- Egyptians valued it as a **rejuvenating** flower.

Calendula's use extends into the creative force for the written or spoken word and can be used to **enhance communication** through this medium.

It is the delicate petals of the calendula flowers which are harvested when they are newly open. Calendula is a gentle herb even for children and old people.

Symptoms improve when lying still or walking, but worsen in damp or cloudy weather or in draughts and after eating.

THERAPEUTIC USES

The Calendula is a pretty flowering herb, though its scent isn't very appealing. It has antiseptic and even anti-cancerous properties. It is used to treat acne, sun-burn and even snake bites. Effective in controlling flu and herpes viruses, they also reduce lymphatic congestion and infections, and swollen lymph glands.

It is an anti-bacterial, can check amoebae infections and worms in the bowels, and is one of the best plants for treating fungal infections such as thrush.

It has been used for pelvic and bowel infections, including enteritis and dysentery and for viral hepatitis.

Calendula has an affinity for the female reproductive system. It can be taken for heavy or irregular periods, chronic uterine pain with a feeling of stretching and dragging in the groin, an enlarged uterus and vaginal warts.

It regulates menstruation, reduces tension in the uterine muscles and relieves menstrual cramps. It has an estrogenic (any of several female sex hormones) effect, which helps relieve menopausal symptoms and reduces breast congestion, which cause tenderness and mastitis.

Its astringent properties help reduce excessivc bleeding and uterine congestion.

Calendula has a reputation for treating tumors and the female reproductive system, such as fibroids and ovarian cysts, as well as cysts in the breast and digestive tract.

During childbirth it promotes contractions and delivery of the placenta.

An infusion of essence has been used for treating conjunctivitis and other eye inflammations or eyewash for sore eyes.

An infusion can be used as a mouthwash for inflamed gums.

Douche or bathe for thrush and vaginal infections.

Calendula is used for injuries where the pain is out of proportion to the injury. As a tincture, it is taken internally.

It is particularly useful for wounds, which may suppurate, and to prevent cuts, injuries and inflammatory problems becoming infected.

Calendula has also been used to treat cramps, obesity, leucorrhoea, muscles pain, swelling veins, hyper acidity.

After tooth extraction, gargling with calendula in cooled boiled water can control profuse bleeding.

For skin conditions, particularly and for catarrh conditions and deafness.

Digestive colic, stomach, and duodenal ulcers. Speeds post-operative healing, and reduces adhesions.

Brings relief to children having infections and fever also as a gargle for sore throats, and tonsillitis.

Wash, apply cream or compress for boils, sports inflamed wounds, painful varicose veins, leg ulcers, sore nipples in nursing mothers, and sore eyes.

Lotion or cream for itchy skin rashes, grazes, cuts, broken chilblains, eczema, and fungal infections.

Other conditions which can be helped by calendula include fever accompanied by agitation; jaundice.

MAKE A CREAM

Add calendula oil drop by drop to any ready-made un-perfumed pure plant cream, and blend thoroughly. Stop adding the oil when the cream reaches a soft usable consistency. Do not worry about adding too much calendula oil.

Note

Calendula cream is easy to make and is a valuable treatment for various skin disorders. Homeopathically prepared Calendula cream is widely available and makes a useful first aid remedy for all kinds of wounds.

POSITIVE QUALITIES

Calendula gives great forces of warmth and benign compassion to the human soul; especially helping to balance the active and receptive modes of communication and receptivity, especially in the use of the spoken word and in dialogue with others.

TRANSFORMATION

Brings understanding beyond words an appreciation for the real meaning of others messages.

10

CALIFORNIA POPPY
(The Flower of Gold)

Botanical Name	:	*Eschscholzia californica*
Family Name	:	*Papaveraceae*
English Name	:	Butter Cup
Hindi Name	:	Poppy

Group

Social influence.

Plant

Its vibrant yellow-orange (gold) flower is the state flower of California, and native to the west of North America. It symbolizes the ephemeral pleasures of life (here one minute, gone the next). In India it blooms in Feb.-March.

Key words

- Believe "all that glitters is gold".

EMOTIONAL SYMPTOMS DUE TO ENERGY BLOCK

- They can fall into the trap of drugs, desire for flashy items, deny the natural way of life because they are fanatic, think some miracle can happen, try to escape from reality.
- At the same time these people are in harmony and honest by nature, but materialistic and crave for money and get fascinated with glamorous things.
- For people who **compare** themselves to others and are wanting some miracle to happen.
- For those who **do not feel worthy, are** restless and seek spiritual experiences.
- For those who feel that their contribution to **life is of no value.**
- For those who have a **disability,** particularly children.
- Their spiritual life lacks discipline and solidity and they may be susceptible to techniques or influences, which open the **psyche too quickly causing inner disharmony.**
- Can be thought of as a gentle balance to the emotions and a **calming remedy** in times of **stress.**
- It is well worth using when trying to withdraw from addiction, be it to alcohol, drugs, orthodox drug or tobacco.
- Non-addictive alternative to the opium poppy acts as a **gentle sedative** and is suitable for **calming children.**
- **To calm restlessness, anxiety, tension and insomnia.**
- The poppy symbolizes the ephemeral pleasure of life-here one minute, gone the next.
- "The need for psychic and spiritual balance" is a major indication for prescribing this essence.

- A sense of inner balance is maintained during **psychic awakening.**
- Past life information and psychic information in general are released and properly integrated. Much of this information is released through dreams.
- **Hyperactive.**

PHYSICAL SYMPTOMS DUE TO EMOTIONAL BLOCK

West Coast Indians used the California poppy chiefly as a pain reliever for toothache. The plant was also prescribed as a sedative and analgesic (an agent that allays pain) for headache and insomnia. Contains low levels of alkaloids that are known to have sedative effects.

PRACTICE

Used over a six-month period, some people would start seeing auras and nature spirits. The recommended dosage is several times a day with up to five or seven drops of the essence being taken in pure water with each dose.

Most people could employ this essence because it is universally applicable in expediting emotional cleansing. But this essence is applicable neither to any specific emotional states nor to releasing emotional traumas that occurred in childhood. Artists' creativity is stimulated with this essence through the release of past life and psychic information.

Note

The saying "all that glitters is not gold" is an apt one to describe the soul lesson of the California poppy. Those who need the California poppy seek spiritual glamour or enticing psychic experiences outside themselves, rather than engaging in a balanced process of spiritual growth. They can be attracted to a vast spectrum of dazzling phenomena, including drug use (especially psychedelic drugs), occult ritual, religious cults, or charismatic teachers. The soul can also be mesmerized by social glamour and fame, and become easily immersed in the life of media stars, and many other fleeting fads or causes. Such souls have the "wide-eyed" expectation that the spiritual goal, which they seek, can be found somewhere outside them.

THERAPEUTIC USES

Its antispasmodic action relaxes muscles through out the body.

For treating colic in the stomach and gall bladder.

For soothing muscles and relieving tension headache, migraine, neuralgia, back pain, sciatica.

It can be applied for local pain, and toothaches.

California poppy also influences the heart and circulation.

It slows down a rapid heart beat and relieves palpitations and helps to lower high B.P. Is used in tincture form for insomnia, slowness of the circulation and general weakness.

"It moderately invigorates the pineal and pituitary glands. On the cellular level, it oxygenates the circulatory system. Moreover, it facilitates the ingestion of vitamin A. Since the psychic qualities in the eyes are strengthened, telepathic and clairvoyant vision is stimulated. The eyes are the physical vehicles involved in clairvoyantly seeing auras and nature spirits".

It is easier to assimilate gold with this essence. This is an important remedy in multiple sclerosis and other nerve diseases in which a lack of gold in the system helps produce the problem. In addition, this essence heals the hearing problems. Middle ear problems affecting balance can be treated with California poppy. It is utilized as spray, especially over the eyes and ears.

Because they do strengthen and develop a solid inner life, they are often susceptible to techniques or influences, which open the psychic faculties too rapidly especially before these energies are balanced with the heart forces.

POSITIVE QUALITIES

Helps to develop a more solid inner life, awakening the light within and enhancing self-reliance spiritual heart forces balance "all that glitters is not gold".

TRANSFORMATION

California Poppy stabilizes the golden light of the heart, encouraging more self-rcsponsibility and quiet inner development. In this way the soul finds the true treasure which it seeks the golden sun force of the awakened human heart.

11

CANNA
(The Flower of Jupiter)

Botanical Name	:	*Canna Indica*
Family Name	:	*Cannaceae*
English Name	:	Indian shot
Hindi Name	:	Sarvajjaya

Group

Absent from present life.

Plant

Tropical herbaceous perennials that were formerly cultivated for their foliage only are now so developed that the flowers are most brilliant and of varied colours. This flower is plain yellow in colour, and blooms from August to October.

Key word

- Over active mind.

EMOTIONAL SYMPTOMS DUE TO ENERGY BLOCK

- For those with **over active mind,** repetitive thoughts, chattering mind, lack of calmness, hard to wind down.
- **Unwanted thoughts** constantly come and go, and they often talk to themselves
- Constant **mental chatter,** head a hall of echoes.
- Often remember unpleasant thoughts and situations which come back to bother.
- **Mentally hyperactive,** therefore lack concentration in every day life, e.g., do not hear when they are being addressed.
- Victims of an **over weaning mental** process that has gained an upper hand over all other personality levels.
- **Sensitive** towards spoken words and continuously grind the words again and again.
- Find it **hard to concentrate** on one subject because mind is constantly at use, because of thinking.
- **Do not listen to others** when they are speaking, so when asked they do not remember the matter because the mind was not listening to what the other person was saying.
- Find it **difficult to meditate,** cannot control the active mind.
- Always over worked, even without physical movement.
- Mind works like a wheel. **Delay in taking decisions.**
- Makes a **mountain of a molehill** by thinking.

PHYSICAL SYMPTOMS DUE TO EMOTIONAL BLOCK

- **Cannot sleep** because of the thoughts going round in their head, particularly in the early hours of the morning.
- **Tired** and **depressed during the day,** head feels full, may have frontal headache, and the eyes hurt.

- Those who find it hard to concentrate and who suffer from **lack of energy** because the mind cannot relax.
- **Mental over exhaustion.**

PRACTICE

Their constant brewing on negative thoughts and words brings pain in the lower jaws and the brain in never cool and clear.

THERAPEUTIC USES

Insomnia, headache, pain in eyes, depression, piles, varicose veins, mouth ulcers, boils and ulcers.

POSITIVE QUALITIES

Peace within themselves and undisturbed by outside influences, and in this quietness and calmness of the mind, comes the solution to all problems. Promotes concentration.

TRANSFORMATION

Thoughts will be of positive form, cool collective and attentive, and will help them to take decisions on their own at the right time.

9. Calendula

10. California poppy

11. Canna

12. Chamomile

13. Champa

14. Corn

15. Cosmos

16. Curry leaf

12

CHAMOMILE
(The Flower of Equilibrium)

Botanical Name	:	*Chamomilla matricaria*
Family Name	:	*Asteraceae*
English Name	:	Chamomile
Hindi Name	:	German Chameli

Group

Indecisive.

Plant

A wild plant with small, daisy-like flowers and feathery pinnate leaves. It is the flowers that are most often used for therapeutic purposes. In the plains the flowering initiates in mid-February and lasts until mid-April. Center of the flower is yellow and the petals are white.

Note

Double flowers are considered more desirable for healing uses.

The centre of a chamomile flower is like a stomach and the plant is thus considered useful for stomach ailments.

KEY WORD

- Moody.

EMOTIONAL SYMPTOMS DUE TO ENERGY BLOCK

- These people are fussy, fretful, changeable, easily get upset, irritable by nature, unable to release emotional tension, whining, never satisfied. Impatient, rude and have an anger.
- Being known as 'the remedy of the sun' Chamomile inserts the energy of the sun into those who feel dull, angry and have emotional problems.
- For **depression, hyperactivity, poor concentration and learning problems.**
- For those who get easily worked up and have **difficulty calming** down again.
- For **nervousness,** emotional instability and **insomnia.**
- For highly strung, over-responsible, churned up states.
- For hyperactive children prone to mood changes and to extreme emotional reaction.

PHYSICAL SYMPTOMS DUE TO EMOTIONAL BLOCK

- For emotional tensions mainly in the **stomach area,** anxiety and fear, gives a deep relaxation.
- Tension accumulates around the **solar plexus** leading to digestive problems and a sluggish gall bladder. It is a sedative and a calming medicine for the stomach.

- For hysteria, nightmares, convulsions, delirium, tremors of alcoholics, melancholy and a whole range of nervous afflictions, especially of women.
- For muscle pain and tension throughout the body.
- For restless or hyperactive children and can be given in a bottle or on a teaspoon to small babies to relieve pain.
- For emotionally based stomach problems, particularly in children.
- For babies who may be teething.

PRACTICE

Brings counsel to children who are "sunshine and showers" and **swallow their hurt, feeling misunderstood.**

Helps those who are sensitive to pain, unable to deal with their discomfort, being impatient, rude or angry when ill. Often the reaction seems disproportionate to the amount of pain being felt. Even slight pain may cause sweats and fainting in women and children. Also good for those who cry in their sleep. Relaxes with good sleep. Bathe to calm irritable or hyperactive children. Chamomile is useful when there is emotional turmoil, which creates stress, sleeplessness and digestive problems. For inner harmony and calm

Note

In the language of flowers, chamomile is a symbol of energy and patience in adversity, because of its great ability to restore equilibrium and support the nervous system. Chamomile was traditionally used in love potions and at weddings, and to wash the face and hair to attract the beloved. Our ancestors also respected it as a grave plant, to ease the passage of the dead into the world to come.

THERAPEUTIC USES

Chamomile has been best known as a calmative. As a nervine chamomile is safe and effective, gentle to the stomach, it can also be used to relieve indigestion.

An infusion of chamomile blossom can be added to the bath to calm irritable or hyper active children.

Chamomile has a powerful soothing and sedative effect which is harmless.

Essence is used to cure diarrhea in children and it is used with purgatives to prevent griping, and as a tonic it helps dropsy.

Good for colic, gastritis, indigestion, peptic ulcers, diarrhea. PMS, period pains, irritable bladder, fluid retention, cystitis, eczema, boil, skin infections, allergies such as pollen and house dust. Headache, migraine, children's fevers, teething, earaches. Menopause symptoms, muscular pain, inflamed joints, sprains, burns. Tension, anxiety, depression, over-excitement, restlessness, insomnia, irritability.

Relaxes and soothes muscles, colic (particularly in babies), abdominal pain, wind and distention, treat both diarrhea and constipation.

Heartburn and acidity, anti inflammatory, peptic ulcers, irritable bowel syndrome. Varicose ulcer on the legs. Cold, sore throats, coughs, gastro-enteritis, bronchial tubes, asthma, sinusitis, douche for vaginal infections. Liver tonic, rashes, cuts, chilblains, insect's bites. Swelling on the face due to abscess or injury.

TONIC, ANODYNE AND ANTI-SPASMODIC

Also good for children's stomach complaints, which are often emotionally based.

Externally it can be applied alone or with other herbs as a poultice to relieve pain, swelling, inflammation and neuralgia.

Its strong antiseptic properties make it an invaluable lotion, the flowers are good for resolving toothache and earache. The herb itself is and ingredient in herb beers. It has extensive healing properties.

POSITIVE QUALITIES

It helps to release tension and resolve inner conflict, enabling inner quiet and encouraging serenity, emotional balance and a sunny disposition.

TRANSFORMATION

Brings emotional objectivity; clears stress and unprocessed emotions out of the solar plexus and nervous system.

13

CHAMPA
(The Flower of Chiron)

Botanical Name : *Michelia champaca*
Family Name : *Magnoliaceae*
English Name : Yellow Champa
Hindi Name : Champabari

GROUP

Social Influence.

PLANT

Champa is an Indian tree. The flowers are used as offerings for Shiva. The plant may reach a height of 20 mtrs in humid climate. It has yellow, green, red or white flowers. Flowering takes place during the hot weather and each flower lasts for 2 to 4 days. It is a very slow growing plant. But for medicine purpose, use only yellow Champa.

KEY WORD

- ✈ Subservient.

EMOTIONAL SYMPTOMS DUE TO ENERGY BLOCK

- ❖ For those who allow themselves to be **dictated** by others. To be the **under dog.**
- ❖ These people are **weak willed** and find it difficult in saying no for any little work even if they don't want to do it.
- ❖ They are timid, easily get **influenced by others,** can easily be imposed upon and have little strength of will.
- ❖ They have close bonds to family or parent. Servile instead of being a **willing helper.**
- ❖ Reacts to the wishes to the others rather than their own.
- ❖ Whatever they do is taken for granted so they receive no appreciation, people take advantage of them and keep ordering them around.
- ❖ Sometime a **martyr,** because they feel they have sacrificed themselves for others by torturing themselves.
- ❖ Unconsciously adopt gestures, phrases and opinions of a stronger personality.
- ❖ They find it difficult to take their own decision, are easily made unsure, and are so sensitive that they get upset and hurt.
- ❖ These people are **extremely sensitive,** particularly to disharmonious energies.
- ❖ Sapped by others because they cannot say no, even if they are not well.
- ❖ Over sensitive and sometimes mediumistic.
- ❖ Out of **fear of hurting** someone and thereby loosing appreciation and love, they show much consideration and often lose their will.

- Loss of appreciation and love strikes so much terror, that they ultimately become slaves.
- For those who feel the need to take care of others.
- Co-dependent types who give away their power and become victims of bullying.
- Children are quiet, sensitive, good natured and pleasant. They are responsive to praise and reproof. They are hardly a problem to their parents. Happy to share and care for their toys, non-aggressive, they do as they are told.
- Charming and considerate, loved everywhere for their kindness and helpfulness.

PHYSICAL SYMPTOMS DUE TO EMOTIONAL BLOCK

- May affect shoulders and back, white faced with rings under eyes.

  Lack of will power, always tired, exhausted, inner frustration, and inner anger. Often a weak handshake.

PRACTICE

Champa is helpful to people when they are ill for a long time and have become weak. For old people who have given up in the face of difficulties.

The effects of a flower essence spray are enhanced if the aura is "brushed clean" before application. Cover the forehead with the fingertips overlapping and brush or stroke down the side of the face, neck and over the shoulder, repeat this seven times. Then cover the crown with both fingertips and brush straight down the back to the coccyx again, do this seven times. It is easier for a friend to do this for you, and you for them. Finally, spray the blend of essences up the front, over the head and down the back, then up one side, over the head and down the other side. Apply in the morning and then as required.

The combination of Walnut, Champa and Peepal can be beneficial.

Combine all the essences into a spray and use as required.

Dosage tips—essence can be taken internally if desired, take 7 drops 3 times a day.

These essences can be added to a bath, in addition to whatever else is being taken in a treatment bottle. Add to oil burner and allow essences to permeate the house.

THERAPEUTIC USES

Bitter, cooling nature, astringent, anti-spasmodic, purgative, ulcers, anti-inflammatory, for eyes, blood purifier, burning in body, less urine flow, poisonous body, worms, acidity, lumps in body, wounds, eczema, joint chronic pain, colitis, pre menstrual syndromes, leucorrhoea, cough, acidity, circulatory conditions, chilblains. Physical weakness after an illness, cough after measles, insomnia, loss of appetite. Anti malarial, bacterial and viral infections. Treats rheumatism and gout, eczema and boils nervous system and tonic in anemia, leprosy, itching.

POSITIVE QUALITIES

Assertiveness, individuality, will, strength, boundaries to mix with his fellows without losing his own individuality or his own opinions. Who serves wisely, quietly and unobtrusively, knowing when to give and when to refuse.

TRANSFORMATION

Get confidence, peace and happiness in inner self. Bring the strength to rise up and brave the situation.

14

CORN
(The Flower of Nature)

Botanical Name : *Zea mays*

Family Name : *Poaceae*

English Name : Corn

Hindi Name : Makka

GROUP

Social influence.

PLANT

Archeological evidence indicates that a type of primitive corn was used as a food in Mexico at least 7,000 years ago. This is one of the three main cereal crops in the world. It produces male and female flowers in long, spike-like racemes with cream coloured flowers. The wild species originated in tropical America. There are now many cultivated varieties. Corn has traditionally been used as a diuretic.

KEY WORD

- Stress due to disorientation.

EMOTIONAL SYMPTOMS DUE TO ENERGY BLOCK

- For sluggishness, blocked energy, unresponsiveness, procrastination, unwillingness, resistance, lethargy due to change of place.
- For those who need to live close to **nature** unrestricted by the constraints of the modern world.
- It helps people to deal with urban, technological or confined living conditions when necessary, and despite physical limitations, to continue to evolve spiritually.
- Ideal for damage resulting from institutionalization (in schools, hospitals, prisons etc.). Protects our psychic gifts.
- Ideal for town-dwellers searching for contact with the earth.
- For those who find it extremely painful to "contract a great deal of spaciousness around" into the modern conditions of living.
- Its seeds display different colors, expressing the goal of seeking balance amongst many diverse races.
- Corn is suitable for people living in large cities and high density housing because it helps people handle living in cramped quarters.
- If you have trouble paying rent take this essence; it clams the person down to handle such problems in an intelligent fashion.
- It can also be used in refugee camps.
- It is good for the people who are living out of their country (mother earth) and they miss their own native place.

- ❖ Daydreamers, overly nervous individuals, or those who cannot focus on various issues would benefit from corn.
- ❖ A child faring poorly in-group tests, and facing peer pressure.
- ❖ This is a wonderful elixir to take when doing long-term planning. This can include buying a house of entering an agreement that will take some years to bear results.

PHYSICAL SYMPTOMS DUE TO EMOTIONAL BLOCK

- ❖ Corn can be used in mild cases of obsession, schizophrenia (several mental disorder), or conditions generating such difficulties.
- ❖ Corn is often the remedy of choice in psychosomatic illnesses known for illness of mind and body including stress-related cancer.
- ❖ It can be used in biofeedback and creative visualization therapies for treating cancer.
- ❖ It helps the individual focus, the body's immune system, including the blood flows of imbalanced areas, and become emotionally detached to deal with problems in an objective manner.
- ❖ Psychological problems causing cancerous tumors or leukemia can be faced with this essence.
- ❖ With regard to androgyny, the acceptance of both male and female halves within an individual is encouraged by corn essence.
- ❖ Individuals who experience food allergy are also often affected with candida. Many common allergies relate to food substances that are taken repeatedly over time. Corn is often one of these.
- ❖ Corn is particularly useful as a remedy for **urinary problems.**

PRACTICE

For people who can project into the future. Occasionally you will meet a person who always seems to have an intuitive understanding of events and knows how to be in the flow of life. This is because they have a balanced body, so they can project into the future. These individuals frequently become very nervous when others offer them too much advice. This is because their information is no longer personalized to them, so it no longer is in tune with their body.

THERAPEUTIC USES

Corn can further be used to treat nightmares, which a weakened astral body can cause. Chinese medicine for treating urinary and kidney problems and stones.

Will benefit the whole urinary system and may help to prevent cystitis.

May be beneficial in the treatment of bedwetting in children, disorders of the prostate and cystitis, and inflammation of the urethra.

Treat nightmares, cancerous tumors, leukemia, and kidney.

POSITIVE QUALITIES

Brings initiative to projects, rekindling enthusiasm and providing unlimited energy to accomplish anything you desire.

TRANSFORMATION

Corn helps to balance and guide the soul in expressing its vast spiritual nature through the limitations of the physical world and physical body.

15

COSMOS

(The Flower of Warmth)

Botanical Name	:	*Cosmos bipinnatus*
Family Name	:	*Asteraceae*
English Name	:	Lace cosmos
Hindi Name	:	Cosmos

GROUP

Loner.

PLANT

Cosmos is a common garden flower native to Mexico. It grows three feet tall with rose, purple, or white flowers and yellow discs. Orange and yellow flowers have also been developed. The plant grows best in warm climate, and the flowers bloom from early summer until mid-autumn.

KEY WORD

- → Intelligent but lack focus.

EMOTIONAL SYMPTOMS DUE TO ENERGY BLOCK

- ❖ Cosmos is for those people whose higher mental faculties are not properly integrated with the speaking and thinking functions of the **nervous system.**
- ❖ Such individuals often feel **frustrated** and **overwhelmed** as they attempt to convey through their thoughts, and especially through their speech, the true inspiration with which the Higher Self is in contact.
- ❖ In some cases the speech may actually become dull and the person becomes an **introvert** when the person feels that he or she can no longer make contact with her or his soul.
- ❖ This essence is more for certain types of people who are introverts, **shy,** or procrastinating individuals. Such people could express more clearly their philosophies on given topics.
- ❖ These type of people have no clarity of mind. Actually they can't explain their mind with the appropriate words. They are intellectual, but confused and introverts.
- ❖ They are impatient, where concentration is needed, that's why they have learning difficulties.
- ❖ They are shy in front of people and get nervous in speaking and have lack of self esteem.
- ❖ They **cannot focus and concentrate** in communication.
- ❖ **Disoriented in thoughts.**
- ❖ Feel **frustrated** as they attempt to convey their thoughts, and especially through their speech and are over whelmed by too many ideas.

- Find it **hard to express** their thoughts and emotions, which may come out jumbled and disorganized.
- They don't interfere in any ones work and they do not like any one else also disturbing in their work.
- They maintain a thin veil between close friends even.

PHYSICAL SYMPTOMS DUE TO EMOTIONAL BLOCK

- **Dullness of mind** and sort of hysteria.
- It allows people to release **emotional tensions** stored in the heart.
- These persons can be flooded by too much information, rendering the speech patterns rapid and inarticulate; or the thoughts may be superficially intellectual but **lacking in deeper concepts.**

PRACTICE

It generates composure before speaking or initiating an artistic expression. It is invaluable for actors, writers, or people in leadership positions. And linguistic abilities increase.

THERAPEUTIC USES

Circulation improves, metabolism is strengthened, sympathetic and parasympathetic nervous system sensitivity increases, and heart and thyroid activity are invigorated.

Relief in their diseases, sore throats, throat cancer, and bronchial condition occurs, but in each case, essence should be taken in combination with remedies.

It assists in the assimilation of iodine, silica, and vitamin E.

POSITIVE QUALITIES

It improves clarity of thoughts and articulation and enables communication of inner wisdom through the personality.

TRANSFORMATION

Cosmos harmonizes the thinking and speaking patterns with the higher soul functions, so that the true spirit can shine forth from the personality.

16

CURRY LEAF

(Flower of Tension)

Botanical Name	:	*Murraya koenigii*
Family Name	:	*Rutaceae*
English Name	:	Curry leaf
Hindi Name	:	Neemda

Group

Indecisive.

Plant

The curry leaf tree is a very popular tree in South Indian homes. This plant is a large perennial shrub, which grows to the height of 30cm. The leaves of the tree, known as curry patta in Hindi, contain a glycoside named koenigin. They are slightly bitter and aromatic and are used as flavoring in Indian cuisine. The curry tree is native to India and Sri Lanka. It grows in all tropical zones, especially in rich soils. It is cultivated in the damp and hot parts of India. The white flowers are found in clusters and from these arise the oval and pointed dark red fruits or berries, which may also turn to purplish-black when mature.

KEY WORD

→ Tension.

EMOTIONAL SYMPTOMS DUE TO ENERGY BLOCK

- For bringing warmth into the lives of those who **feel alone** in this world.
- Because of tension, they cannot take decisions.

PHYSICAL SYMPTOMS DUE TO EMOTIONAL BLOCK

- For healing ulcers and hyperacidity caused by **mental tension** and an imbalanced diet (which may include a lot of meat and alcohol).
- Curry leaves possess the qualities of a **tonic.** They **strengthen the stomach** and regularize its action. They also act as a mild laxative.

PRACTICE

They are tense by nature.

THERAPEUTIC USES

Cures eruption on the skin, dysentery, diarrhea, piles, vomiting, bruises, fevers, leucoderma, relieves renal pain.

Used as a tonic, carminative, for strengthening and toning the stomach, for purifying the blood, for tuberculosis, worms, burning pain, hemorrhoids or a mass of dilated veins in the swollen tissue near the anus soft tissue, acute abdominal pain and swellings in various parts of the body.

Good for diabetes, constipation, asthma and burns. Eye disorder, insect bites, kidney disorder, digestive disorder, obesity, blood pressure, premature graying and falling of hair. Used also as a mild purgative.

The leaves, bark and root of the curry plant are used as a tonic, stimulant and anti flatulent.

POSITIVE QUALITIES

Essence produces greater relaxation as well as a balanced awareness and concern about diet and life style.

TRANSFORMATION

Curry leaf brings warmth, love and happiness in life. Brings a glow to the aura, which helps to attract the right people.

17

DRUMSTICK

(The Flower of Serenity)

Botanical Name	:	*Moringa oleifera*
Family Name	:	*Moringaceae*
English Name	:	Drumstick
Hindi Name	:	Sahjan

GROUP

Indecisive.

PLANT

A middle sized tree with gray bark and brittle branches. A special tree which can be seen through out India. It has rounded leaves, white flowers and typical long fruit pods, with 3-sided seeds. Long pods are used as vegetable.

KEY WORD

- ✈ Bitterness.

EMOTIONAL SYMPTOMS DUE TO ENERGY BLOCK

- They harbour resentment and desire revenge. They feel victimized.
- For belief that one is not good enough due to inferiority complex.
- For dispelling bitterness, regarding a happening.
- These people are either on top or totally in a low.
- They are intelligent and confident yet charred with negative thinking.
- They suffer from an inferiority complex and find everyone better than themselves.
- Mind gets stuck with difficult emotional feelings because of negativity.
- Too much of negative thinking.

PHYSICAL SYMPTOMS DUE TO EMOTIONAL BLOCK

- Mind gets closed from all the sides, you feel as if you are not breathing.
- Drumstick is helpful for **reducing the desire to smoke.**
- They see the negative in every situation and feel the pain.
- Opens up the chakra centers, bringing a new spiritual awareness.

PRACTICE

There is a lot of pain in the mind due to life's problems, they develop anger thinking about the old history which has given them unhappiness, then the anger changes into bitterness. Or they go into a shell and will not open up in front of public. Flowers and fruits contain-amino-acid, glucose and sucrose, citric acid, mallic acid, succinic acid, fumaric acid, oxalic acid. Good for solving difficult emotions.

Note

It is good for reducing weight. In ayurveda it is known as sweet bitter and has all the qualities for vitality, developing the taste buds and removing gasses.

THERAPEUTIC

Generally drumstick is good for all parts of the body, especially for stomach ulcers and gastritis, eye problem, night blindness, acidity, cough, weakness, asthma, swelling, stones, kidney, arthritis, digestive, constipating, expectorant, purgative, antifungal, carminative, cardiac stimulant, liver protective, sore throat, mouth ulcers, hiccough, breathing problem, running nose, paralytic affections, intermittent fever, epilepsy, spleen, worm, edema, unripe abscess, itching, urinary stones, piles, sexual vigor, anti-inflammatory, anti-tumour and to increase resistance.

Good for bronchitis. Helps in reducing weight. **Also helps in relieving night blindness, weakness.**

POSITIVE

It helps to love oneself and brings a sense of peace, calmness and a feeling of well being by building up positive feelings.

TRANSFORMATION

After taking this essence a person's thinking goes into a positive mode, because fear subsides and he is able to face the reality.

18

EUCALYPTUS
(The Flower of Purification)

Botanical Name	:	*Eucalyptus globules*
Family Name	:	*Myrtaceae*
English Name	:	Blue Gum
Hindi Name	:	Neelgiri

GROUP

Exhaustion due to lack of oxygen.

PLANT

While native to Australia, this tree is now found in many parts of the world. Known as the blue gum tree, it reaches heights of almost 40-50 feet making it one of the tallest trees in the world. The flowers are solitary, axillary, and white with no petals. Blooms in March and April.

KEY WORD

- Feel claustrophobic.

EMOTIONAL SYMPTOMS DUE TO ENERGY BLOCK

- For "People experiencing **grief,** especially over the demise of a loved one".
- For those people who are **unable to listen to others.**
- For the people who do not accept their present situation and are **not happy.**
- For those who are **scared** to be alone.
- For children who **feel they are unwanted** and are a hindrance in others' life.
- For those people who leave a group of people because of their emotion but at the same time are afraid of being alone.
- For those adults who claim that they do not need anyone's help.
- In attuning to another's energy, it sometimes appears necessary to shield your understanding, your sensibilities, and most importantly your emotional response. Eucalyptus relaxes this process.

PHYSICAL SYMPTOMS DUE TO EMOTIONAL BLOCK

- People who **do not breathe** well from any cause, individuals who almost drown, and people who suffer from inhalation of smoke in a fire.
- Eucalyptus **oxygenates** the system and improves the lung functioning of people who have smoked for a long time.
- It can be prescribed in any form of radiation sickness, particularly plutonium poisoning.
- For those feeling **tired** and **sluggish,** in mind and body, often a consequence of chronic catarrh in the head. Such people

have a desire for exercise, and their symptoms tend to be worse at night.

- ❖ These emotional people can face respiratory problems, cold, lack of oxygen.

PRACTICE

The balancing capacities of the **heart chakra** are activated. This **stimulates the thymus** because it is associated with the heart chakra. In the first seven years of life, the thymus gland produces some hemoglobin. **Disagreements in marriages or partnerships,** and even sharp hostilities between people can be resolved with eucalyptus because it helps you understand the other person's position. Expansion of energy in the physical body can sometimes be necessary in moving through the grieving process.

Iron and hemoglobin, which carry radiation in the system, are strengthened and cleansed, so parts of the body lacking oxygen are replenished. The entire circulatory system is activated to better carry nutrients and oxygen to various parts of the body, particularly the pancreas.

THERAPEUTIC USES

The most popular use of eucalyptus is as a cleanser for the lungs and lymph systems. A classic remedy to clear the nose and help dry mucus conditions is to inhale the vapors of hot eucalyptus leaf tea, or infusion.

The eucalyptus is also known as the **fever tree.** It exhales an aromatic odour, which exerts an antiseptic effect in the area in which it grows, so sometimes it is deliberately planted to purify these areas.

Recent research suggests that eucalyptus may **lower blood sugar.**

It increases circulation, promotes sweating and thereby relieves fevers.

It eases inflammations in the kidney sand deterioration, liver, lungs, and nasal passages.

It is quite effective in treating jaundice and malaria.

For acute infections, including typhoid and influenza fevers, measles, as well as catarrhal conditions throughout the body and congestive headaches.

Good for asthma with thick phlegm, bronchitis, ease croup, whooping cough, emphysema, and for sore throats and enlarged, ulcerated tonsils. It also increases the action of the heart, tuberculosis.

Good for intermittent fever, nervous system, gastric and intestinal sluggish digestion, dyspepsia, offensive wind and an empty feeling in the stomach. Eating disorder, acute diarrhea and dysentery relieve gastric pain with colic, blood and mucus discharge in the stools, with a feeling of heat in the rectum.

In the urinary system, symptoms indicating eucalyptus include blood in the urine, spasmodic stricture of the urethra, pain on urination and when urine has the odor of violets.

For flu, stiff and painful joints, pain in the limbs on walking, stiff weary feelings, gout and pricking sensations in the muscles followed by painful aching.

Herpes and varicose ulcers also respond well to it.

POSITIVE QUALITIES

Eucalyptus augments the capacity of the lungs, to breathe more efficiently, thereby shaping people in mind, body and spirit.

TRANSFORMATION

Eucalyptus essence contributes to the formation of our respiratory system and emotional body. There is a direct link between our lungs and emotional body, which creates emotional equilibrium.

19

FEVER FEW

(The Flower of Relief)

Botanical Name	:	*Chrysanthemum parthenium*
Family Name	:	*Asteraceae*
English Name	:	Bachelor's Button
Hindi Name	:	Guldaudi

GROUP

Fear.

PLANT

A wild hedgerow plant found in many areas of Europe and Great Britain. Feverfew is a pretty member of the daisy family composite. Fever few has other names, which indicate, its usefulness for women. The name bachelor's buttons comes from the tradition of young men who wished to gain the love of a lady by carrying the flowers in their pockets. Fever few also derives its name from its ability to bring down fevers. Color is white and yellow in center. Fever few grows in any soil and seeds itself easily.

KEY WORD

→ Hysterical.

EMOTIONAL SYMPTOMS DUE TO ENERGY BLOCK

- These people are nervous by nature, fretful and have mental disturbances.
- It is also considered valuable for a variety of problems including **hysteria,** and it is interesting that these emotions are commonly ascribed to women. It relates to the womb, (indicated by words such as hysterectomy for surgical removal of the womb).
- It is used specifically for **highly nervous** people who are **oversensitive to pain,** and prone to sudden fits of irritability or anger.

PHYSICAL SYMPTOMS DUE TO EMOTIONAL BLOCK

- It is prescribed for **convulsions** and for soothing fretful children.
- More recently, fever few has gained fame as an excellent remedy for headaches and migraine.
- It helps relaxing tension and lifting **depression** and **promoting sleep.**
- It has also been used to relieve nerve pain, as in neuralgia and sciatica.
- The herb is planted around dwellings to purify the atmosphere and ward off disease.
- Fever few is highly valued for malaria, as well as colds and catarrh. It is frequently used for menstrual problems and other women's complaints.

PRACTICE

Fever few essence for mental work. It is prescribed for a range of nervous symptoms including convulsions, twitching, restlessness, and delirium.

The flower essence fever few is taken for headaches and migraines, particularly those experienced in a cyclical pattern by women, according to their cycle of hormonal changes.

THERAPEUTIC USES

It is employed in hysterical complaints, nervousness and low spirits as a general tonic.

It acts as a tonic for the nervous system. Fever few has a bitter taste, and has a beneficial action on the liver and digestion, enhancing the appetite and digestion, allaying nausea and vomiting and helping to clear heat and toxins from the system.

It will help relieve the pain and inflammation of arthritis and reduce symptoms associated with a sluggish liver.

This essence helps in reducing fevers, convulsion, hysteria, and low spirits.

It will also act as a decongestant, clearing phlegm, chronic catarrh and sinusitis.

It has also been used for asthma, and other allergies such as hay fever-research suggest that it inhibits release of substances, which trigger allergies and migraines.

Studies show that fever few extracts may delay the onset of migraine.

It is employed in hysterical complaints, nervousness, as a general tonic.

POSITIVE QUALITIES

It helps to balance the temper of women and brings peace in children.

TRANSFORMATION

Nerves get strengthened to face all situations easily.

20

FRENCH MARIGOLD
(The Flower of Genes)

Botanical Name	:	*Tagetes patula*
Family Name	:	*Astraceae*
English Name	:	French Marigold
Hindi Name	:	Jafri Gainda

Group

Absent from present life.

Plant

This is a decorative annual which originated in Mexico. It's orange, red-brown, yellow or striped flower's blooms from the summer and winter both.

Key word

- Difficulty in learning.

EMOTIONAL SYMPTOMS DUE TO ENERGY BLOCK

- For those who find it difficult to grasp things the first time and it needs to be explained a few times for the mind to understand.
- They repeat the same mistakes again and again.
- They are slow learners.
- Their IQ level is lower than normal children.
- French marigold helps one develop **psychic abilities.** Or it can be used when one is not really in touch with what people are saying and when there is difficulty learning, perhaps because of trauma in childhood.

PHYSICAL SYMPTOMS DUE TO EMOTIONAL BLOCK

- French marigold eases **inflammation in the inner ears and pancreas.**
- It eases the inflammation or other problems in the **muscular system.**
- Eases viral inflammations.
- It stimulates the pituitary gland and certain antibiotic properties in the thymus, particularly in the first seven years of life.

PRACTICE

Slow in learning when confronted with a situation for the second or third time, these people do not draw on their experience of the first incident.

THERAPEUTIC USES

Flower essence helps in reducing inflammation in the inner ear, in the pancreas, diabetes, and viral inflammation.

Helps deal with genetic deterioration of the spinal column, pituitary glands.

POSITIVE QUALITIES

It opens the doors to intuitive understanding.

TRANSFORMATION

"French Marigold" increases the senses particularly of hearing as the supplement to spiritual forces so that the person could understand others in a better way.

17. Drumstick

18. Eucalyptus

19. Fever few

20. French marigold

21. Garlic

22. Geranium

23. Ginger

24. Gooseberry

21

GARLIC
(The Flower of Power)

Botanical Name	:	*Allium sativum*
Family Name	:	*Liliaceae*
English Name	:	Garlic
Hindi Name	:	Lehsun

GROUP

Fear.

PLANT

Garlic is a member of the lily family and a wonderfully impressive remedy used in healing for thousands of years. While native to Siberia, this herb is now a common food crop worldwide. It flowers in May, especially in Latin countries. It produces white, sturdy, and strongly scented flowers.

Garlic belongs to the onion family, and is one of best-known and most-used medicinal plants. Garlic has been shown to lower total serum cholesterol as well as cholesterol in human clinical trials.

KEY WORDS

- Fear of a known thing.

EMOTIONAL SYMPTOMS DUE TO ENERGY BLOCK

- For week people garlic has stimulating and energy-giving properties.
- It strengthens positive thought forms, to destroy **negative thought,** and to bring such energy particularly from the flower essence into people.
- It is for impotent men to give them vigour and youth.
- Garlic people tend to be **anxious and impatient, full of fears,** such as fear of not recovering, or fear of being poisoned.
- Garlic gets rid of any fears or **paranoia** because it crystallizes objectivity in the mental and emotional bodies.
- These people may be **sensitive** and **sad, weep during sleep,** and have an **impulse to run away.**
- It is recommended particularly for those who are **plagued by fears and anxieties** and are **emotionally drained** as result.
- In a depleted state they are prone to **chronic nervousness, insecurity,** and are **vulnerable to negative influences.**
- Garlic also eases anger. Garlic can be applied for **all type of fear.**

PHYSICAL SYMPTOMS DUE TO EMOTIONAL BLOCK

- It can be used for stage fight or to relax a person facing a difficult therapy such as surgery. Even if someone were afraid to release hidden fear or anger, these insecurities could be gradually released and faced with garlic.

- This may manifest as a **poor immune response** with a tendency to parasitic or viral infection or a tendency to fall prey to emotional or psychic parasites in one's life. This leads inevitably to further draining of vital energy; the face may be pale, the eyes vacant, and there may be a feeling of being scattered.
- This is partly associated with its legendary ability to banish superstitious creatures.

PRACTICE

Garlic like many other strong-smelling herbs was believed to possess occult magic and initiate spiritual experiences.

A symbol of strength-athletes at the Olympic games chewed it before taking part to improve their chance of victory.

Throughout garlic's use in healing there run three main themes-it is strengthening and energy-giving, detoxifying and an antidote to poisoning, and it lends protection against a whole host of evil influences both physical and metaphysical.

Note

Recent research has shown that garlic acts as a powerful antioxidant and its sulphur compounds have anti-tumour activities, while it is also said to protect the body against the effects of pollution and nicotine.

In confirmation of the ancient use of garlic for heart disease and high blood pressure, recent research into the heart and circulation has shown that garlic can significantly lower the level of harmful blood cholesterol-particularly important for those suffering from arteriosclerosis and high blood pressure.

Garlic flower essence is a **very important healing agent for those souls who become too diffused and** face a wide spectrum of disturbances.

Garlic addresses many forms of nervous fear, which arise from the overly intense activity of various elemental beings in the body. In all of these cases there is a characteristic vacancy in the eyes and paleness of features, with the impression that soul-color and vitality is being drained from the individual.

THERAPEUTIC USES

Garlic has a stabilizing and harmonious effect.

For antiseptic, diaphoretic, diuretic, expectorant, stimulant, antioxidant, decongestant, headaches, physical weakness, throat infections, asthma, jaundice, toothache, heart disease, high blood pressure, skin problems and as an antidote to poisons. It is an effective antibacterial, anti fungal, antiviral and anti parasitic remedy. Rejuvenation, colds, skin disease, parasites, infections and gangrene of lungs, joint problems and arthritis, cysts and growths, bone healing, fluid retention, worms and as an antidote to poisons, sore throats, flu, excellent remedy for acute and chronic bronchitis, whooping cough and bronchial asthma, as well as sinusitis, chronic catarrh hay fever and rhinitis. By causing sweating it helps resolve fevers. It is beneficial to diabetics and cancer patients. It may help to reduce attacks of allergic asthma and hay fever.

It is a remedy for colds and other respiratory infections to relieve gas pains and to rid the body of intestinal worms.

Cleanses the blood and helps to create and maintain healthy bacteria and acts on the intestinal mucus, and will relieve colitis and diarrhea with pathological flora in the gut, with dull pain the lower abdomen.

It may prevent stomach cancer, treats infections of the stomach and respiratory system.

Garlic improves digestion, relieves wind and distension, and enhances absorption and assimilation of food. It also benefits the pancreas enhancing the production of insulin, making it an excellent remedy to lower blood sugar in diabetics.

Thus garlic helps to slow down the ageing process, verifying our ancestor's use of garlic as a rejuvenate tonic. By clearing the body of toxins and diseases it helps to maintain a youthful vigor, and with such energy one is able to fend off disease.

Garlic also reduces blood pressure and a tendency to clotting, helping to prevent heart attacks and stroke, it also reduces the risk of arteriosclerosis.

POSITIVE QUALITIES

Brings awareness to the individual of his states of fear, and motivates him to deal with them accordingly.

TRANSFORMATION

Garlic calms the body and gives confidence and courage which restores wholeness and strength for such souls, helping them to consolidate and to bring into greater harmony the physical bodies with the spiritual realm.

22

GERANIUM

(The Flower of Constancy)

Botanical Name : *Pelargonium graveolens*

Family Name : *Geraniaceae*

English Name : Geranium

Hindi Name : Rosha

Group

Indecisive.

Plant

There are many varieties of wild geranium. This non-hardy garden geranium came from the South Africa species of Pelargonium and was introduced into Europe in the 17th century. They become increasingly popular because of the brightness of their flowers and varieties of color, Geranium means stead fast piety. In medicinal times geranium was used as a protective herb to ward of evil influences. Color is red.

Potted geraniums have long history of medicinal use. Over 700 varieties exist, and their essential oils differ depending on where the plant is grown. Fresh and floral in fragrance, geranium was traditionally regarded as feminine oil, a powerful healer, and a valuable insect repellent.

KEY WORDS

- Unhappy in life.

EMOTIONAL SYMPTOMS DUE TO ENERGY BLOCK

- These people are not happy in their day to day life.
- It has a balancing effect on the **nervous system, helping to alleviate apathy, anxiety, stress, hyperactivity, and depression.**
- **For those who are confused and have no strength to project plans into action.**
- It helps to get things started systematically by providing the energy and clarity that is needed. Depressed, sad, exhausted, and confused.

PHYSICAL SYMPTOMS DUE TO EMOTIONAL BLOCK

- It is helpful for aversion to food or even too much hunger, it **balances the hunger.**

PRACTICE

Geranium is **mentally uplifting and refreshing.** With no interest in life these people are not interested in doing daily work. This type of nature changes and these people start to enjoy work.

THERAPEUTIC USE

Muscular pain, diarrhea, PMS, grazes, cuts, piles, varicose veins, chilblains, burns, eczema, ulcers, skin getting blue.

The anti-inflammatory, soothing, and astringent properties of geranium account for its success in treating arthritis, acne, diaper rash, burns, blisters, eczema, cuts and congested pores. Antiseptic properties make it useful for cuts and infections, sore throats and mouth ulcers.

It is also a diuretic, used to relieve swollen breasts and fluid retention, and to stimulate sluggish lymph and blood circulation. Geranium helps to stop bleeding, and acts as a tonic for the liver and kidney problems and stones. Good for diabetes and tonsillitis, depression, anxiety, over-excitement, mood swings, diabetes, urinary and respiratory infection, greasy skin, menopausal problems, PMS, irregular periods, fluid retention, diarrhea, kidney stones, neuralgia, externally to heal cuts and wounds.

Positive Qualities

It has a balancing effect on mind and body to lift the spirits and comfort the heart.

Transformation

Geranium helps to lift the spirits of those who are depressed and lack colour in their life, and are nervous and tense.

23

GINGER
(The Flower of Paradise)

Botanical Name	:	*Zingiber officinale*
Family Name	:	*Zingiberaceae*
English Name	:	Ginger
Hindi Name	:	Adrak

GROUP

Unhappy.

PLANT

The tick, tuberous roots of this reed-like plant have been used as a culinary spice and medicine since antiquity. It is native to southern Asia and widely cultivated in the tropics. A large proportion of prescriptions in oriental medicine contain ginger.

The name comes from ancient Indian Sanskrit sringa-vera, meaning horn body, probably referring to the root. The word was later adapted by the Greeks aszingiberis, leading to gingibar in Latin. Family name is Zingiberaceae. Flower color is purple.

KEY WORD

- Shock and trauma.

EMOTIONAL SYMPTOMS DUE TO ENERGY BLOCK

- For people who have **anger, irritability, hate, frustration, swinging** from love to hate.
- In the shock state they are unable to see, to walk, to hear, to touch, and have a problem in swallowing.
- Ginger has a warming and releasing effect.
- For those people who are in a state of trauma or shock, and have cut themselves off from their emotions.
- These types of people **build a wall of invulnerability** around them.
- They may appear **cool, haughty, aloof,** and even cold but for relationships they are too intense.

PHYSICAL SYMPTOMS DUE TO EMOTIONAL BLOCK

- Ginger helps the body to fight off infections before they become entrenched by activating the circulation, producing perspiration and stimulating the digestion to eliminate toxins.

PRACTICE

Brings **clarity in the mind, intelligence and determination, as well as courage.**

Medicine ginger's pungent and warming properties **enhance the 'fire' in the body,** responsible for proper digestion, body heat, visual perception, hunger, thirst, the luster of the skin, the softness of the body, the light in the eyes.

Note

Ginger along with Garlic significantly reduces blood glucose and serum lipids.

Traditionally a healing herb that is considered diaphoretic and slightly diuretic.

Long intake is good for people who can't pass full urine or flush the kidney. Slowly the quantity will increase.

It invigorates the stomach and intestines, stimulating the appetite and enhances digestion by encouraging secretion of digestive enzymes. It moves stagnation of food and subsequent accumulation of toxins, which has a far-reaching effect throughout the body, increasing general health and vitality and enhancing immunity.

Take ginger to rectify the defective humorous or fluids of the body.

THERAPEUTIC USES

It is found helpful in eliminating mucus, nausea, hangover and general debility. Slightly diuretic and it strengthens the kidneys, bladder and uterus by warming them and increasing their vital energy. Women with delayed menstruation or menstrual cramps commonly drink ginger tea. Strengthens the lungs and kidneys.

Good for people with respiratory disorder, alcoholic, cholera, piles, blood in urine, allergic rashes, impotency, menstrual disorder, pains, travel sickness, **chest congestion, colds, flu, bronchitis and other complaints. It has a history in treating kidney problems, arthritis and rheumatism.** Asthma, whooping cough and tuberculosis of the lungs. Sickness during pregnancy, over-eating, nervousness and infection.

It settles the stomach, soothes indigestion and calms wind. Its pain-relieving and relaxing effects in the digestive system relieve colic and spasm, abdominal pain, distension and flatulent indigestion, and help relieve griping from diarrhea and dysentery.

It is an aid to cure hangovers.

As a curc of for colds, constipation, dyspepsia, painful and scanty periods, insomnia, kidney problem, snakebite, flatulent colic, alcoholic gastritis, stomach and alimentary canal, vomiting, toothache, weak eyes, to strengthen the heart and as an aphrodisiac. Morning sickness, dizziness, vertigo, stomach flu. In the uterus it promotes menstruation, useful for delayed and scanty periods as well as clots.

It relaxes spasm and painful ovulation in periods, and is recommended to invigorate the reproductive system and treat impotence caused by deficiency of vital warmth in the body.

So ginger makes a useful preventive remedy against winter chills and ills, such as tonsillitis and bronchitis, as well as infections in the digestive tract. In the East it has been used for epidemics such as cholera.

POSITIVE QUALITIES

Ginger unthaws the frozen feelings of such people, and relieves tension and fear. It increases sensitivity, magnifies perception, and enhances sensory awareness through sight, touch and hearing, bringing one into the presence.

TRANSFORMATION

It has a comforting and uplifting effect on those feeling insecure, fearful, lethargic or depressed.

24

GOOSEBERRY

(The Flower of Rejuvenating)

Botanical Name : *Phyllanthus emblica*

Family Name : *Euphorbiaceae*

English Name : Gooseberry

Hindi Name : Amla

GROUP

Indecisive.

PLANT

A small sized or middle sized deciduous tree with small leaves, feathery branches. Male and female flowers are born on the same tree, flowers are pale green, usually in dense clusters below the leaves on small stalks. Fruits 1.5 to 2.5 cm diameter, fleshy, round and rather indistinctly marked into 6 lobes, pale green or yellow seeds. General rejuvenator, at the cultivated farms the fruits are larger in size.

KEY WORD

- Insecurity for new happenings.

EMOTIONAL SYMPTOMS DUE TO ENERGY BLOCK

- **Mentally irritated, want their** way every time and they **demand love.**
- These people are **impatient** by nature.
- Get annoyed in the surroundings which are not according to their liking.
- They want to **come in the lime light** and be noticed by people.
- **For appreciation** they want to shout and tell the world forcefully to look at them and appreciate them.
- They are **full of fear** and have too much of **anger.**
- They are too dry by nature and find it **difficult to understand** others' problems.
- A lot of desire and longing for what might have been, no enjoyment in life at present moment.
- Find it difficult to adjust with circumstances.
- They only enjoy a situation which is to their liking and perception.
- They are **introverts, fearful,** and **insecure.**
- Fear for the new or inability to assimilate the new.

PHYSICAL SYMPTOMS DUE TO EMOTIONAL BLOCK

- These people can develop problems due to being emotionally upset, like throat irritation, stomach upset and skin problems

PRACTICE

These type of people may be having a fear but they try to show their ability and have a desire to be noticed. It is a health promoter and prevents aging.

THERAPEUTIC

It is cool by nature, hair tonic, complexion enhancer, strengthens nervous system and bone marrow, useful in diabetes though it is diuretic, cardiac tonic, loss of taste and anorexia, acid peptic diseases, uterus tonic, nervous system, heart, cholesterol, circulatory disorder diseases, T.B., asthma, bronchitis, diarrhea.

Goose berry has the property to keep the body and mind light, cool and dry, helps to increase appetite, stops nausea and vomiting, irritation of stomach, takes care of the heat of the body and thirst, calms the fever and its heat.

Colic pain, hoarse voice and good for cough, dry cough, dysentery, skin diseases, vomiting, nausea, rumbling in the stomach, flatulence, constipation, acidity, phlegm, obesity, high blood pressure, indigestion, thirst, hyperacidity, loss of sense of taste, nasal infection, arrests bleeding, white spots on the nail, anemia, bleeding piles, white discharge, Health tonic – Vit. C, generally to prevent infections, tone up the body.

It is an anti acid and is helpful in controlling liver related problems.

To stop bleeding is a special quality, removes mucus and reduces body fat.

It is excellent in cases of mucus and acid formation.

Removes edema and helps in joining broken bones. Like nectar it removes tiredness, good for urine problems.

General rejuvenator. Improves potency.

POSITIVE

The thought comes in them that life agrees with me, I assimilate the new every moment of every day. All is well !

TRANSFORMATION

This person responds only to love and to loving thoughts. All is peaceful.

25

HARSHRINGAR
(The Flower of Flexibility)

Botanical Name	:	*Nyctanthes arbor-tristis*
Family Name	:	*Oleaceae*
English Name	:	Night Jasmine
Hindi Name	:	Harshringar/Parijat

Group

Exhaustion due to rigidity.

Plant

It is a small tree, goes up till the height of 15-20 feet, the flowers are aromatic and flower petals are white and stem is orange. The stem colour is used for Mahaveer Ji. The stem is also used in food for flavour. This tree flowers twice in a year, February-March and September-October. The tree sheds its flower in early morning hours, making a carpet at the base of the tree. It looks like a shower of flowers.

KEY WORD

- Rigidity of the mind.

EMOTIONAL SYMPTOMS DUE TO ENERGY BLOCK

- These people are **rigid** in their behavior with every one.
- These people do **not change** according to the circumstances, they withhold their old things and want to live with them permanently
- Old rules and regulations are better and in modern life they find it difficult to adjust with their children and do not allow them to live their way and get upset.
- They **expect perfection** in all that they do and dislike shoddiness, laziness, or a similar attitude in others.
- They openly **criticize** people's shortcomings, showing their disapproval.
- They are **self-righteous** and generally proud to enjoy their stringent life-style.
- They would need the remedy if, as is often the case, their high standards **become so harsh** and inflexible that they deny themselves even the simplest pleasures of life.
- Their **idealism** often tends towards **fanaticism.** They are inclined to become members of extremist sects or groups in order to be heard and convince others of their ideology.
- Harshringar is quite frequently given for those whose **personality** is consciously or unconsciously suppressed.
- They want to prove to people that their principles are correct by applying on them selves and showing in day to day life.
- They get into an **argument** with any body, and believe that their own thinking and words and routine are the best.
- These people are **cold with their children** and turn a 'deaf' ear.

- ❖ They disturb others in their work and **teach righteousness** with their behavior.

Physical Symptoms Due to Emotional Block

- ❖ This type of people can develop problems such as pain, stiffness extra, due to their rigid emotional feelings.

Practice

Harshringar is often taken to increase the face glow and to remove dandruff from hair. It also help in improving the hump at back and any de-shaping of the body.

Therapeutic Use

It is a diuretic, tonic and astringent.

Good for constipation, cough, expectorant, stimulant, antipyretic, dysentery, menorrhea, ulcers, dandruff, chronic fever, sciatica, rheumatism, asthma, arthritis, diabetes, blood circulation and mouth ulcers.

It is useful for urine diseases and mal functioning of the gall bladder.

Positive Qualities

Rigidity gets relaxed, mind gets cool, and brings a positive adjustment and acceptance in life.

Transformation

It helps in relaxing the mind and body and to adjust according to the circumstances.

26

HIBISCUS

(The Flower of Emotional Release)

Botanical Name	:	*Hibiscus rosa-sinensis*
Family Name	:	*Malvaceae*
English Name	:	China Rose
Hindi Name	:	Gudhal

GROUP

Unhappy.

PLANT

(Java) has large number of hybrid varieties of colours, size of flowers also varies from 5-12 cm. Height goes above 1.2 to 1.7 mtr. The flower is red and flowers throughout the year.

KEY WORD

- Extreme despair.

EMOTIONAL SYMPTOMS DUE TO ENERGY BLOCK

- Hibiscus is the remedy for those who feel so **stressed,** even tortured, that they have reached the limits of their endurance and feel in a state of **utter despair.**
- The mind and the body are **completely exhausted** from uncomplainingly fighting difficulties, either mental or physical, until a **sense of hopelessness** and complete darkness sets in.
- In this **'dark night of the soul'** sufferers may come face to face with themselves and this may prove to be the catalyst for entering a new stage in life.
- For healing all **traumas** connected with mental and psychical shocks. Restores balance and realignment to the body.
- One of the most tragic assaults to the soul dignity of women is the **exploitation and commercialization of female sexuality.**
- This deeply **wounds the souls** of many women so that they no longer feel a warm connection with their sexuality.
- Often the sexuality is divorced from deeper feelings of love and warmth, which come from the heart.
- It many cases the sexual expression becomes cold and unresponsive, because the soul can no longer contact this part of the self and infuse it with love and caring.

PHYSICAL SYMPTOMS DUE TO EMOTIONAL BLOCK

- Hibiscus essence helps women to reclaim their sexuality, and vitality.
- It can aid many women who have been sexually traumatized, and is also generally beneficial for all modern women who have unconsciously absorbed media images and other stereotypes of dehumanized sexuality.

- ❖ This remedy is sometimes also indicated for men who need to develop a stronger relationship to feminine warmth and positive sexuality.
- ❖ For enhancing compatibility between people in on -to-one relationships, thus evoking warmth and responsiveness.
- ❖ For women who have lost all contact with their sexuality.
- ❖ Frees-psychological blocks of sexual origin.

PRACTICE

For healing all traumas connected with psychic and spiritual shocks. Restores balance and realignment to the body. Has a connection with the female uterus.

THERAPEUTIC USES

Analgesic, diuretic, demulcent, anti-pyretic, cardiac, emollient, aperients, refrigerant, aphrodisiac, emmenagogue, contraceptive.

Used in boils, indigestion, menstrual disorder and diabetes.

Used for whooping cough, in early stages when cough is dry, violent and spasmodic.

It is also given for diarrhea accompanied by severe abdominal pain rumbling which is relieved by a bowel movement.

It helps in colds, fever, menorrhagia.

It is an anti-inflammatory, muscle relaxant, anti-bacterial, anti-fungal, anti viral, anti-spasmodic.

Also useful in polyuria, piles, leucorrhoea, gonorrhoea, catarrh. Gentle laxative and a softener of inflamed parts.

Soothes internal and external wounds and sores; also soothes the alimentary tract and relieves inflammation.

Lowers body heat.

Helps to combat irregular menstrual cycle and menopause related problems.

Hibiscus for **healthy heart—controls cholesterol levels.**

POSITIVE QUALITIES

Women feel comfortable with their sexuality; particularly those who have suffered trauma in the past. Promotes spontaneity, brings harmony to the mind, so creating an emotional sense of well-being, the feeling (in mind, body and soul) is good to be alive.

TRANSFORMATION

It enhances the process of transformation that is possible in such a state of despair and helps to prevent us from simply going to pieces and deriving little or no benefit form the experience. It brings love and warmth to women who have been abused in any way.

27

HIM WATER
(The Healing Water)

English Name : *Ganges Water*
Hindi Name : Gangajal

GROUP

Over care.

PLANT

This is not a plant, but the holy water from the Ganges, containing healing properties; it works at a different level. The Ganges water is potentized when the sun is at its greatest strength. Incidentally, any spring which is still left free and in its natural state, can be used for the remedy.

KEY WORDS

- Live with their own principles.

EMOTIONAL SYMPTOMS DUE TO ENERGY BLOCK

- Those of this nature are so **strict with themselves** that they tend to live a rigid regime or set of standards without harming others.
- They may be **very religious** or have certain other **ideals, which govern their lives,** and they **strive to achieve** these ideals or follow their particular faith.
- They chastise themselves if they should stray from their determined path.
- They do not convince others of their ideals, they often try to be **role models.**
- They focus on their principles and on **'doing the right thing'** without harming others.
- Through the practice of yoga, they aspire to understand the 'Self'.
- Life is made subject to dogmatic theories and sometimes exaggerated ideals.
- Hard on themselves, do everything possible to achieve top form and stay there.
- Sets highest standards for himself, almost to the point of self-abandonment, and will enjoy denying himself many of the things of daily routine.
- These people feel like misfits in society.
- Unaware of the compulsions they are living under.
- Concept of spirituality – they cling to a particular aspect that is accessible (meditation technique, special diet etc.).
- **Want to be in top form both mentally and physically** and will avidly pursue any course that might lead them there. The man appearing in the swimming pool at 7 a.m. having jogged

the woods, and who thereafter sits down intently to a specially prepared breakfast! They are **workaholics.**

- ❖ Believe that worldly desires inhibit spiritual development, want to be **saints** while still on this earth. Fall into their own trap when meditating, because of overdoing.
- ❖ Suppress important physical and emotional needs, are self-denying.
- ❖ Do not interfere in the lives of others, being completely preoccupied with seeking personal perfection. Great perfectionists.
- ❖ Reproach themselves if unable to maintain **self-imposed discipline.**
- ❖ **Highly crystallized,** the personality freezes in certain decision, by ignoring the demands of reality. They absolutely want to be what they consider to be good and in no way what they have identified as not good.
- ❖ They believe that self made **principles** are better than the society principles for their development. It is possible that the things they consider good are not yet destined to come up in the present life cycle.
- ❖ The error lies in excessive **self-wildness** and a totally wrong material approach.

PHYSICAL SYMPTOMS DUE TO EMOTIONAL BLOCK

- ❖ After delivery when a woman does not succeed in feeding, and feels angry at her inadequacy.
- ❖ Children **demand perfection** in their work and may cause mental rigidity, tension, lack of sleep, stress and strain. May help the **panicked eater.**

Often relates to a food fetish, those over concerned with a diet, purity of living, strict morality, wherever a rigid fixed self-discipline may cause suffering.

PRACTICE

The continuous suppression of libido leads in time to a total loss of love for life. It has been found that Him Water in baths made a person loosen up and relax. If there is too much fixation, drink this water every day.

THERAPEUTIC

Dysmenorrheal, muscle pain, joint pain, arthritis, cholesterol, High blood pressure, heart problem, stiffness of the joints and arteriosclerosis

POSITIVE QUALITIES

They become little understanding and try to adjust with the situation.

TRANSFORMATION

Mind gets relaxed and flexible. While still maintaining their principles, they let go of the rigidities, just as a stone's texture smoothens with the constant pouring of water.

25. Harshringar

26. Hibiscus

27. Him water

28. Holly hock

29. Jasmine

30. Kachnar

31. Lemon

32. Lotus

28

HOLLY HOCK
(The Flower of Softness)

Botanical Name	:	*Althaea rosea*
Family Name	:	*Malvaceae*
English Name	:	Holly Hock
Hindi Name	:	Gulkhaira

GROUP

Indecisive.

PLANT

Mild plant, grows in salt marshes and damp fertile places. Likes full sun. Originates from China, grows in winter in India. **Colour** – red, dark red, pink, light pink. It is also known as Marshmallow.

KEY WORDS

- Lack of trust and problem in making a commitment.

Imbalance: Depression from a known cause, temporary set back. Gloom and sadness.

EMOTIONAL SYMPTOMS DUE TO ENERGY BLOCK

- Used as a flower essence to engender **warmth** and **openness.**
- For those who **feel isolated, lonely, cut off** and unable to give or receive warmth and friendship.
- May stem from **insecurity, fear** or **lack of trust** related to incidents in early life.
- The feelings may give rise to problems making or keeping friends, or in making a commitment to a relationship.

PHYSICAL SYMPTOMS DUE TO EMOTIONAL BLOCK

- Hollyhock is a wonderful remedy for any kind or **irritation** or **inflammation** inside or outside the body, because of its great soothing and healing properties.
- The demulcent mucilage **soothes the digestive, respiratory** complains.
- Hollyhock will help relieve **heartburn** and indigestion.
- A **mild expectorant** and an immunity enhancer, it is **helpful for dry, irritating coughs and chest infections.**
- In the urinary system, hollyhock acts as a **soothing diuretic,** useful in cystitis and irritable bladder, and was the traditional remedy for easing the passage of **urinary gravel and stones.**
- Hollyhock has a cooling effect and should be thought of whenever there is **excess heat and inflammation.**

PRACTICE

They find a logical explanation for their negative attitude. Cannot cope up with even small difficulties and are often depressed. Cooling for upper part of the body.

THERAPEUTIC USES

It helps in digestive, respiratory, urinary stones inflammation, ulceration of the mucous membranes. Also in heart burn, indigestion, mild expectorant, for dry cough and chest infection, cystitis, irritable bladder, tooth cleaner.

Hollyhock was traditionally added to ease childbirth and has also been used to improve production of breast milk.

Teething babies were given a Hollyhock to cool their inflamed gums. Adults used the root as a tooth cleaner.

The leaves can be applied to wasp and bee sting and insect bites, scalds and burns, sunburn and inflammatory skin problems such as eczema and acne.

For boils, carbuncles and draw out thorns, bruises sprains and strains, joints, muscular aches.

POSITIVE QUALITIES

Lifts the spirit and gives the encouragement needed to the preserver to try again. It restores the understanding that there is no failure when one is doing one's best, whatever the apparent result, and that there is no obstacle too great or too big.

TRANSFORMATION

Helps to over come barriers to friendship, and to warm and caring relationships. Helps to soothe and ease communication.

29

JASMINE
(The Flower of Luxury)

Botanical Name	:	*Jasminum officinale*
Family Name	:	*Oleaceae*
Common Name	:	Jasmine
Hindi Name	:	Chameli

GROUP

Absent from present life.

PLANT

The native land is Persia and India. They produce sweet-smelling white flowers that bloom from June to Oct.

Known in India as Queen of the night, the delicate jasmine flower has one of the loveliest and most distinctive perfumes, particularly intoxicating at night. The common white Night Queen is a native of Northern India and Persia, while the flower is a native of the

Himalayas and has slightly larger, highly perfumed flowers grown for use in perfumery. There are between two and three hundred species of this flower, mostly native to Asia.

KEY WORD

- Surrender to God after failure.

EMOTIONAL SYMPTOMS DUE TO ENERGY BLOCK

- For the realization that the future is healed now.
- For lovers, those who **rebel against authority** and find it difficult to get on well with others.
- For those who have a **low-esteem** or a **poor grade in school, especially in philosophy.** The individual might also be an agnostic. It stimulates a sense of practicality and mental clarity.
- Replaces feeling of alienation with diplomacy.
- Helps you to find peace in your environment.
- For those who cannot face the day ahead, it gives strength of mind to over- come all kinds of **negativity.**
- For those going through great suffering from **painful, debilitating diseases.**
- **For those who only come alive as dusk falls,** finding it hard to communicate during the day because they are drained by the hum drum way of life.
- For calming the **nerves** and **soothing emotional problems.**

PHYSICAL SYMPTOMS DUE TO EMOTIONAL BLOCK

- They may be **prone to accidents** such as bone fractures due to weakness in skeletal structure.
- Eases bursitis and cartilage, bone tender disease.

- It can also be utilized to improve the **sense of smell,** nervousness and congestion.
- It increases awareness of innate famininity and the wisdom that this brings.
- It is excellent for **stress relief** and is uplifting during times of lethargy.

PRACTICE

In the language of flowers white jasmine symbolizes deep affection, happiness and elegance.

It stimulates the brain, increases perception and allows the mind to grasp deep questions about the essence of all life and our purpose on this planet.

For loss of your soul's purpose or a misunderstanding of it and lack of ambition towards it's realization.

Note

In China jasmine has been a symbol of feminine sweetness and beauty, and Indian jasmine a scared flower, known as 'moonlight of the grove' and is traditionally woven into bridal wreathes, and is worn as scented ornaments by women.

The flower oil has been a favourite scent and hair oil of Indian women. Jasmine is held scared to Vishnu and Indira.

In Ayurveda jasmine is used for calming the nerves and soothing emotional problems, relieving period pain, P.M.S. and tension related headaches.

THERAPEUTIC USES

This essence is to ease diseases associated with mucus problems such as lung congestion, especially during pneumonia or a common cold.

It dissolves and discharges viruses, eliminates excessive acidity, and removes toxins from the digestive tract, particularly the colon.

Cures diseases associated with protein deficiency like hypoglycemia, and is good for vegetarian people.

The astringent properties of the flowers treat inflamed eyes and skin, and as gargles and mouthwashes relieve sore throats and mouth ulcers.

Jasmine is recommended for people with problems of excess mucus clogging the nose, respiratory tract, throat and chest and causing a feeling of cloudiness and sluggishness.

It is widely known as an aphrodisiac.

Jasmine's antiseptic properties are useful for treating a range of infections including respiratory infections and problems in the genitor urinary system, including cystitis.

Excellent for pneumonia, bursitis and cartilage, bone tender disease calming the nerves, sense of smell, uterine tonic, which can help with menstrual cramp and disorders of the uterus.

Are used to treat conditions as diverse as liver cirrhosis and headaches.

Its pain-relieving properties add to strengthen contractions during childbirth.

It is also believed to strengthen male sex organs and oil as a massage has been used for prostate problems.

Oil is relaxing and its antidepressant effect helps to clear postnatal depression with massage.

POSITIVE QUALITIES

Jasmine clears the passageways in the head and promotes mental clarity.

TRANSFORMATION

It brings acceptance and transformation of suffering into positive love, kindness, and sensitivity to others. Relieves the burden of fear, nightmares and pain.

30

KACHNAR
(The Flower of Ice)

Botanical Name : *Bauhinia variegata L.*

Family Name : *Fabaceae*

English Name : Mountain Ebony

Hindi Name : Kachnar

Group

Absent from present life.

Plant

Bauhinia is a medium size ornamental tree. Its bark is grey or brown from outside and pink to dark yellow from inside. The leaves have a shallow cleft at the tip. The flowers are white with light yellow spots or pink with red spots or purple-mauve and are orchid like in shape. They flower when the tree is in a leafless condition from February to March. This herb is found in sub-Himalayan forests of India, Burma, and several other countries. Taste is acrid.

KEY WORD

→ Digging old thoughts.

EMOTIONAL SYMPTOMS DUE TO ENERGY BLOCK

- Makes his own body like a dumping ground, keeping and **restoring all the problems,** and does not speak it out to people.
- Is **fearful, needs protection all the time,** runs away from feelings, experiences insecurity and self-rejection, feels life is empty, needs fulfillment.
- **Inability to breathe** for himself feeling stifled and choked. Suppressed crying.
- Fears rejection, has an **inferiority complex,** and believes that he is not good enough.
- Thoughts are always rotating in his mind.
- Assimilation of **inflamed thoughts. Anger of the past,** afraid to let it go, **feels burdened.**
- Wasting away from **selfishness and cruel thoughts is burdened by possessiveness and thoughts of revenge.**

PHYSICAL SYMPTOMS DUE TO EMOTIONAL BLOCK

- They may face these problems: breathing, stomach, skin problem and sore throat.

PRACTICE

Too much brewing of thoughts of anger, but keeps them to himself.

Bauhinia holds the wealth of medicinal properties in it. It is a useful antiseptic wash for a variety of minor skin infections. Kachnar essence in hot water a gentle laxative, and a gargle mixed with pomegranate essence is an excellent remedy for sore throat.

Note

Bauhinia tree, which is mentioned in Sanskrit dramas of the famous poet Kalidasa, and also some popular songs, is a real treat for the eyes. All over northern India, when the flowering of Bauhinia tree takes place, its leafless branches get covered in a blaze of pink-white blossoms and marks the advent of spring, a delightful but short season followed by a hot summer. This flowering coincides with the festive harvest time, which is also the time when the village women go out in the jungle and collect the flowers and buds of the Bauhinia, which they usually dry and store for medicinal purposes.

THERAPEUTIC USES

Flower essence is good for frequency of passing stool or Irritated Bowel Syndrome. It reduces body heat and is used to cool the eyes.

Has laxative properties and is useful as a tonic.

Also good for Malarial fevers and as an antidote to snake poison.

For obese people, useful for breaking down fatty deposits in the body.

Regularize menstrual dysfunction and glandular problems, especially of the throat.

Astringent, cough, expectorant, inflammation, leprosy, scrofula, prolapsed rectum, diabetes, controls metabolism, skin disease, ulcer, intestinal worms, asthma, tuberculosis gland, piles, dysentery, diarrhea, goiter, bleeding hemorrhoids, cough, heart burn, indigestion, haematuria, menorrhagia, skin diseases, sore throat, tuberculosis, worms, gonorrhea, edema.

It is a blood cleanser also good to increase the white blood cells.

It gives strength in intestines, (sangrehni) lever swelling, bleeding piles, P.M.S., blood in urine, When the body is de-shaped (Kubdapen) of the child.

For excessive menstrual bleeding.

For ulcer and stomach pain—put 15-30 drops of essence in the bath tub, and take a bath for 15 minutes daily for 48 days.

It is good for dysentery, chronic disorder of the bowels, liver and worms in the intestines.

POSITIVE

This essence easily and comfortably releases thoughts which the person does not need in life any more.

TRANSFORMATION

Comes to peace with his own feelings, and feels safe and creates the courage for his own security.

31

LEMON
(Flower of Clarity)

Botanical Name	:	*Citrus medica var.*
Family name	:	*Rutaceae*
English name	:	Citrus Limon
Hindi Name	:	Neembu

GROUP

Indecisive.

PLANT

This short thorny shrubby fruit tree, 5-10 feet high, ovate leaf with winged petiole while native to India, is now widely grown throughout the world. The white, deep pink, and highly perfumed flowers 3 to 10 in axil of leaf, bloom in the spring.

KEY WORD

→ Hazy mind.

EMOTIONAL SYMPTOMS DUE TO ENERGY BLOCK

- The **powerful energies** observed moving through people when smelling the flower have a **very nourishing, cleansing effect.**
- Its scent was a very important component in rituals, and its similarity to other scents such as lemon balm was known.
- Lemon is often seen for its **holistic properties;** it works on multiple levels at once, particularly as a flower essence.
- Lemon has a strong impact on the mental body, creating clarity of thought in the individual.
- People needing this essence usually have **mental blocks,** a **lack of humor,** or extreme **emotional** states.
- Although often displaying a high I.Q., they cannot make decisions. There is an inability to link up issues or think clearly.

PHYSICAL SYMPTOMS DUE TO EMOTIONAL BLOCK

- Students studying for exams would like this essence.
- Lemon does not increase eloquence, but improves vocal capacity by enhancing your pronunciation. For example, it alleviates stuttering.
- It aids many parts of the physical body because there is a general release of stress.
- The muscles are relaxed, the lymphatic system is cleansed, and the skin tissue is invigorated because of increased blood flow to the area.
- Lemon can be applied to teeth that decay from the inside. But the person's ability to transfer the lemon's tooth enamel characteristics to the inner depths of the tooth through creative visualization will be very important to make it effective for this purpose.

PRACTICE

The **left-hand portion** of the brain is stimulated so that mathematical or computer skill and the ability to learn languages are activated. Skills based on mathematical principles such as architecture can be learned with greater ease. Other essences that can be utilized here include lotus.

Lemon aids in the production of certain enzymes, and it assists in the assimilation of protein, calcium, zinc. Its high vitamin C content makes this a valuable fruit in preventing scurvy, ascorbic acid, fructose, glucose, sucrose, flower bud contains-amino acid. It could be used as a supplement in mega-vitamin therapy or when specific vitamins are needed such as vitamin A in certain eye diseases or vitamin E for the skin.

Lemon is another common fruit tree that is quite valuable as a flower essence. In some cases lemon can be applied externally.

THERAPEUTIC USES

Lemon essence is good for kidney stones pain, nails and cores, hair fall, dandruff, lice, baldness and to regenerate hair, heart beat, back pain, joint pains.

For throat pain, laryngitis, redness in throat, increase the eyesight, dyspepsia, appetite, mouth bad odour, sour taste, gasses, ulcers in mouth, nose bleed.

For acidity, sour burp, stomach ache, constipation, vomiting, morning sickness, naval Shifting, diarrhea, amoebiasis, cholera, piles.

Jaundice, abortion, obesity, high B.P., heart problem, fever, malaria, cold, sinus, asthma, insomnia, headache, water bound diseases.

Dry skin, oily skin, itching, increases the blood, pimples, acne, for beauty.

It is a good mouthwash, more natural than fluoride, it removes plaque and strengthens the enamel on the teeth. Put three to seven drops of the essence in one or two ounces of pure water and drink that amount each day until the problem is solved. Also good for gum and tooth bleeding, and as a tooth whitener and cleanser.

For smoking, sun stroke, foot perspiration, giddiness, vitality, spleen, stuttering, stammering, lisping, liver trouble, scorbutic, burning sensation, cough, throat disorder, tuberculosis.

Good for arthritis, and weakness and particularly good for new arthritis.

It is the best preventative drug for scurvy and is also very valuable in fevers and allying thirst.

It is recommended in acute rheumatism and may be given to counteract narcotic poison such as opium.

It is used as an astringent gargle in sore throats, for uterine hemorrhage after childbirth, as a lotion in sunburn and as a cure for severe hiccoughs.

Good anti-periodic drug and can be used to replace quinine in malarial injections, or to reduce the temperature in typhoid fever.

Lemon is good to rub over the arm after an injection. Some of the effects of the injection will be reduced and healing will happen more quickly.

It dissolves scar tissue in the body.

It reduces cholesterol in the system.

POSITIVE

Emotional blockage is taken care of and humour sets in life.

TRANSFORMATION

Creating clarity of thoughts and taking the mind in the right direction.

32

LOTUS
(The Flower of Light)

Botanical Name : *Nelumbo nucifera*

Family Name : *Nelumbonacaeae*

English Name : Lotus

Hindi Name : Kamal

GROUP

Loner.

PLANT

Lotus plant is there on the earth since 160 million years. This is one plant, which has not undergone many changes, it loves to live on still water, Lotus is native to Egypt, Florida and several tropical regions of Asia. The light pink flower native to India is the best species and location to use as a flower essence. It produces a large flower on top of water. The pink, purple, red or white fragrant flowers appear in the summer. Lotus is the national flower of India.

KEYWORD

- Spiritual pride.

EMOTIONAL SYMPTOMS DUE TO ENERGY BLOCK

- Lotus in its normal state resonates easily with the crown chakra. There is a great similarity in the pattern of the crown chakra and the physical make up of lotus.
- The universal flower which kindles **harmony** in all areas.
- It always act like a **booster** to other remedies when combined with them.
- All **emotional problems** are eased. It brings all the nadis and subtle bodies into a temporary state of alignment.
- Opens the crown chakra to **higher energies.**
- A universal essence for all aspects of the human being.
- For blossoming and spiritual harmony. Encourages reception and spiritual openness. A spiritual elixir and aid to meditation
- **Harmonizes** the soul forces and purifies the emotions.
- Gently releases **negative emotions,** correcting imbalances.
- It **eases fears,** which usually relate to future lives.
- Obsessive state can be treated with lotus and it helps one develop telepathy and other psychic powers.

PHYSICAL SYMPTOMS DUE TO EMOTIONAL BLOCK

- **Hastens recovery from illness.** Aligns and balances and clears the entire system of toxins.
- **General tonic.** For spiritual pride.
- **Calms the mind** and improves concentration.
- Lotus also helps distinguish between soul and **delusional messages,** and it can be used externally as a salve and spray.

PRACTICE

It synchronizes the elemental energies in the human body. For children it brings deeper **meditation,** cleansing the entire system. Lotus attunes one's future life in the spiritual direction.

It brings any disease including AIDS to the surface, so these forces can be expelled from the system. It is very helpful when added with other flower essences. It is recommended during period of stress when relaxation seems necessary.

HISTORY

Brahma, the creator of the universe appeared from the Lotus and created the universe. In the famous story during 'Amrithmanthan' when the ocean of milk was churned by the devas and asuras, Goddess Laxmi emerged from the waves with the Lotus in Her hand. The relation between Laxmi (Goddess of wealth) and Lotus is immortal. The Lotus is the symbol, which opens up our foray to the universe with all it's divine power.

THERAPEUTIC USES

This energizes heart, liver, spleen, pineal glands, diabetes, constipation, menopause, baldness, painful urination, cardiac tonic and fever.

It can be used extensively in all forms of tissue regeneration.

Past live information stored in the genetic code is released and longevity increases.

This gives relief from palpitation of heart, biliousness, vomiting and giddiness, diarrhea, dysentery and stomach upset, ringworm and skin diseases, and smallpox.

Used as diuretic, de-worming agent and is used to treat skin disorders as also a general tonic.

It is useful in cough, and fever.

Has cholesterol reducing effect.

It is a good coagulating agent to prevent any type of bleeding disorder in the body. The lotus helps to keep the circulation of two vital organs in the body that is—heart and brain.

POSITIVE QUALITIES

Lotus opens an expansive spirituality, meditative insight and synthesis.

Harmonizes inter personal relationships.

TRANSFORMATION

They understand the future without fear. Lotus balances, cleanses and strengthens the aura.

33

MARJORAM
(The Flower of Consolation)

Botanical Name	:	*Origanum majorana L*
Family Name	:	*Lamiaceae*
Common Name	:	Marjoram
Hindi Name	:	Marwa

GROUP

Loner.

PLANT

Native to Portugal and grown as an annual plant through the rest of Europe and Great Britain. Most ancient and versatile healing flower. It is from one of the groups of Basil. The leaves are double the size of Basil. Colour of the flower is white. The flowering time is in summer. By nature the plant has warming properties.

Marjoram has traditionally symbolized youth, beauty and happiness.

KEY WORD

A person who feels lonely.

EMOTIONAL SYMPTOMS DUE TO ENERGY BLOCK

- ❖ Mind is upset due to **tension.**
- ❖ There is too much **anxiety** in the mind.
- ❖ Feels too **lethargic** to work when the work is in front of him.
- ❖ To calm unwanted **desire of sex.**
- ❖ Feels too **lonely in old age,** always wants company.
- ❖ **Marjoram** is for those who have lost someone. Also provides inner strength to those grappling with their aging process.
- ❖ A person who has **grief, sorrow** and **depression,** Marjoram will relieve him.
- ❖ Emotionally warming, calming properties for lonely people, who live alone.

PHYSICAL SYMPTOMS DUE TO EMOTIONAL BLOCK

- ❖ It helps to minimize damage from radicals and to protect the body from the impact of the ageing process.
- ❖ Marjoram is used extensively in medicine, notably to **nourish the brain** and the digestive organs, for relief from narcotic poisoning, convulsions and dropsy.
- ❖ Marjoram symbolizes consolation. **Nervous** by nature and those affected by nerve problem are aided by its use.

PRACTICE

It has a relaxing effect on both, the mind and body, offers warming properties to ease tense muscles, easing anxiety, restlessness and internal trembling and encourages circulation. When treating an old person try to interact with him with patience and love so he can open out to you and tell you his feeling of loneliness.

Marjoram is still used as a nervine and calmative—It is indeed one of the most sedative herbs, soothing for people who cannot sleep owing to the pace of life today, soothing for those suffering from pangs of love, for jagged nerves and for feverish excitement.

THERAPEUTIC

Sweet marjoram is widely used in cookery and aids digestion of food

Marjoram is used to alleviate **painful and delayed menstruation, tension** and **anxiety,** which are the part of premenstrual syndrome, and is also good for **insomnia** and irritability.

Some types of **infertility** may be treated with this flower remedy, as it has an effect on the pituitary function. It is used to promote **urination,** to relieve **injuries** and **bruises** and treat **conjunctivitis** and other eye diseases. Useful for arthritic conditions, it helps to clear **toxins** from the **joints.**

Hot infusion of Marjoram can be inhaled to clear the **respiratory** passages during a bout with a cold or flu. Gargles for **sore throats** or mild **mouth infection.**

Infusion can be placed on top of nose and **sinus** areas to relieve sinus problems and **hay fever.**

Effective against **bacteria** and viruses. It will protect against infection in the winter and **clearing phlegm,** soothing **cough, sinusitis, fever, sprains, strains, poor circulation, chilblain, diarrhea, gout, antispasmodic, indigestion, improve appetite, wind, colic, nausea, diarrhea, constipation, depression, insomnia and high blood pressure. Intestine pain, lethargy, P.M.S., low B.P., migraine, hysteria, leucoderma, constipation and nervousness.**

POSITIVE

Is comforting, calming, soothing and greatly supportive in times of grief, sorrow, and vulnerability.

TRANSFORMATION

It helps one let go of the fear of being vulnerable, of being alone, and helps one to be more self-reliant and find inner strength. Relaxes the body and mind.

34

MORNING GLORY
(The Flower of Keys)

Botanical Name	:	*Ipomoea purpurea*
Family Name	:	*Convolvulacae*
English Name	:	Railway Creeper
Hindi Name	:	Morning Glory

GROUP

Absent from present life.

PLANT

This is a tropical American vine that has become a popular garden flower. Its sky-blue flowers usually bloom from early in the spring until the fall. In India flowers in March-April-June.

KEY WORD

- Negative living habits.

EMOTIONAL SYMPTOMS DUE TO ENERGY BLOCK

- This essence can be useful when leading an erratic life style, often requiring stimulants to stay alert. Morning glory essence gently regulates the body clock.
- For those who rely on stimulant to help them through the day.
- For those who find it difficult to wake up in the morning.
- Helps us become conscious of our **negative living habits** and **addictions.**
- Supports withdrawal and **rehabilitation.**
- For **loss of spiritual faith** and certainty that you were created in the creator's likeness.
- For liberating one self from **harmful habits** such as dependence on **alcohol, coffee, tobacco, addiction to opiates** and **nicotine.**
- Benefiting those trying to **give up drugs** at any stage of treatment.

PHYSICAL SYMPTOMS DUE TO EMOTIONAL BLOCK

- Good for **restlessness** at night.
- Helps you get up and **greet the morning with** enthusiasm.
- For **"night owls"** with **erratic eating** and sleeping rhythms who have **difficulty getting up in the morning.**
- Balances vital strength and tones the nerves and improves immunity.
- Dull, toxic, or "hung-over", unable to incarnate into the body, especially in the morning, addictive, erratic behavior, escapism, exhaustion, fatigue, dreams and sleep.

PRACTICE

It encourages attunement with rhythms to restore natural energy and sparkling life force so that we are refreshed and in touch with life.

Regularizes the rhythms of daily life.

Morning glory has some influence on the emotional body. Display of nervous irritability, including grinding of the teeth and jitteriness exemplified by talking too much or restlessness at night to the point of insomnia, are all states treatable with this remedy.

It is good for restless nights. It helps one get up in the morning and maintain stamina and vitality throughout the day. This is primarily because it strengthens the mental body. With morning glory, one breaks nervous habits such as smoking or using opiates. The essence removes opiates from the sympathetic nervous system.

THERAPEUTIC USES

For uric acid accumulation and bowel problems. Aids circulation and eliminatory systems.

Used as a liberating remedy for drug abuse and addiction (ranging from opiates to tobacco) its key purpose being to break destructive habits and cleanse the body of associated side effects (restlessness and nervous hypertension).

Restores the nervous system to its original balance and vitality.

Many levels of physical illness will set into the body, especially compromised immune response, nerve depletion, and disturbances in vital organs such as the liver.

Can treat advanced manic-depressive states or schizophrenia when the individual has lost complete touch with reality. Also helps bring people out of comatose states, particularly when this condition is caused by shock.

Good for nervousness, addiction, insomnia, tonic for the entire nervous system. Helps to maintain stamina and vitality throughout the day. It strengthens the mental body. Addiction of opiates and nicotine, trying to give up drug use, withdrawal symptoms.

POSITIVE QUALITIES

Sparkling vital force, awake and refreshed, in touch with Life.

TRANSFORMATION

Morning Glory helps the soul come to greater awareness and respect for life and the life processes of the body. The individual learns to adjust its rhythm so that it is more in tune with the cycles of Nature. Through Morning Glory, the soul learns to experience more natural states of energy, and thus the gift of life itself.

35

MULBERRY
(The Flower of Goodwill)

Botanical Name	:	*Morus nigra*
Family Name	:	*Moraceae*
English Name	:	Mulberry
Hindi Name	:	Shahtoot

GROUP

Social influence.

PLANT

The mulberry is a native of oriental parts, more particularly Persia. It is a deciduous tree up to 30 ft in height. The fruit is oblong, red; shot stalked berry, which turns purple when ripe. The flowering time is June and July. Flower colour is white. It grows more in Karnataka.

KEY WORDS

- Jealousy and hatred.

IMBALANCE EMOTIONAL SYMPTOMS DUE TO ENERGY BLOCK

- For those people who have **irritation, hysteria** and **mental problems.**
- Alleviates long held **prejudices, hatred and deep disharmony.**
- Good for dealing with the legacy of **negative patriotism** and **social conflict.** Brings reconciliation.
- **Heart is hardened,** complains about others.
- They are **discontent, unhappy, frustrated,** often without cause.
- **Jealousy, distrust, revenge, malice, fear** of being deceived.
- Suspects a negative aspect to every thing, easily suspicious of others, **anger** towards fellowmen.
- Frequently feels hurt or injured. **Belittles** others in his heart.
- **Absence of love, presence of misunderstanding, various types of vexation.**
- These people are **super sensitive** to real or imagined plights.
- They always believe that they have no jealousy against any body, and that they are very tolerant
- These people **sap the energy of others** and are **resentful, angry and find fault in others.** Have a **violent temperament.**
- Children who are jealous of the second child. These type of children are **bullies, pinching others, biting, throwing things, destroying toys, like twisting the head of the doll, or beating or cutting a toy in an artificial way.**

- ❖ They are moody, feeling cut off from love, blaming others, get outbursts of anger, become violent, and are mildly paranoid.
- ❖ Mulberry people are restless, irritated, lose control, complain about others, always find fault in others, for their own mistakes also they blame others, and all this manifests in physical expressions.

PHYSICAL SYMPTOMS DUE TO EMOTIONAL BLOCK

- ❖ They suffer from acute violent illness, e.g., fever, inflamed burning or itching, skin rashes, allergies, gall bladder disease, and coughing.
- ❖ They are the "do not breathe on me" type of people. Have phobias like "this makes me sick".

PRACTICE

When in practice if there is a little conflict that medicine is not affecting the patient then give this medicine for ten days then start the old prescription again.

When the case does not respond to the other remedies, use Mulberry and Rose.

Active intense type—give Mulberry.

Weak despondent type—give Rose Red (low key, passive type of persons and anemic).

HISTORY

Our forefathers ate mulberries to gain good appetites. The bark being steeped in vinegar helps the toothaches.

THERAPEUTIC USE

Mulberry is helpful for acidity, arthritis, high fever, meningitis, mentally retarded, blood purifier, throat irritation, sore throat, diphtheria, laryngitis, laxative, pharyngitis worms, mouth ulcers and good as a tonic; application of essence is helpful in itching and eczema on the skin.

For sore throat gargle with hot water twice or thrice till the pain subsides.

Inflammation of throat and mucus leads to increase in heat in the stomach and burning in the urine, which are controlled by Mulberry essence.

Mulberry helps in controlling diabetes and blood pressure.

Lowers body heat, it is a laxative, it expels worms from the body and is used for convalescents and for anemic people.

POSITIVE QUALITIES

They are able to rejoice in the success of others and bear the vexations of life with understanding and tolerance.

TRANSFORMATION

Mulberry heals the soul by reversing psychic currents of energy which are directed too strongly toward the self. The Mulberry soul becomes self fulfilled rather then self absorbed.

36

MUSTARD
(The Flower of Fire)

Botanical Name	:	*Sinapis alba L.*
Family Name	:	*Brassicaceae*
English Name	:	Mustard
Hindi Name	:	Sarson

GROUP

Absent from present life.

PLANT

Mustard is an annual plant cultivated as spice all over the world. It has been used for centuries as a pungent condiment and healing herb. A very common annual 30-60 cm in height, growing in fields by the wayside. The brilliant yellow flowers appear from May to July.

KEY WORD

- Mind gets blank for unknown reasons.

EMOTIONAL SYMPTOMS DUE TO ENERGY BLOCK

- They are in despair, depression, without obvious cause with gloomy look, deep sadness, suffer periodic affliction from a malefic star.
- Reduced energy, frequently leading to physical slowness, mental blockage, and dampened spirit.
- Instead, the feelings are much deeper and more overpowering, especially because the consciousness finds it difficult to penetrate to the cause or meaning of such **depression.**
- The reason for this experience lies deep within the **subconscious memory,** and often points to karmic circumstances beyond the present life.
- If the events preceding the depression are carefully reviewed the individual can usually be helped to identify an image, a word, a person, or a place, which served as a trigger point for the unconscious to activate this darker material of the psyche.
- Mustard assists this healing response, helping one to come to terms with deep, un-reconciled parts of the past.
- For the kind of depression, which descends like a dark cloud and hides the sunshine and joy of life.
- The mood then sinks into a melancholic misery, the heart feeling like the weight of lead.
- People who suffer from the Mustard state are very unhappy but when asked why they feel that way, they cannot find a reason.
- They will often say that they have everything they want, a loving family, a comfortable home, holidays, no financial worries, yet they feel so low, and cannot understand why,

until it eventually lifts as suddenly as it came, only to return again and again in a fluctuating cycle.

- Something **heavy, black, unknown descends; the soul is in mourning.**
- **Gloomy depressive** feelings come out of blue, enveloping the personality like a black cloud.
- Feels excluded form normal life.
- Can see no logical connection between this condition and the rest of life.
- Completely introverted, caught up in gloom, all energies are at a low.
- Unable to cover up this mood before others.
- Unable to overcome the mood with common sense arguments.
- At the mercy of this feeling until it goes of its own accord; then feels as though set free from prison.
- Afraid of these attacks, because unable to do anything about them.
- **Unrecognized anger** at a situation or another person may be a contributory factor.

PHYSICAL SYMPTOMS DUE TO EMOTIONAL BLOCK

- These type of people will often complain using these words "I am in a blanket of awful depression with bad headaches, nothing I can think of can cheer me up, and nothing seems worth while."

PRACTICE

The soul in need of this essence feels suddenly **overwhelmed** with feelings of gloom and despair. These feelings do not appear connected with obvious episodes or situation surrounding the person's life.

Poor circulation, chilblains and lethargy.

Well known folk remedy for sore and acting feet and for dispelling chills and colds.

Chest infection, rheumatism and arthritis.

An infusion can also be used as a gargle for sore throats and tonsillitis.

Pain killing properties, it relieves toothache (to apply).

Headaches, catarrh and sinus problems.

Bronchitis and pneumonia and other respiratory infections.

Lumbago, gout, sciatica, neuralgia pain and spasm.

Plasters were made with 1 part mustard to 4 parts whole-wheat flour mixed in water into a paste. An egg added to the mixture stopped any blistering of the skin.

A hot infusion of the seed is a stimulating footbath and aids removal of colds or headaches.

THERAPEUTIC USES

Mustard is diuretic, to relieve acute local pain, easing congestion of the organs, headaches, neuralgia and spasms.

Good for cold, poor circulation, chilblains, lethargy, flu, chest infection, rheumatism, arthritis and toothache.

It helps in headaches, catarrh and sinus, bronchitis, pneumonia and other respiratory infections, lumbago, gout, sciatica, neuralgia pain and spasm.

It is antiseptic, warming, carminative, antibacterial, antiseptic, and antiviral.

Mustard aids digestion and ease gastric distention, and a laxative.

It acts as an irritant, encouraging blood flow toward the surface of the skin in cases of rheumatism, sciatica, peritonitis, and neuralgia, and for various muscle aches.

Antidepressant, P.M.S., stress, insomnia, virus, bacteria, tonic, heart, circulation, liver, stomach, uterus, regulate appetite, prevents and relives digestive spasms, constipation, nausea, soothes cracked, chapped, sensitive, dry skin, encourages wound healing. Broken veins, aging, coughs and hay fever.

Good for backache, joint pain, digestive upsets, hiccups, and as a laxative. Mustard eases constipation, minor aches and pains, and muscle stiffness.

Practice for Children

Usually there is a reason for a child's depression, in which case "Gentian" might be more appropriate, but some times it descends like a dark cloud, as if from nowhere, and is more common during puberty and adolescence than in younger children.

Positive Qualities

Mustard helps to dispel the dark cloud, which overshadows the life of these people, and thus allows the sunshine to fill their lives once again.

Transformation

It brings equilibrium and equanimity by helping the self to balance extreme polarities of light and dark. Rather than experiencing light as separate from darkness.

33. Marjoram

34. Morning Glory

35. Mulberry

36. Mustard

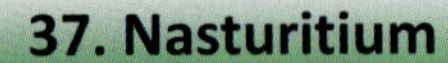

37. Nasturitium

38. Neem

39. Onion

40. Ox eye daisy

37

NASTURTIUM
(The Flower of Patriotism)

Botanical Name	:	*Tropaeolum majus*
Family Name	:	*Tropaeolaceae*
English Name	:	Nasturtium
Hindi Name	:	Jalkumbhi

GROUP

Exhaustion due to over mental work.

PLANT

This lovely bright orange, red, or yellow annual is one of the easiest and most rewarding flowers to grow from seed. Nasturtiums come from tropical South America, where they are perennial. Flowers blooms from Jan. to March.

KEY WORD

- Overly dry intellectual people.

EMOTIONAL SYMPTOMS DUE TO ENERGY BLOCK

- For **narrow-mindedness, compulsiveness, nervousness, or obsession** with an issue.
- **Hunger pangs during a fast exemplify** this.
- For those who tend to live too much in their heads, for **intellectuals** who neglect their **emotional** and physical lives.
- For students or those in phases of **life demanding strong mental activity,** whose vitality and health is depleted.
- Their struggle and suffering brings them to a point of indifference towards the trivialities of life. They become cold towards others' problems, physical or mental.

PHYSICAL SYMPTOMS DUE TO EMOTIONAL BLOCK

- Is applicable in deterioration of the nervous system, especially when the eyes are weakened.
- **Disinfectant.**
- It dissolves **respiratory congestion during colds** and aids in forming red blood cells.
- This **imbalance predisposes** the individual to many forms of physical illness, from colds and congestion in the head, to immune dysfunction and general hardening of the body.
- This essence mildly influences in the strengthening of the nervous system, enhances the assimilation of the B vitamins, and stimulates the mental body.

PRACTICE

Nasturtium may be indicated for fatigue after meditation or channeling. A deeper connection to the center of the earth may result when using Nasturtium flower essence. One's interconnection to the earth gets lost in the meditative process, and a sense of loneliness and tiredness develops.

THERAPEUTIC USES

Nasturtium is used for urinary problems, including infections such as cystitis, stones and gravel.

Good for chest congestion, bronchitis, cold, catarrh, chronic bronchitis, antibiotic, congestion.

As a natural antibiotic it will not destroy the normal bacterial population of the intestines.

Being high in iron it is helpful when feeling tired because of anemia.

Its strengthening effect was used in the past as a rejuvenative and an aphrodisiac,

Externally, nasturtium has an old reputation of retarding balding. The tincture of nasturtium was massaged regularly into the scalp- so Nasturtium helps 'keep you hair on'.

A good blood cleanser, aiding the body's elimination of toxins.

It also broadens one's horizon and aids meditation.

It invigorates the digestion, improving appetite and absorption of its nutritious contents.

It acts as a tonic for weak digestion and food stagnation, which, lead to toxicity and poor absorption.

It increases the circulation, carrying the absorbed nutrients around the body to where they are needed, giving a sense of well-being and strength.

The bitters are also detoxifying, stimulating the liver, pancreas and gall bladder activity and the secretion of digestive enzymes.

The bitters in the seeds stimulate the bowels and ensure elimination of toxins via this route.

Nasturtium acts on the kidneys and bladder, increasing elimination of waste products in the urine.

Nasturtium also has anti-microbial properties.

It is used particularly for chest infections, and because it also has decongestant properties it is well worth using to clear the phlegm that accompanies bronchial problems.

Energy tonic, eye problems, hyperactivity, metabolism (re-balancing), intellect (IQ booster), mental harmony, over-intellectual behaviour, procrastination, trapped (feeling), meditation aid, vision.

Note

It influences the pituitary chakra, and it is mild tonic for the entire endocrine system. Initiations received through the third eye or pituitary chakra make you a less narrow individual

Vitality, sensitivity, broadmindedness, joy of life force, very warming, flaming, radiant energy and warmth.

To be used during "funny spells" – when loaded by work or pre-influenza state.

Who tend to over-indulge the intellect to the detriment of their physical well being.

Revives a feeling of aliveness with vital energy.

For intellectuals who think too much and deplete their life force.

Restores warmth, vitality and radiant energy.

Restores vital physical life energy during times of intense mental level focus.

For those who know they need to make changes in their lives but seem unable to make the first move.

When the soul over-uses or over-extends thinking forces, so that they are no longer in alignment with the lower, metabolic forces of life.

Helpful for students, whose careers demand strong intellectual activity or any phase of life where the intellect predominates.

POSITIVE

This essence will ultimately provide greater levels of joy within individuals which will take root as courage within most people.

TRANSFORMATION

Nasturtium brings balance between intellectual, emotional and physical activity. It restores emotional warmth, physical vitality and earthly practicality.

38

NEEM
(The Flower of Durability)

Botanical Name	:	*Azadirachta indica*
Family Name	:	*Meliaceae*
English Name	:	Margosa
Hindi Name	:	Neem

GROUP

Absent from present life.

PLANT

Neem is a very well known tree of India. The Margosa is a very popular tree, which grows to a height of over 20 meters. The white flowers are found in branched panicles. The green fruits turn bright yellow when ripe and are one seeded. In olden days the stem was used for cleaning teeth.

KEY WORDS

- Difficulty in concentrating.

EMOTIONAL SYMPTOMS DUE TO ENERGY BLOCK

- For those who have a **strong inner life;** the ability to imagine and dream is particularly well developed.
- They are so strong that they **overwhelm** and **distort the soul's connection** with the body and the concrete physical world.
- These people are always **dreaming** and lack a vibrant emotional and physical presence in the here and now.
- His self esteem becomes vulnerable and susceptible due to physical illness. Once his ego warms up a bit he regains his spirit.

PHYSICAL SYMPTOMS DUE TO EMOTIONAL BLOCK

- For those who have **difficulty in concentrating.**
- Helps in times when there is a great need to focus such as when giving exams, tests and so forth.
- Helps integrate body, mind and spirit, creating wisdom.
- Good to take after meditation sessions.

PRACTICE

Observe the patient well, for skin problems and concentration.

Neem is useful for life. Neem is planted at the gate to clear the air.

Neem kills insects, mosquitoes. Have bath with leaves for skin disease.

THERAPEUTIC USE

It expels worms from the body, burning sensation near the heart, fever, and cough, ulcers, inflammation and leprosy.

Used as an insecticide, inflammation in the liver and skin diseases.

Bitter tonic, astringent and anti periodic, worms, tuberculosis, jaundice, inflammation, gout, arthritis, measles, chicken pox, hyper acidity, piles, heart problem, diabetes, nose, cures gases, obesity, acidity.

It is cooling also. It is for people who are heavy in weight.

For washing aching ear and eye problems.

Is used on pimples and boils to reduce the heat and pain.

Note

Flower essence is made from the flowers of an old Neem tree besides the temples of Khajuraho.

POSITIVE QUALITIES

Alertness develops and practical living takes its own shape without any ego.

TRANSFORMATION

For bringing overly cerebral people into their hearts, making them more loving, intuitive, understanding and giving, and less judgmental.

39

ONION
(The Flower of Acceptance)

Botanical Name : *Allium cepa*

Family Name : *Liliaceae*

English Name : Onion

Hindi Name : Pyaaz

GROUP

Social influences.

PLANT

Onion is a biennial or perennial plant that produces greenish-white flowers in a round ambulates cluster from Jan. to March. It originated in Asia but is now a common vegetable grown in many parts of the world with many cultivators.

KEY WORD

- Those who have suffered domestic violence.

EMOTIONAL SYMPTOMS DUE TO ENERGY BLOCK

- For **emotional liberation** and **'letting go'.**
- For a person who is **undisciplined, illogical, or irrational.**
- A skilled psychologist, of course, peels away these barriers one at a time, hopefully gradually reaching the root cause of the problems to release them, just as one peels away layer after layer of the skin to reach the sweet core of the onion.
- Another function of onion is the alleviation of emotional states in the sense that its volatile oils stimulate the eye ducts, which purges the emotions.
- For those who are **narrow-minded,** holding one-sided opinions and becoming critical of other' views and habits.
- Onions cause the body to **"weep"** which helps to release toxins.

PHYSICAL SYMPTOMS DUE TO EMOTIONAL BLOCK

- For a few individuals onion will ease pre menstrual syndromes.
- On the physical and cellular levels it works mostly on the skin, increasing the capillary action there.
- This essence is a liquid form of therapy that, during counseling sessions, slowly strips away barriers that may exist between the therapist clients.
- It aids the counselor in gradually removing barriers the mind has built around itself for protection.

PRACTICE

Cultivates tolerance, compassion and ability to listen. It also stimulates the liver. Whenever a flower essence does this, it creates a more positive emotional outlook on life, and any toxicity that can block vibrational remedies from working are weakened or discharged from the system.

THERAPEUTIC USES

Whooping cough, common cold, bronchitis, old asthma, tonsillitis, hiccup, menstruation, piles, enlargement of spleen, liver, biliousness, catchall, jaundice and excessive itching in the anus due to pin worm infection.

It cures sperm, premature ejaculation, impotency, thickens watery semen, sterility due to weak sperms, poor retentively etc.

Constant urge to pass stool with passing much mucous, indigestion, flatulent colic, gastric infections. Stimulate digestion and cleanse the intestines.

It stimulates sweating and expels worms to calm jittery nerves to relieve high blood pressure and to induce urination.

A diuretic to help eliminate fluid in heart and lung sacs.

Cures blood clotting even in horses leg.

Onion essence is given to people with fatty diets, and apparently increases the body's ability to reduce blood clots.

Helps treat viral infections and fevers. Remedy for chest, expectorant.

It warms the body and stimulates the circulation.

Onion increases blood circulation and can relax the muscles.

It is a nerve tonic, to relieve epileptic fits, tooth decay, indigestion and food poisoning, laryngitis with hoarseness, antibiotic, draws out infection.

It may provide some protection against cancer.

Strengthens the lungs.

Cleanses the intestines and helps to maintain balance of bacteria.

It acts as a digestive, it strengthens the heart, it restores sexual potency weakened by disease.

To cure ear ache caused by exposure to cold winds.

POSITIVE QUALITIES

This creates increased clarity and patience which eases the process of introspection and the emergence of repressed emotions in psychotherapy.

TRANSFORMATION

"This essence helps you to get adjusted with the domestic problems and to find the way with logic."

40

OX EYE DAISY

(The Flower of Innocence)

Botanical Name	:	*Chrysanthemum leucanthemums*
Family Name	:	*Asteraceae*
English Name	:	Ox eye daisy
Hindi Name	:	Guldaudi

GROUP

Absent from present life.

PLANT

The common daisy, known throughout the world for its cheerful face that flowers from early spring to late autumn, has always been favorite of children. Great ox-eye-daisy is found in fields throughout Europe and Northern Asia. The flowers have white petals and are golden yellow inside.

The name comes from day's eye, because the flower opens in the morning when the sun rises and closes when the sunsets.

KEY WORD

→ Vision in life.

EMOTIONAL SYMPTOMS DUE TO ENERGY BLOCK

- ❖ For those who have no clarity of mind, and the ability to absorb information and organize themselves in relation to it.
- ❖ They cannot concentrate to bring together information from different sources into a focused whole.
- ❖ It is particularly for those who suffer from the recurrent problems related, for example, to money, relationships, or learning skills, with out understanding why.
- ❖ It is also a good remedy for people involved in planning and organization.
- ❖ For vision and the visionary.
- ❖ Dissolves the blockage of fear, which prevents clear sight.

PHYSICAL SYMPTOMS DUE TO EMOTIONAL BLOCK

- ❖ Develops better vision.
- ❖ Benefits the eyes and ears.
- ❖ Chakra-third eye.
- ❖ Imbalance brings relief from nightmares and night sweats and nervous excitability.
- ❖ Daisy is a good remedy for both children and adults.

PRACTICE

In the olden days, it grew in battlefields and was used to stop bleeding and reduce bruising and shock. The cheerful little daisy is a symbol of innocence, because of its association with children, and of survival.

THERAPEUTIC USES

Ox eye daisy is helpful for antispasmodic, tonic, whooping cough, asthma and nervous excitability.

An infusion of ox-eye daisy flowers is good at relieving bronchial coughs and catarrh. It is also used as a lotion for wounds, bruises and ulcers.

It would benefit inflammatory skin conditions such as acne and boils.

It can be applied on varicose veins and haemorrhoids.

It is useful for diuretic properties, aiding the elimination of toxins, thus providing a ready remedy to detoxify the body, useful when treating arthritis and gout.

Its astringent properties are useful in curbing diarrhea and bleeding and can be used for heavy periods.

In fact the ox eye daisy used to be a popular remedy for women's problems, given for swelling in the breasts, and swelling and heat in the reproductive system.

The Ox eye daisy resembles an eye and so should be given for problems affecting the eyes. It was used for making eye baths to treat inflamed or irritated eye conditions including black eyes.

The astringent properties of the daisy would be helpful here. Ox eye daisy will staunch bleeding from cuts and wounds and taken internally and used locally it should be thought of wherever there is shock or bruising from a knock or fall.

This remedy is also a heart protector and kidney savior.

POSITIVE QUALITIES

It helps us to survive the knocks of life, like the ox eye daisy constantly which despite being trodden on, comes up smiling.

TRANSFORMATION

It brings a greater perspective when we cannot see the woods of the trees.

41

PANSY

(The Flower of Thoughts)

Botanical Name	:	*Viola tricolor*
Family Name	:	*Violaceae*
English Name	:	Pansy/Heartsease
Hindi Name	:	Gul Sosan

GROUP

Fear.

PLANT

Hardy perennial herbs, useful in borders. It is known as 'heart ease' as it's shape resembles the heart. Annual flower blooms from January to March. Colour blue, violet, yellow or two colour.

KEY WORD

→ Fear of Viral.

EMOTIONAL SYMPTOMS DUE TO ENERGY BLOCK

- For those experiencing a deep-seated **sense of grief** over the loss of a loved one. Affects adrenal and kidney function. Brings transcendence over grief, pointing the way to new outlets for our loving nature and generosity. Helps in the elimination of toxins.
- It stimulates the mental body by propagating and magnifying the essence of thought forms.
- It is effective in the **right-hand portion of the brain,** where the intuitive faculties reside.
- Pansy looks like the diaphragms or psychic membranes associated with the chakras.
- Pansy is for **thoughts.**
- Wild pansy or heartsease has close association with the affairs of the heart in myth and legend. It is so called for its ability to **heal the heart** and ease a broken heart.
- It soothes the pain of separation from loved ones.

PHYSICAL SYMPTOMS DUE TO EMOTIONAL BLOCK

- No particular emotional states are associated with this essence because viruses are not influenced by intense emotional factors, except on occasion when there is lung congestion.
- This is an **exceptional remedy** against most **forms of viruses** from the common cold or AIDS to **herpes or hepatitis.**
- Sudden tiredness may sometimes be the initial effect of interaction of viruses with the immune system. Use pansy, but if possible, rest within half an hour.

- ❖ If **tiredness** develops after meditation, it is the immune system kicked into aching from the meditative process.
- ❖ Pansy is quite useful in treating bovine leukemia and the new forms of AIDS characterized as HTLV II as well as HTLV I.
- ❖ Hardy resistance for any one feeling low or vulnerable or susceptible to frequent viral illness. It balances the immune system, encourages strength resistance and the will to over come illness.

PRACTICE

Heartsease (pansy) is used for healing the heart. It is for disappointment in love, in separation, and when broken hearts cause symptoms in those previously happy and healthy.

Note

The flower's common name pansy comes from the French pansies meaning thoughts. In Hamlet Aphelia says, "There is pansies– that's for thoughts". In the Victorian language of flowers heartsease means 'you are in my thoughts'. People also believed that if they carried a pansy it would ensure the love of their sweetheart. Adrenal glands also get better with pansy.

THERAPEUTIC USES

Heartsease has cooling, cleansing and anti-inflammatory properties.

In the respiratory system, the mucilage in heartsease is soothing, while an expectorant action making it good remedy for harsh irritating coughs, asthma, croup and bronchitis.

It reduces fevers and swollen glands, and acts as a soothing diuretic for fluid retention and cystitis.

Pansy relieves inflamed joints in arthritis and gout.

It also reduces blood pressure and arteriosclerosis, helps strengthen blood capillaries, and thereby stops bruising.

Helps in the elimination of toxins, also effective for clearing the painful itching of cold sores/herpes.

Heartsease is used similarly for skin problems, particularly cradle cap, eczema of the scalp, impetigo and scabby skin complaints. Symptoms tend to be worse in winter and cold air. It is indicated for people with swollen cervical glands, coughs, and phlegm in the throat, for rheumatism, gout and itching eruptions around the joints.

It is also prescribed for bedwetting in children who have vivid or disturbing dreams, and whose urine smells particularly strong.

It is also taken for conditions relating to the heart-anxiety and palpitations on lying down.

It also reduces blood pressure.

POSITIVE QUALITIES

These type of people get strength to face the viral and think positive.

TRANSFORMATION

They enter a "free mind" mode and are able to think clearly and take care of themselves.

42

PEEPAL

(The Flower of Sensitivity)

Botanical Name	:	*Ficus religiosa*
Family Name	:	*Moraceae*
English Name	:	Ficus
Hindi Name	:	Peepal

GROUP

Fear.

PLANT

Peepal is the only tree of nature, which always gives oxygen unlike other trees, which leaves nitrogen in the night. Generally near the temple and old village houses there was always a Peepal tree for clean environment. Peepal is an old plant of India. In olden days for any occult fear people used to sit under the tree. In India people pray under this tree. A huge tree with grayish bark. Leaves smooth skinning, broadly ovate, apex long and narrow 12-18 cm long. The tree is indigenous in Bengal and Burma and is cultivated all over India. Peepal doesn't flower but has fruits and in the fruits the flower is there when open. It is very strange that wherever bird droppings fall Peepal will grow and the roots will come on the roof also. It is called 'Ghuie Pushpak.'

Note

Gautam Budhha achieved nirvana and enlightenment after great meditation while sitting under a peepal tree. Sine then the tree has been named as Bodhi-tree. To remove the danger of snakes in the house put some branches of peepal tree.

Peepal leaves are the staple food of silk worms. These white silk worms are in Assam. Small twigs and bark are eaten with relish by the elephants that is why in Sanskrit peepal is called "Gaj Patra" "Gaj Bhaksak".

KEY WORD

- Anticipatory fear.

EMOTIONAL SYMPTOMS DUE TO ENERGY BLOCK

- For those who develop goose flushes, vague anxiety, hidden fear and apprehension.
- For those who suffer **vague or acute fears** for no apparent reason.
- Such people are more **sensitive** than most– they rustle even in the slightest breeze like the leaves of the tree.
- They are easily affected by the collective **unconscious** and by **superstition, myth** and **legend,** and by concepts of life and death and religion.
- **Anxiety** and **apprehension** can creep up on Peepal type of people both during the night and day.
- They may wake up in the night with **terror,** and may dread going back to sleep again.

- ❖ Their fears are often connected with **thoughts of death** or religion or a sense of disaster.
- ❖ Creepy sensation of fear, as if bewitched.
- ❖ Self deceptive, delusions, over imaginativeness.
- ❖ Fearful fascination with occult phenomena, superstitious. Magical concept, panic in the dark with no explanations.
- ❖ Fear of persecution, of punishment. Fear of an invisible force or power.
- ❖ Nightmares, waking in fear and panic and not daring to go back to sleep.
- ❖ Afraid of thoughts and dreams on religious subjects, darkness and death.
- ❖ Afraid of fear, but doesn't dare to talk about it with anyone.

PHYSICAL SYMPTOMS DUE TO EMOTIONAL BLOCK

- ❖ The fear can be so-intense, so as to become terrifying and cause **trembling,** sweating and butterflies in the stomach.
- ❖ For enhancing the **sense of smell** which has been blocked by mucus or shock.
- ❖ One is caught up in subconscious anxieties. Have been born without a protective skin layer.

PRACTICE

It is good for newborn children and old people too.

Note

Tree leaves give such a soothing sound that when you sit under it and meditate, it helps you in relaxing your mind. It is very hygienic, clear and cooling.

In The Vedas it is written that Peepal increases your intellectual level and alertness.

Sitting under the tree keeps you healthy and gives long life.

This is the only tree through which the rays of the sun can penetrate down to the bark; therefore there is always light under the tree.

Leaves are always moving in stillness of air, that is why Peepal is called 'Jal Patra' that is continuous walking, implying that you have to do deeds in life.

THERAPEUTIC USES

Peepal is for all types of urinary problems, blue urine and sexually transmitted diseases like Gonorrhea etc.

It is helpful for impotency, diabetes and good to increase the breast milk.

Good for those ladies whose babies do not survive.

It is good for vomiting, nausea, thirst and mucus.

Good for blood related problems and acidity; it increases the taste for food and digestion.

Good for health, rejuvenation, memory, life threatening diseases and longevity.

When there is lack of oxygen, this essence will help.

It is good for controlling excess hunger.

Good for asthma, leprosy, breathing problem, bronchitis, diphtheria, tuberculosis, acidity, diabetes, boils, pimples, heavy wounds, venomous bites, night blindness, malaria, earache, deafness, cold, irregular periods, headaches.

POSITIVE QUALITIES

The flower remedy increases inner strength and confidence, and helps to still fears and anxieties.

TRANSFORMATION

It enhances the awareness of a higher power behind and above all existence, and the ability to trust more in the divine power of love, encouraging one into a wider range of experiences and adventures without fear holding one back.

43

PEPPERMINT
(The Flower of Refreshment)

Botanical Name : *Mentha piperita*
Family Name : *Lamiaceae*
English Name : Peppermint
Hindi Name : Podina

GROUP

Indecisive.

PLANT

One of the most popular herb teas in the world, easily grown in gardens, but is a rather invasive plant. Try growing it in a bucket buried in the ground, with the bottom knocked out.

KEYWORDS

- Stuck between two things.

EMOTIONAL SYMPTOMS DUE TO ENERGY BLOCK

- For those who feel **lethargic,** and **mentally cloudy** or **apathetic,** often related to digestive or metabolic imbalances.
- They may crave for food, which then makes them feel sluggish or sleepy afterwards.
- **Getting stuck between two things. Oscillating to and fro.** Whether I should do this or that.
- Peppermint imparts alert clarity and mental vibrancy.
- Those who need this remedy have a soul struggle between the lower and upper parts of their being especially between the metabolic/digestive forces and the thinking/creative forces. In these cases, the life or metabolic forces overwhelm the consciousness with too much warmth, making the mental capacity dull and lethargic.
- Peppermint is at once **cooling and warming**. It cools down the lower organs, especially the liver, so that the consciousness can be freed for higher activity.
- They may crave the stimulation of food, only to find themselves sluggish and mentally incapacitated afterwards.
- It is as though two parts of the Self are warring for attention.
- For those who live in **fear of losing loved ones.**
- They fear and are acutely emotional regarding the loss of possessions, health, and security of their loved ones.
- May suffer inner conflict related to an incomplete relationship with their mother.
- Builds confidence and a sense of control; fosters the ability to visualize a future in which their desires are fulfilled making life feel safer.
- Develops mental clarity and a quick wit, encourages active and awakened thought processes.

- ❖ Good for students and intellectuals.

PHYSICAL SYMPTOMS DUE TO EMOTIONAL BLOCK

- ❖ It stimulates the thinking forces so that they have a "digestive capacity" of a higher nature, making the thinking livelier, vital, and penetrating.
- ❖ Many people who need Peppermint have profound issues around eating and consciousness.
- ❖ Also aids protein digestion and treats gastric ulcers.

PRACTICE

It has been recognized by orthodox doctors as being useful in the treatment of liver and gall-bladder disorders. It promotes the flow of bile. One of its traditional functions is to dispel gas.

THERAPEUTIC USES

It relieves indigestion, flatulence, spasms, diarrhea, nausea, colic, wind, vomiting, depressed appetite, menstrual cramps, and gall bladder pain, stomach cramps, and travel sickness.

The antiseptic qualities of peppermint make it a useful gargle for **sore throats.**

It also helps to **open the skin pores and cause sweats** and tone the liver, intestines, and the nervous system.

It is a valuable expectorant in the treatment of bronchitis, colds, sinus, blocked nose and flu, and it can reduce fevers by inducing sweating and cooling the body.

Peppermint is a painkiller, is beneficial for toothaches, headaches, and some migraines. It is a good inhalant to clear **catarrh** and **blocked sinuses.**

It relieves itching, is a useful antiseptic for acne and congested skin, and is an emergency remedy for shock.

Muscle and mental fatigue are both relieved by peppermint.

It clears our palate and stimulates our senses.

POSITIVE QUALITIES

Peppermint brings clarity, and mental alertness.

TRANSFORMATION

Peppermint brings great healing and balancing energy, freeing the mind for higher thought, and helping the digestive life forces work in their proper sphere.

44

PERIWINKLE

(The Flower of Patience)

Botanical Name : *Vinca minor L.*

Family Name : *Apocyanaceae*

English Name : Periwinkle

Hindi Name : Sadabahar

GROUP

Loner.

PLANT

An erect plant, 30-60 cms high, with simple opposite leaves and white or rosy flowers. It is a perennial and annual shrub found in the Himalayas. There are over six hundred species, and they belong to the *Balsamaceous* family. The color which is used in essence is dark pink. The flowers bloom in summers. They can grow any where; do not need care, are very common.

KEY WORD

- Impatience.

EMOTIONAL SYMPTOMS DUE TO ENERGY BLOCK

- Those who are **quick in implementing thoughts** into action and who wish all things to be done without hesitation or delay.
- **Impatience, irritability, nervous indigestion.**
- For **deep emotionalism** concerning family, nation and race.
- They are **upset** when the link is broken.
- Bestows the need for humility and an increasing capacity for compassion.
- For **insomnia,** cools the mind bringing peace.
- Always in a **hurry** to finish the work.
- For those who feel like taking work away from those people who are very slow.
- Tend to take words out of others mouth when they are slow in speaking.
- They hurt themselves while walking because they are in such a hurry that they can't see.
- Find it hard to wait for things to take their course.
- Spontaneous, active, energetic, impatiently take things into their own hands.
- Cannot stand fools gladly. Great desire for independence.
- Extreme **inner tension** makes them accident prone, though the **anger** passes just as quickly.
- Excessive self-willedness and self-imposed limits on their personality.
- These people are extroverts. If they do not relieve their state in words, they resort to frequently gesturing, drumming their fingers on the table.

- ❖ They can alienate people by being brusque and unsympathetic, speaking their mind quickly and without thought.
- ❖ It is for an emotional state of irritation, for tension and pain.
- ❖ When ill they are anxious for a hasty recovery.

PHYSICAL SYMPTOMS DUE TO EMOTIONAL BLOCK

- ❖ **Short term exhaustion, sudden hunger** because energy resources depleted by fast pace.
- ❖ Nervous indigestion. Hot flushes.
- ❖ Due to impatient nature they can develop cramps, sudden pain, tension in back.

PRACTICE

For those people who are fidgety and find it hard to sit still when they are sitting and talking. Indigestion problem and nervous tension.

Note

This remedy is one of the five remedies in 'I rescue' remedy. It removes the stiffness of the body. This essence has the quality of balancing the central nervous system.

THERAPEUTIC USES

Good as a laxative, astringent, tranquilizer.

Periwinkle is good for treating cancer specially leukemia, breast and bladder. Diabetes, fistula, sprained ankle, skin eruption, sudden excessive or prolonged menstrual bleeding, pediatric tumour, cardiotonic pains, cramps, tension in back, neck, jaws, shoulders, rashes, skin irritation, fistula, diabetes and low blood pressure.

Mild constipation, ringworm, insomnia, stimulates liver activity.

It has thus been used as an adjunctive treatment for jaundice and some hepatic – related ophthalmic conditions.

External treatment for hemorrhoids and other varicose conditions.

POSITIVE QUALITIES

It helps to be less hasty in action and thought; more relaxed, tolerant, and gentle towards shortcomings of others and 'upsetting conditions'.

TRANSFORMATION

The goal is patient acceptance, flowing with the pace of life and others.

41. Pansy

42. Peepal

43. Peppermint

44. Periwinkle

45. Petunia

46. Pine

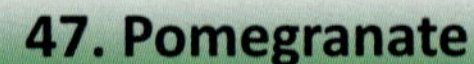

47. Pomegranate

48. Poppy Red

45

PETUNIA
(The Flower of Peace)

Botanical Name : *Petunia hybrida*

Family Name : *Solanaceae*

English Name : Petunia

Hindi Name : Petunia

GROUP

Fear.

PLANT

This popular garden flower is native to South America. The flowers come in mauve, pink, purple, white, or yellow colors, often speckled striped or veined in various shades.

KEY WORDS

✈ Mischievous and hyperactive.

EMOTIONAL SYMPTOMS DUE TO ENERGY BLOCK

- These people have an uncontrolled temper and staring eyes. They remain agitated and desperate, and get bouts of hysteria.
- **Impulse to do harm** to other people or themselves, suffers from long periods of **anxiety or depression.**
- Feeling of no longer being able to keep the inner control mechanism going.
- Toy with the idea of **putting an end** to it.
- If taken internally or externally, it eases **nervous tensions.**

PHYSICAL SYMPTOMS DUE TO EMOTIONAL BLOCK

- Petunia is rapidly assimilated into the body through the skin.
- It can be used to treat **speech impediments** such as stuttering and most ailments associated with the **left portion of the brain.**
- Petunia increases blood flow to specific parts of the body, which assists healing.
- Anything that increases the blood flow to a region of the body stimulates that area. So petunia could be considered a mild aphrodisiac. It could be rubbed over erogenous zones.

PRACTICE

This negative state is not always easy to diagnose from external appearances. More extreme states often betray themselves by eyes that are wide open, staring and blinking less than normal.

Note

Helps when the mood is of an acute or sudden nature and is indicated wherever there is a lack of emotional control such as sudden outbursts of irrational and uncharacteristic rage or violence or hysteria.

THERAPEUTIC USE

Increases blood flow, relieves nervousness, tension, stuttering, it treats left side of the brain, bruises, scars, inflammation of the frontal sinuses, pain across the cheekbones, blinding and persistent headaches, feeling of desperation.

It is an antidepressant, and has a calming effect on hyperactive children.

POSITIVE QUALITIES

Bestows a quiet calm courage and endurance and the ability to face all unhappy and distressing experiences of life bravely, never losing control of their emotions.

TRANSFORMATION

Mind becomes cool and controlled.

46

PINE

(The Flower of Assurance)

Botanical Name	:	*Pinus strobus*
Family Name	:	*Pinaceae*
English Name	:	Soft pine
Hindi Name	:	Cheed

GROUP

Unhappy.

PLANT

It grows to a height of about 36 meters. Bark is brown-red towards the bottom, and orange-brown and flaky in the upper crown. Male and female flowers appear on the same tree, yellow and red respectively. Flowers from May to June.

KEY WORDS

- Self-blame and guilt.

EMOTIONAL SYMPTOMS DUE TO ENERGY BLOCK

- For the feeling of guilt, often using apologetic terms in phrases and conversation.
- **Tend to blame oneself for past and recent mistakes.**
- Introvert.
- Find little joy in life.
- Feel's partly responsible for the mistakes of others.
- Set's the highest standards for himself – more than others – and feels guilty at heart if unable to live up to them.
- Even if successful, feels he could have done this, or that even better.
- Look more to limits than potential, self-destructively undermines self with **negative image.**
- Feels **unworthy, inferior, an underdog waiting for the stick.**
- Psyches himself about being ill and lands up feeling **depressed** or **exhausted.**
- In their heart of hearts, they consider themselves **cowards.**
- **Undervalues self-extremely, negative narcissism.**
- Finds it difficult to accept anything, unconsciously feels he does not deserve anything.
- The child tends to be the **scapegoat** in class, taking the blame for the mistakes of others, accepting punishments without complaining.
- Mother who feels guilty about not being able to successfully breast-feed straight away, feels she has failed and has let herself and her baby down.

PHYSICAL SYMPTOMS DUE TO EMOTIONAL BLOCK

- It can be given to those suffering mental, physical or sexual depletion and adrenal insufficiency as it has a stimulating effect on the adrenal medulla and cortex.
- It helps in infections and the discomfort that accompanies cystitis, by aiding the elimination of toxins via the kidneys.

PRACTICE

Broadens one's outlook. For those who are discontented, critical, over-conscientious, apologetic and over humble. The constant effort to improve themselves may lead to fatigue and depression. Pine + Mulberry or Willow is good.

Pine is for perfectionists, not for ordinary people. They may be outstanding in their field but never seem quite content with themselves or their endeavors. They can be overly conscientious and strive to live up to the high standards that they place upon themselves. This state of being can lead to overwork and/or a constant effort to improve them selves.

Pine is for those who feel remorse concerning past actions that have led to their current financial state. These feelings would include guilt or being overly hard on oneself. For eating yourself up or for the intense desire for perfection at all costs.

THERAPEUTIC

Remedy for the lungs, liquefies and helps to expel bronchial phlegm, clears the head of congestion and is an anti-inflammatory.

Its antispasmodic action in the chest will help relieve asthma and a harsh tight cough.

It is an antiseptic, good for catarrh, colds, sinuses, eases breathing (inhaling), hay fever, rheumatic and muscular pains, headaches, toothache, flu, sore throats, pneumonia, tuberculosis, poor circulation, digestion, tiredness, weakness, excessive perspiration, tonic revitalizing, arthritis, gout and is beneficial for the urinary system.

To prevent and secure the infestation with lice, fleas and scabies.

Remedy for chronic skin diseases such as eczema.

It has a beneficial effect on the bladder and kidney systems and **fluid retention.**

POSITIVE

Willing to take the responsibility and bear the burdens of others and accept their faults and not cling to them. They have great powers of perseverance and effort and are rightly humble about their gifts.

TRANSFORMATION

The confidence and clarity leads to not feeling guilty about others' behaviour and to accept it is their fault.

47

POMEGRANATE
(The Flower of Growth)

Botanical Name : *Punica granatum*
Family Name : *Punicaceae*
English Name : Pomegranate
Hindi Name : Anaar

GROUP

Unhappy.

PLANT

A deciduous shrub or small tree young branches four angled and spiny at apex leaves, oblong, glabrous flowers dark red, fruits hard out side and fleshy in side. It is a native of Iran and Afghanistan. It spread early around the Mediterranean and eastwards to India, China, and Japan and is cultivated mostly around Pune, Gujrat, Uttar Pradesh. It has several varieties which differ from one another in colour of the rind and seeds and size of the fruit. The sweet ruby and the sour varieties are most popular. The plant was developed partly so that its flowers would create a powerful symbolism for people at deep levels relating to the ultimate purpose of the root chakra particularly its highest spiritual nature.

KEY WORDS

- Emotional problems and insecurity of women.

EMOTIONAL SYMPTOMS DUE TO ENERGY BLOCK

- It is to provide the ability to tap into deep levels of **courage** and **strength** whenever necessary.
- It is very important in allowing the transition to flow easily and smoothly.
- This is a remedy for women.
- It can universally apply for any **emotional problems,** but particularly for problems women are experiencing.
- It is a love potion for women, and if they have trouble accepting their **femininity,** it helps them overcome such insecurities.
- It creates a sense of nurturing within the individual.
- Feels unloved from childhood.

PHYSICAL SYMPTOMS DUE TO EMOTIONAL BLOCK

- They may have diarrhea, styptic, dysentery, stomach ache, eye and throat problem.
- Irregular menstruation, constipation, root chakra energy problem, yeast infection in the vaginal tract and excessive dryness in the entire physical body in women are also assisted.
- It has some beneficial effects on the cardiovascular system.

- It increases blood flows to the cervix, clitoris, fallopian tubes, ovaries, uterus, and vaginal lining.
- It is a marvelous remedy for treating tumors and cysts in these areas.
- It is used as a brain tonic especially during over work and exhaustion.

PRACTICE

- Men who have trouble developing the maternal aspect of their personality would also benefit from it.
- A woman could **conceive** sextuplets with this essence.

THERAPEUTIC USES

It is a cooling astringent, anti-diarrhea, styptic, anti-dysentery, stomachic, brain tonic, appetizer, blood purifier, anthelmintic, ophthalmic, aphrodisiac, pharyngitis.

It acts on the liver, heart, kidneys, tones up their functions, beneficial in digestive disorders.

It binds the stools and tones up the intestines, results in bilious vomiting and nausea, burning in chest due to excessive secretion, flatulence and maiming sickness, asthmatic fevers, dysentery, weakness, piles of any type, tapeworms, eye ailments, conjunctivitis, eye pain due to strain, preserves eyesight, kidney stones, bladder, gums bleeding, prevents pyorrhea, anal itching, cough, throat problem, astringent, prolapsed of anus, cure of anal itching, spleen disorder, anemia, gastric disorder, applied on gums to stop bleeding and bleeding piles.

POSITIVE

Relaxes the mind and initiates a sense of positivity in the midst of problems.

TRANSFORMATION

This essence creates a sense of recognition for the need to nurture one self.

48

POPPY RED
(The Flower of Underworld)

Botanical Name : *Papaver somniferum L*
Family Name : *Papaveraceae*
English Name : Corn poppy
Hindi Name : Posta

GROUP

Absent from present life.

PLANT

In Greek mythology the opium poppy was an attribute of the goddess Demeter. They are red in color and in India they grow in winters as an annual, flowering from Feb. to March.

KEY WORD

- Day dreamer.

EMOTIONAL SYMPTOMS DUE TO ENERGY BLOCK

- Poppy is for those who do not have **balance in their daily life** between activity and rest, the spiritual and the physical, evolution and being.
- For escapists who find it hard to face up to the realities of life and tend to live in the world of **imagination and dreams.**
- For those who are **fearful of expressing strong emotions** such as **anger.**
- For men who mistreat women sexually, seeing them merely as objects.
- Enhances past-life recall in those consciously seeking it.
- Can increase forgiveness of our own past-life actions and those of others.
- For dependent, selfish people who can be jealous and covet others belongings.

PHYSICAL SYMPTOMS DUE TO EMOTIONAL BLOCK

- Poppy natured people can develop colitis and constipation
- It takes away the awareness of pain.
- It also affects the muscles of the body in small doses, causing relaxation.

PRACTICE

In small amounts this has a transitory exhilarating effect as the mind floats free and the imagination has full play.

THERAPEUTIC USES

For mucous colitis, constipation and tuberculosis

It is used for pain relief, particularly post-operatively and in cancer.

It acts on the circulation by engorging the blood vessels of the brain.

It is used for insensitivity of the nervous system, painless symptoms, sleepiness, lethargy, lack of vital reaction, even stupor.

It has also been used for cases of typhoid, cholera in infants, stroke, T.B. and diabetes.

The poppy red has been employed medicinally over the ages as a mild sedative to induce sleep in babies.

The flowers contain traces of alkaloids that would act as a sedative, but no scientific studies have been carried out to prove this effect.

It is used to ease pain. It may be used for chest complaints, e.g., pleurisy and as a pediatric cough syrup.

POSITIVE QUALITIES

❖ It lends courage to assert yourself, to express your feelings in their entire color and to shine like the bright red poppy. They try to cultivate generosity and service to others.

TRANSFORMATION

It brings a caring responsibility and love back to sex without diminishing physical arousal or pleasure.

49

RADISH
(The Flower of Confidence)

Botanical Name : *Raphanus sativus*
Family Name : *Brassicaceae*
English Name : Radish
Hindi Name : Muli

GROUP

Unhappy.

PLANT

It is a tuberous root vegetable, which grows through out the year. It has too many varieties, round, red, long white. One of the best-known and most used medicinal plants is the long thin bitter white radish. The white colour flowers bloom in March.

KEY WORD

→ Find it difficult to cope in life.

EMOTION SYMPTOMS DUE TO ENERGY BLOCK

- They are tired and confused with lack of confidence, self-censorship, and a negative mental attitude.
- For any one suffering from **bereavement.**
- People suffering from a sense of being **unable to cope.**
- Feel **too confused** to organize their work and finish it.
- Feel **exhausted** when work is in front of them.
- If there is a demise, these people find it difficult to handle the situation and they get upset about the future.
- Mind become **negative** when problems come in front of them.
- Their objective is not clear.
- These type of people have lived in comfort and therefore they don't know how to handle problems, because they have never seen all this in life.

PHYSICAL SYMPTOMS DUE TO EMOTIONAL BLOCK

- It is a good remedy of scurvy, gravel and stone, and has been beneficial in preventing the formation of gallstones.

PRACTICE

They are lazy and not ready to struggle in life, they are scared in facing problems with confidence.

THERAPEUTIC USE

It is good as an appetizer, digestive, carminative, diuretic, laxative, anti-calculi.

Used in diarrhea, cystitis, swelling, asthma, cough, earache, urinary disease and bleeding piles.

Increases fertility, gent's semen, helps in avoiding miscarriages.

Skin colour gets better and face becomes beautiful, removes dryness.

Cleans the face from acnes, pimples, and pigmentation.

Helps in toothache, good for bones, exhaustion, worms, ulcers, piles, blood circulatory problem, stiffness, heart problem, jaundice, obesity, diabetes, cold, cough, skin problem and itching.

It clears sinuses and sore throat.

Radish takes out carbon dioxide from the body and gives oxygen.

Helpful for urine problems, flatulence and obesity.

Reduces lice from hair, if massaged daily.

POSITIVE QUALITIES

Specifically strengthens and reorders the mind, affording mental objectivity, and general well being.

TRANSFORMATION

Brings comfort after the death of some one very close and integrates the mind after shock and trauma or bereavement.

50

RANGOON CREEPER

(The Flower of Stability)

Botanical Name : *Quisqualis indica*

Family Name : *Combretaceae*

English Name : Rangoon Creeper

Hindi : Madhu Malti

GROUP

Loner.

PLANT

A large scan dent shrubby climber, goes up to the height of 15-20 feet, with simple opposite leaves, flowers terminal in drooping spikes. It is a climber whose flowers are white-rosy-scarlet, blooming in October.

KEY WORD

✈ Gets influenced by other people.

EMOTIONAL SYMPTOMS DUE TO ENERGY BLOCK

- They are restless, mentally confused and have uncertainty; doubting oneself; invalidating own sense of truth and seeking inappropriate advice from others.
- **Fear of rejection, running away from life.**
- **Anger** always burning within, heated thoughts.

  Emotional malnutrition, lack of love and security
- These people get **influenced by other people** and follow them.
- They don't want to struggle in life.
- Want an **easy way of life** and want to run away from realities.
- **Will power is weak,** they get carried away by powerful gurus.
- Cult leaders **easily capture their soul** and they move with these people leaving their families.
- For **restless wanderers** who are willing but are unable to settle down.
- These types of people are **not bitter, but confused.**
- They are very simple, **sweet to talk to** and of pleasant behavior, but are unsatisfied.

PHYSICAL SYMPTOMS DUE TO EMOTIONAL BLOCK

- Allergy on skin.

PRACTICE

Their insecurity and desire for love and attention, makes them vulnerable and they take to gurus and cults.

THERAPEUTIC USE

Diarrhoea, fever, rickettsia (negative micro-organism which spreads to men from lice, fleas, ticks), parasitic skin problems.

POSITIVE QUALITIES

Frees those who are entangled in gurus and cults and bestows them with the courage to root themselves and surrender the urge to wander.

TRANSFORMATION

Brings coolness, peace and love and calms the expression on the face.

51

ROSE RED
(The Flower of Love)

Botanical Name	:	*Rosa indica*
Family Name	:	*Rosaceae*
English Name	:	Rose
Hindi Name	:	Gulab

GROUP

Exhaustion due to demands.

PLANT

The birthplace of the cultivated rose was probably Northern Persia, now Iran, from where it was taken to Turkey, Greece, Italy and the rest of Europe. In India flowers bloom from Nov. to March. It flowers through out but the size and frequency is less.

KEY WORD

- Demands love.

EMOTIONAL SYMPTOMS DUE TO ENERGY BLOCK

- They **demand love** and are **never satisfied.**
- They are **possessive, domineering, excessively interfering and manipulative.**
- They always feel **insecure, have fear of being alone,** or **loosing friends,** family or possessions.
- Take pleasure in constantly commenting on things, of loved ones, correcting and **criticizing** them.
- Have to have "loved ones around them like a court, in order to monitor and guide their lives."
- They are always **over concerned** about their loved ones and can force them into things which may harm them.
- Selfish **conditional love.**
- **Saps their victim's vitality.**
- Finds it **hard to forgive** those for whom he is concerned.
- May escape into illness on occasion to gain sympathy or achieve ends with the dear ones.
- Gets angry or **starts weeping** if not getting attention from the dear ones.

PHYSICAL SYMPTOMS DUE TO EMOTIONAL BLOCK

- In men they have been used to treat **impotence.**
- For women who feel **insecure** about their sexuality, and lack confidence in loving, intimate relationships.

PRACTICE

The rose is the **symbol of love.** The red rose increases confidence in those feeling insecure about their sexuality and who suffer from feelings of shame or timidity about their bodies. It helps you to open up to love and bring your desires into action.

THERAPEUTIC USES

Rose acts as a tonic for the heart, circulation, liver, stomach, and uterus, and helps to detoxify the blood and organs.

It regulates the appetite, and prevents and relieves digestive spasms, constipation, and nausea soothes cracked, chapped, sensitive, dry, inflamed, or allergy-prone skin, stops bleeding, and encourages wound healing.

Broken veins and aging or wrinkled skin also benefit.

Rose has an affinity with the female reproductive system, helping to regulate the menstrual cycle and alleviate PMS or post-natal depression.

It benefits stress-related conditions such as insomnia and nervous tension, and is a powerful antiseptic against viruses and bacteria.

Rose is also useful in treating headaches, earache, conjunctivitis, coughs, and hay fever.

In the digestive system this helps reduce hyperacidity and over activity bringing excessive hunger and thirst and often mouth ulcers.

Rose can relieve cold and flu symptoms, sore throat, runny nose, as well as blocked bronchial tubes.

It cures spitting of blood and elimination of wastes through the urinary system.

It has been used for stones and gravel in the kidneys and bladder.

An infusion makes a useful remedy for diarrhea, enteritis and dysentery.

Note

Brides and bridegrooms were crowned with roses; they were scattered on the marriage bed, and worn as garlands at feasts, apparently to prevent drunkenness.

POSITIVE QUALITIES

The rose is the remedy of independence. It is traditionally said to mean 'pleasure and pain' as it brings pleasure to the eyes and heart when found blooming, but pain from its sharp prickles if you try to pluck it.

Inspires selfless love given freely, respecting the freedom and individuality of others.

TRANSFORMATION

Rose red warms the heart and softens the emotions, engendering an easy-going feeling to enhance sensuality.

52

SALVIA
(The Flower of Immortality)

Botanical Name	:	*Salvia chinensis*
Family Name	:	*Labiatae*
English Name	:	Chinese Sage
Hindi Name	:	Salvia

GROUP

Unhappy.

PLANT

It is an annual plant, seeds are sown is November or late October and flower blooms in February-March. Colour is red.

KEY WORD

- Phobia for cleanliness.

SYMPTOMS

- ❖ Always doubt of poison in body and feels infected.
- ❖ It paranoid about cleanliness.
- ❖ **Cleaning remedy,** for those having the feeling of having been soiled, e.g., by disease, pollution, touching a dirty object or dealing with an infected material.
- ❖ They must **wash their hands again and again** for hygiene. They will repeatedly inspect, say for instance a knife, in a restaurant.
- ❖ **Self-disgust on negative thoughts, unkind words spoken,** egoistical towards others.
- ❖ **Self-condemnation** for having done something not in accord with own inner nature.
- ❖ **Perfect housekeeper,** showing her cleanliness.
- ❖ Feels everything has to be **as neat as a pin.**
- ❖ **Sensitive** to lack of order in both public and private life.
- ❖ They **feel ugly** in feeding a child.
- ❖ For those who do not like them selves, so become "rebels",
- ❖ For **selfishness,** intellectual hostility, defiance, criticism of others and life in general, irresponsibility.
- ❖ Feels disgust with, e.g., skin eruption, sweaty feet, spots and warts.
- ❖ Children are fussy about their toys if they are dirty, or dislike cleaning their own stool and playing in dirt. Girls at their puberty feel ugly.

PHYSICAL SYMPTOMS DUE TO EMOTIONAL BLOCK

- ❖ The feeling of ugliness due to having pimples on face will go, and Salvia will also clean the face.

PRACTICE

Urge to be perfect; they often fall into fanatic tidiness and perfectionism. Conscientious and tidy. Students who must complete their homework in an ideal manner. Sensitive to any kind of disorder and find inner peace only when everything is in its proper place.

THERAPEUTIC USES

Improves moles, birthmarks, constipation, warts, skin disease, pimples, pigmentation and rashes. (For external use apply cream.)

HOW TO MAKE A CREAM

Take 100 gm pure cream, without essence and perfume, and add 30 drops of mother tincture and mix well.

POSITIVE QUALITIES

To get rid of any thing we do not like either in the mind or the body, e.g., rash or warts or growth.

TRANSFORMATION

- These people now maintain complete control of their thoughts and have the wisdom to see things in their correct proportion. Brings constructive changes to one's self image.

49. Radish

50. Rangoon Creeper

51. Rose Red

52. Salvia

53. Snapdragon

54. Sunflower

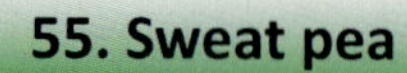

55. Sweat pea

56. Tamarind

53

SNAPDRAGON
(The Flower of Positivity)

Botanical Name	:	*Antirrhinum Majus*
Family Name	:	*Plantaginaceae*
English Name	:	Snapdragon
Hindi name	:	Dog Flower

GROUP

Exhaustion due to mental brewing.

PLANT

This plant, which is native to the Mediterranean, is now widely cultivated as a garden flower. It blooms in winter from Feb.-March with orange, pink, purple, red, white, or yellow-colored flowers.

KEY WORD

- Misdirected libido energy.

EMOTIONAL SYMPTOMS DUE TO ENERGY BLOCK

- **Abusive nature, aggressive behavior, too much anger, talks with authority, blames others.**
- **Creative** by nature yet **destructiveness.**
- They are **honest people** with strong instincts yet are irritable and can harbor hatred.
- **Think low** about themselves, **negative** thinking.
- The positive Snapdragon type, possesses strong physical presence.
- Such persons are **highly energetic,** with powerful will and libido.
- In some cases, these energies are so pronounced that they over-ride the other chakras of the body.
- In other instances, these forces may have been culturally repressed, causing the energy to be improperly released elsewhere in the body.
- With both these **patterns of imbalance,** the individual will **miss-direct** digestive and sexual forces, which rightly belong in the lower energy centers, distorting them through expression in the communication center.
- The **spoken word is misused in a harsh or destructive way,** with the tendency toward **biting sarcasm or lashing criticism.**
- There can be **extreme tension in the jaw and mouth,** grinding of the teeth or the need to eat foods, which stimulates continuous biting, crunching, and chewing activity.
- Snapdragon helps such persons re-direct their powerful metabolic and sexual energy into the right channels.

- For powerful people with strong will and high energy, who misuse their energy through verbal aggression and criticism.
- It helps to redirect 'lower' energy to be expressed through its natural channels, such as through sex and digestion, releasing tension and allowing greater creativity.
- For those who find it difficult to express their feelings.
- Any time there is mental irritation or an inability to speak or to express feelings.
- While it is not associated with acts of violence, there can be a real release of suppressed emotions, which can include rage and screaming.
- **Eating disorders.**

PHYSICAL SYMPTOMS DUE TO EMOTIONAL BLOCK

- Good for any irritation in the throat or voice or tightness in the face (lips and jaws).
- Stuttering is an excellent example and this can be associated with a problem with one's parents.
- Grinding teeth, pain in jaw, ear, and sore throat, stuttering or damage of speech.

PRACTICE

This essence improves logic.

Helps us to recognize what brings us into alignment with others and defines guidelines so that we can clarify and refine plans with reasonable expectations.

THERAPEUTIC USES

The flower essence helps greatly in such visualization. It strengthens the enamel in the teeth, and the connective tissues and joint structures are also enhanced.

It aligns the mental, emotional, and causal bodies to formulate the ability of speech. Damage to the brain's speech center could be treated.

Snapdragon reconstructs the larynx on the genetic level. If some larynx tissue still exists, in combination with hypnosis you could re-grow its tissue. The concentration of energy in the throat can be very useful in many different processes.

It is not just the tissue itself that is important but the person's ability to visualize the complete healing of that part of the body.

The flower essence helps greatly in such visualization. On the cellular level it strengthens the enamel in the teeth, and the connective tissues and joint structures are also enhanced.

The name and shape of snapdragon's flowers show that it is predominantly associated with treating the vocal cords, lips, jaw, and facial tissues, and muscles.

All the cranial plates are aligned. It treats tetanus, Bell's palsy, lip cancer, some forms of arthritis, especially if associated with the jaw, TMJ (temper mandibular joint) disorders, and imbalances in the throat region, including laryngitis and streptococcal infections.

Inflammations in the esophagus and bronchial tubes can also be treated with Snapdragon.

The essence treats allergies that have tendency to cause spots on the skin. Snapdragon should generally be used in the active stages of these diseases.

It can be used externally to treat these problems, and it is effective against the radiation with bitter stimulant.

This stimulates the throat and kidneys, aid in the development of speech and the larynx, and tumours and ulcers.

POSITIVE QUALITIES

Lively, dynamic energy, healthy libido, verbal communication which is emotionally balanced.

TRANSFORMATION

For allowing clear expression of negative feelings and knowing they are valid. Encourages us to give voice to our repressed emotions.

- ❖ At its deepest level, the Snap Dragon helps the soul to distinguish its use of creative forces-especially those, which radiate from the lower energy centers, and those, which are used for the spoken word. By harmonizing the relationship between these energy centers, the soul evolves in its use of creative power.

54

SUNFLOWER

(The Flower of Incarnation)

Botanical Name	:	*Helianthus annuus*
Family Name	:	*Asteraceae*
English Name	:	Sunflower
Hindi Name	:	Suraj Mukhi

GROUP

Exhaustion due to masculine ego.

PLANT

This annual herb grows to twelve feet. Its large, golden-yellow flowers are composed of small tubular flowers arranged compactly on a flat disk. It originated in Mexico and Peru.

KEY WORD

- Egoism.

EMOTIONAL SYMPTOMS DUE TO ENERGY BLOCK

- These people are aggressive by nature and their ego demands that the whole family should listen to them.
- They are the authority and children should depend on them.
- Their confidence level is so high that they conflict their own version of what they are judging because of their power pride.
- Their personal relationship with their children is very low because of their leadership masculine quality.
- Some people mask their true sun-nature with feelings of self-effacement and low self-esteem. This condition darkens the true luster of self.
- Others want their brilliance to shine too strongly, glaring others with pompous self-glory and ego-aggrandizement.
- Just as the soul absorbs from the mother the moon-like qualities of receptivity and nurturing, so does the soul learn from the father the sun-like qualities of the shining, expressive Self.
- Sunflower heals disturbances or distortions in the soul's relationship to the masculine, often associated with a conflicted or deficient relationship with the father in childhood.

PHYSICAL SYMPTOMS DUE TO EMOTIONAL BLOCK

- **Poor posture,** strains in the spinal column, spinal degeneration, and heart diseases can be treated with this remedy.
- Sunflower also eases sunburn, particularly if there is heat exhaustion or toxicity in the skin from an excessive discharge of uric acid.

- It also alleviates the radiation caused by overexposure to the sun or exposure to nuclear fusion involving hydrogen and skin cancer eases.
- Sunflower dissolves **fatty tissue.** This is one of the more powerful effects of sunlight energy that is easily bridged into a person.
- It is particularly useful to take this upon wakening and concentrate the effect by creative visualization in the physical body.

PRACTICE

Sunflower helps in protecting the health of the nerves and brain, as well as the skin and digestive tract. It remove sickness resulting from a lack of vitamins.

All sunflower seed nutrients are transferred to the flower essence. Thus, taking this essence increases these nutrient properties in the system. It can also be applied externally.

Sunflower tempers and spiritualizes the male ego. Lessening the impact of the overbearing male ego, it awakens the male's maternal instinct and desire to have children.

THERAPEUTIC USES

This flower contains vitamin A and D. All the diseases, which are caused due to lack of exposure to the sun's rays get cured with Sunflower.

This attunement can assist with obvious cases of sunburn or excessive exposure to heat.

It helps the heart and other muscles as well as nervous tissues.

Helpful in reducing cholesterol deposits on the walls of arteries.

It is diuretic, expectorant, can cure laryngitis, tonsillitis, influenza and cough, cold.

Medically it is prescribed for rheumatism and numerous respiratory problems.

Used to heal wounds, bruises and ulcers.

Used in pulmonary diseases, bronchitis, cough asthma, dysentery, whooping cough and colds.

Relieves headache and is a treatment for nervous conditions.

Note

This is an interesting essence for atheists. People demonstrating anger or hostility toward their father experience increased understanding with this essence.

When people have trouble with their intuition, and want to know if their perception is correct, or if it is just the idle chatter of material mind, sunflower essence resolves this problem.

POSITIVE QUALITIES

Balanced sense of individuality, spiritualized ego forces, sun-radiant personality.

TRANSFORMATION

This healing of the masculine self is equally important for both men and women. The message of the Sunflower is so universal and foundational, that it is beneficial at nearly every stage in the human life cycle.

55

SWEETPEA
(The Flower of Fairy World)

Botanical Name	:	*Lathyrus odoratus*
Family Name	:	*Fabaceae*
English Name	:	Sweet pea
Hindi Name	:	Matar

GROUP

Indecisive.

PLANT

This climbing perennial is native to Southeastern Europe. It is a wild flower now common in many parts of the United States. The rose-red or purple flowers appear on elongated peduncles in July and August. While this is not used by herbalists, in homeopathy it alleviates nerve disorders such as polio.

KEY WORD

- ✈ Wandering.

EMOTIONAL SYMPTOMS DUE TO ENERGY BLOCK

- ❖ A wanderer unable to form bonds with community or place on earth, social alienation.
- ❖ Many souls are **like pilgrims,** searching and seeking for their place on earth. When this condition is **over-emphasized,** the individual is lost in wanderlust, unable to form true social bonds of caring and commitment.
- ❖ Such people **move from one place to another,** or from one community of friends to another, without becoming truly involved.
- ❖ They **become hardened** in their stance as "outsiders", and are deprived of true soul growth by being unable to establish roots in family or community life.
- ❖ At the heart of the suffering of one who needs sweet pea is a **deep feeling of homelessness.** Such persons do not have within themselves "a sense of place", or love for the earth.
- ❖ Men who have trouble developing the **maternal aspect** of their personality.
- ❖ This alienation can come from the experience of literal homelessness, or for those who were required to move a great deal during childhood.
- ❖ This imbalance is also related to urban and suburban living conditions, like high rise apartment complexes, urban ghettos, or anemic suburban developments which rob the soul of its natural feeling of interest and connection to the earth and the forces of nature.

- For those who have fear, alienation or confusion about relating to others.
- They are always **day dreaming,** this can be a difficult process.
- Sweet pea draws people out of their **fantasies.**
- It can universally apply for any emotional problems, but particularly for problems which women are experiencing.
- It creates a sense of nurturing within the individual. It lies in a lack of love as a child.

PHYSICAL SYMPTOMS DUE TO EMOTIONAL BLOCK

- It is a love potion for women, and if they have trouble accepting their **femininity,** it helps them overcome such **insecurities.**
- Sweet pea creates emotional stability because it calms the emotional body, and it awakens the pancreas.

PRACTICING

Sweet pea creates a sense of social responsibility, so certain adolescents need it. Anyone exhibiting antisocial behavior could benefit from this essence.

People experience the present and therefore develop a social commitment to life. If they are always daydreaming this can be a difficult process. Sweet pea draws people out of their fantasies.

Antisocial behavior could benefit from this essence and get commitment to community, social conceitedness, and sense of place on earth.

They will work together more harmoniously and will combine their forces to assist each others. This is specially true when companions get fairly complicated or a dozen people are working together.

This essence is valuable in physically tight group situations such as people living in big cities. Scientists have already proven that congested living conditions cause antisocial behavior. Families having trouble living together, especially from overcrowded conditions, benefit from sweet pea.

The influence of the essence on tight living conditions is expressed by the numerous pods bound tightly together in the pea. The pod looks somewhat like the colon, which this essence also augments.

THERAPEUTIC USES

Change of hormones, pancreas, nerve disorder, polio, gonorrhea.

A woman could conceive sextuplets with this essence.

It has some beneficial effects on the cardiovascular system.

It increases blood flows to the cervix, clitoris, fallopian tubes, ovaries, uterus, and vaginal lining.

It is a marvelous remedy for treating tumors and cysts in these areas.

It is used as a brain tonic for those who have a slow brain or too much work, and when exhausted.

POSITIVE QUALITIES

It creates emotional stability and calms the body. It stimulates the nervous system on the physical level.

TRANSFORMATION

The sweet Pea helps such persons to come in contact with their feelings about "home", by acknowledging and experiencing this pain, which has numbed the Self, the soul can begin to heal, and find its true connection to the earth and to other human beings.

56

TAMARIND
(The Flower of Generosity)

Botanical Name	:	*Terminalia indica*
Family Name	:	*Leguminosae*
English Name	:	Tamarind
Hindi Name	:	Imli

GROUP

Loner.

PLANT

It is a large tree which goes up to the height of 30-40 feet. Wood is very hard, stem is black. Fruit is shaped like beans, sour in taste, grey in colour, and brown when ripe. In north India it is called Imli. It is used in food for jam, sauce, and chutney. Flowering time is January-February, colour is light pink.

KEY WORD

→ Self-centered.

EMOTIONAL SYMPTOMS DUE TO ENERGY BLOCK

❖ Over-talkative in a self-absorbed manner, over-concerned with one's problems.

❖ For those who become too **absorbed in their own problems and worries.** Such persons are deeply lonely and in great pain, but they seek contact with others in a dysfunctional manner.

❖ They feel **empty inside,** and hope to assuage their hunger by "feeding" off the psychic attention and sympathy of others.

❖ Excessive **self-concern** repels others from forming a truly sympathetic bond, leaving such a soul increasing lonely and dysfunctional.

❖ These people are **chatter boxes.**

❖ They enjoy talking about themselves, their family and friends.

❖ Their audience has difficulty contributing to the conversation, and even when they do, they are not given a listening ear by these characters.

❖ Thoughts entirely centered on personal problems, take themselves terribly seriously, are **hypochondriacs.**

❖ They feel a compulsive need to talk about themselves. Long chatter on phone.

❖ They will **monopolize a group conversation,** cleverly bringing the topic around themselves.

PHYSICAL SYMPTOMS DUE TO EMOTIONAL BLOCK

❖ Frequent colds induced by weather change.

❖ Possible appearance of white patches on the skin.

PRACTICE

In extreme cases, such an individual can learn to manipulate psychic energy so that others are compelled to listen to and attend to their problems.

THERAPEUTIC USE

Helps in urinal disease, leucorrhoea and cold.

POSITIVE QUALITIES

Promotes inner tranquility and emotional self-sufficiency. These people find a way to selfless understanding, and become willing to listen to others. It create a space within them from which a love to share and listen arises.

TRANSFORMATION

As they become stronger within themselves, the soul realizes that compassion is the key to experiencing love, and they are healed from their own suffering by learning to care for and perceive the suffering of others.

57

TUBEROSE
(The Flower of Strength)

Botanical Name	:	*Polyalthia Single Tuberose*
Family Name	:	*Amaryllidaceae*
English Name	:	Tuberose
Hindi Name	:	Rajnigandha

GROUP

Exhaustion due to involvement in many things.

PLANT

This small perennial is native to Mexico. It produces waxy, funnel-shaped, white flowers from July-November. This flower has no stem and foliage and is like a sword. It is one of the most fragrant flowers in the world and is white in colour; thus, it is used as a perfume.

KEY WORD

- ✈ Multifarious activity.

EMOTIONAL SYMPTOMS DUE TO ENERGY BLOCK

- For those who find it difficult to take conclusive decisions.
- When a person gets confused between too many things at a time.
- For anxiety created by conversation revolving around diverse topics.
- For those who get tired doing different types of work at one time.

PHYSICAL SYMPTOMS DUE TO EMOTIONAL BLOCK

- Its intense fragrance symbolizes the fact that it stimulates the **crown chakra.**
- Most flowers with a strong scent have this ability when prepared as a flower essence, of augmenting the subtle bodies.
- The impact on the spiritual body **aligns the emotional body,** which creates increased **sensitivity** in the emotions and physical body, especially the **neurological** system.
- It also works as a **general tonic.**

PRACTICE

Tuberose can be used in conjunction with aroma therapy. This is partly because it augments the body's membranes and tissues. Sometimes intense or synthetic smells such as perfume or camphor block homeopathic remedies from working. It helps in allergies caused by any medicine. Tuberose prevents or overcomes these problems.

THERAPEUTIC USES

Tonic, high blood pressure, blood purifier, ear pain and hair fall, allergies, neurological problems.

Used for skin disease, burning sensation on skin, headache.

POSITIVE QUALITIES

The alleviates laziness and balances the physical and spiritual body.

TRANSFORMATION

Tube rose helps to overcome problems relating to too much work of different categories being handled at the same time. The mind can take decisions easily while sorting things out individually or one at a time.

58

WALNUT

(The Flower of Comfort)

Botanical Name : *Juglans regia*

Family Name : *Euphorbiaceae (Castor family)*

English Name : Walnut

Hindi Name : Akhrot

Group

Exhaustion due to change.

Plant

A beautiful tree reaching up to about 30 m. Grows well in orchards and other protected places. The male catkins and small green female flowers appear on the same tree. Blooms in April and May before or just after the ear-buds burst.

Key words

- Link breaker.

EMOTIONAL SYMPTOMS DUE TO ENERGY BLOCK

- These people feel frustrated when in need of protection from outside influences and helps them in adapting.
- For those who have difficulty settling into a **new environment,** new job or new routine, a different country or a new home.
- For those who find it difficult to **break the link** with the past so that life can start afresh, can never be free from old ties and memories.
- Normally know exactly what they want, but now tend to vacillate in a specific new situation with grudges.
- Have made a major decision affecting one's life, only the last step remains to be taken which they are not able to take.
- Finally want to leave behind all restrictions and influences, but do not quite succeed.
- Those who are often sensitive people and are easily disturbed by such disruptive environmental influences.
- Find it hard to escape the influence of a dominant personality when making decisions relating to ones own life – parents, partners, teachers etc.
- Affected by an unexpected outside event which forced one to rethink ones whole approach to life.
- Those going through crucial changes in life – change of occupation, divorce, retirement, move to another town, move to an old people's home etc.
- Finally want to be really clear in their mind, concerning a change.
- Have given up a relationship, but despite physical separation, still feel under the old partner's spell. Finds it hard to take that final step.

- Still being caught up consciously or unconsciously in old decisions and the bonds of the past. Mentally they are strung with the past.
- They prefer to fall back into old habits, sentimental thoughts, conventional ideas, and old family traditions.

P··ICAL SYMPTOMS DUE TO EMOTIONAL BLOCK

- Major biological changes are about to occur – menopause, pregnancy, puberty, teething, and terminal stages of illness.

CHILDREN

Helpful during the various milestones of a child's development (teething, starting school and puberty for instance).

Walnut can help with adjustment to other changes, e.g., staying away from home for the first time (with grandparents perhaps) or when the child is suffering as the result of parental divorce or a major move. The remedy provides the necessary protection.

Know what they want or want to do, know correct answer to a question or the way to play a certain game, but whose conviction falters and sways when an alternative idea is presented to them. They may then be persuaded to do something, which they don't want.

PRACTICE

Walnut is the **Remedy for change.**

Some practitioners use Walnut to screen themselves from their patients energy's radiation.

For breaking **bad habits** related to eating, (such as over eating). Helps protect a person from influences that can disrupt a diet – others wanting to feed you or situations where you are surrounded by food.

Smoothens the transition caused by moving, career change, school change, divorce, change of religion, retirement, recovery from a long illness, disability, teething, puberty, menopause, mid-life crisis, birth, death.

The remedy helps to guide us through these events in life so that we do not lose our way.

Walnut state is normally only temporary, and genuine Walnut types are not too common nowadays. These people are innovators in the sphere of ideas. Yet being open at heart, they may face a temporary risk of losing their original direction through pressure from others.

Walnut is particularly helpful for providing an insulation against bad media reports or other people's opinions concerning the economy.

Walnut is good for transitional periods such as – being out of work, starting new jobs, additional responsibilities and worries etc.

Used for stress that comes from any sort of transition or change, as well as giving a tangible feeling of protection to those who feel greatly influenced by peers, one particular person, the media, or society's attitudes in general.

Walnut is for those with 'pioneer' mentality – those who are life's trailblazers and trendsetters, going against normal expectations.

THERAPEUTIC USES

Treats gum disease, is an anti-inflammatory, astringent and is also used for cleansing. Good for rheumatism and sore and aching muscles and joints, swelling and skin problems, e.g., scrofulous diseases, herpes, eczema and for healing indolent ulcers.

It is mildly laxative, prevents worms, is soothing and is also a natural digestive.

To relieve fatigue and generally strengthen the body.

Encourages circulation and keeps the heart healthy, helps to soothe colic and dispel gas in the abdomen.

Good for heartburn and diarrhea.

Used as a gargle for sore and ulcerated throats.

For hereditary asthma and baldness.

It is helpful during change in life, of teething, puberty and menopause and can help with the adjustment to childbirth and to the late changes during the menstrual cycle.

Can be helpful during the transition from being overweight to thin and adjusting to a new body image.

The remedy has also been found to have a stabilizing effect with chiropractic manipulation of the spine and with dental problems.

Walnut essence is used in hair tonics and as a poison antidote and also to prevent madness.

TRANSFORMATION

The person remains true to himself, follows life's goals undeviatingly despite adverse circumstances and is not influenced by outside factors and changes.

POSITIVE QUALITIES

The positive aspect of this remedy is constancy and determination. Those who carry out their belief, their life, unhindered by adverse circumstances or the opinion or ridicule of others.

59

WATER MELON

(The Flower of Surety)

Botanical Name	:	*Citrullus vulgaris*
Family name	:	*Cucurbitaceae (Pumpkin family)*
English name	:	Water Melon
Hindi name	:	Tarbooz

GROUP

Unhappy.

PLANT

Watermelon, a favorite in the hot summer months, is an annual, which is grown on the sandy bed of the river. Each fruit weights between 5-15 kg.

The flowers are yellow; the fruit is large, round or oval. A thick or thin ring of white surrounds the red flesh or pulpy part in which numerous flat black seeds are embedded. The plant is known everywhere, especially in tropical countries. It produces greenish-yellow male and female flowers. It is native to the Middle East and India.

KEY WORD

- ✈ No energy for work.

EMOTIONAL SYMPTOMS DUE TO ENERGY BLOCK

- ❖ These people have an inferiority complex, feel low in front of groups of people.
- ❖ Weak convictions due to lack of confidence.
- ❖ They nurture resentments because they find it difficult to speak and express their feelings; this leaves them with a sense of despair.
- ❖ Due to a fear of speaking up in public they are unable to find the right choice of words, yet they always speak with authority.
- ❖ There is an easing of obsessive and depressed states, especially manic depression, and there is more understanding of psychic phenomena.

PHYSICAL SYMPTOMS DUE TO EMOTIONAL BLOCK

- ❖ It is best that the male takes the male flower essence and female takes the female flower essence, but this feature is not essential. It **stimulates fertility** in the female and potency in the male.
- ❖ Even if a person has been taking birth control pills, watermelon overcomes the long-term effects of birth control pills to aid conception.
- ❖ It helps people develop a proper attitude before, during, and after conception.

- ❖ The mother's emotional body is very important during pregnancy because it is vitally involved in creating the body of the fetus.
- ❖ On a psychological level, a deeper attunement and understanding is established between a couple desiring to have a child.
- ❖ Watermelon has a mold aphrodisiac effect, so sex appeal between the couple increases. But this is only in relation to giving birth.
- ❖ An attempt to develop sexuality with watermelon outside the progeny process would not work.
- ❖ One interesting effect from this essence is that during pregnancy the pain the woman experiences eases, and some of it can be transferred to her partner. This is part of the sympathetic bond that this essence establishes between the couple.
- ❖ Watermelon conditions and tones the male and female sex organs, so it eases imbalances in these parts of the body.

PRACTICE

The emotional body is balanced so there is less emotional stress during the pregnancy.

Furthermore, the initial **emotional relationship** between the mother and the infant is created in the womb.

The ability of this plant is to retain powerful energies.

In the female, you may see a slight weight loss especially in the stomach and waistline. And the hips and breasts may slightly expand. In the male you, you may see an increase in muscular tone, the chest may expand, and there may be increased sensitivity in the area of the penis. Many of these things are accomplished by increased blood flow to specific parts of the body and by certain hormones being activated. While it is best that this essence be taken by a couple, if a single woman took watermelon it would still work, but the effects might be slightly less.

THERAPEUTIC USES

Treatment of diminished urination, kidney and bladder-stone, excessive discharge of phosphates in the urine metabolic acidosis such as ketosis encountered in diabetes and starvation.

Effects in the treatment of cardio-vascular and renal disorders associated with sodium and water retention.

Is a mild laxative, promotes flow of urine, fertility; helps in rheumatism, accumulation of liquid in abdominal cavity, painful inflamed joints, excessive protein in blood, fevers, chronic bronchitis, pulmonary diseases, arthritis, indigestion, obesity, mouth and throat disease, arterial hypertension and constipation.

Also for contagious skin diseases, kidney and bladder stones, inflammation of the urinary tract and prostate.

POSITIVE QUALITIES

It provides an inner strength, not simply relating to the physical body, but also its mutability to people so that they can use it as energy storage for many different healings.

TRANSFORMATION

But while the emotions can be balanced, there can still be some mental tensions during pregnancy because watermelon has no impact on the mental body.

57. Tuberose

58. Walnut

59. Water Melon

60. White Rose

61. Willow

62. Yarrow

63. Zinnia

64. Asparagus

60

WHITE ROSE
(The Flower of Grace)

Botanical Name : *Rosa wichuraiana*
Family Name : *Rosaceae*
English Name : White Rose
Hindi Name : Safed Gulab

GROUP

Social influence.

PLANT

A small thorn bush growing to a height of 3 feet. The flowers are pure white. Common in western countries. Flowers from February to April or May, and again in winter. It can be grown in a pot.

KEY WORD

- Uncultured.

EMOTIONAL SYMPTOMS DUE TO ENERGY BLOCK

- These people find it **difficult to adjust** in society.
- They have **no manners,** are of confused mind and often irritated.
- They **are complex.**
- These people belong to a **peer group** and believe in their own small world as a frog of a small pond thinks that to be the entire world.
- They find it difficult to understand the shortcomings of others
- They are **critical, shortsighted, foolish,** and **arrogant** and therefore often **lack tolerance.**
- Appear patient and calm, yet are often seething with irritation from inside.
- **Irritated people,** who complain about others, and suffer from bouts of **petty anger.**
- Annoyed at all small habits, mannerisms, idiosyncrasies and gestures of others
- See the speck in another's eye but not the log in their own.

PHYSICAL SYMPTOMS DUE TO EMOTIONAL BLOCK

- Indigestion, and tension in jaws.

PRACTICE

White rose helps the people from remote areas whose habits are very rustic and who are very simple, straight forward and honest in their thoughts and actions.

The urban modern society finds it very difficult to accept their presence amongst themselves since they are not refined (that's what they feel) in their mannerism and etiquette. Elite society finds these people speaking bluntly and offensively and feels repelled by their disgraceful appearance. All this is in the mind of society people who ignore the simplicity of these people.

This attitude gives the rural people a great mental discomfort and they do not understand the reason for the society people behaving in such a fashion and it gives them a complex, which finds a vent in irritation, and petty anger. Such apathy suppresses their soul, and cuts off the individual from his or her inner sources of vitality and healing.

Rose essence can be given to infants and children to encourage them to grow out of the small group mentality and blossom.

THERAPEUTIC USE

Indigestion, skin disease, eyes, blood cleanser.

POSITIVE QUALITIES

For grace and the regenerating, inspiring and strengthening influence in your life.

TRANSFORMATION

This essence teaches that life is a sacred and precious opportunity which the soul must make every effort to embrace, if it is to find the true meaning of love and caring.

61

WILLOW
(The Flower of Courage)

Botanical Name	:	*Salix vitellina*
Family Name	:	*Salicaceae*
English Name	:	Willow
Hindi Name	:	Bunlong

GROUP

Unhappy.

PLANT

A small tree reaching up to 10m found growing on moist and low-lying ground. The young, pliable shoots and branches are used for basket making and wicker furniture. In winter, the twigs turn a bright orange-yellow. The male and female catkins grow on different trees opening in April and May.

KEY WORDS

- Self-pity.

EMOTIONAL SYMPTOMS DUE TO ENERGY BLOCK

- Unspoken resentment, bitterness, complaining that life is unfair, inflexibility 'poor me' or 'victim of fate' attitude.
- **Sulky, selfish,** embittered with self-pity and ungrateful for help.

  Constant **frowning, grumbling,** spread a **gloom** and a feeling of **negativity,** a difficult patient since nothing pleases him and he is reluctant to admit any improvement.
- Dislike flexibility, lack forgiveness, garner **hatred and inner child irritability, prone to** negativity.
- They also lack perfectionism, easily rejecting people, they carry resentment and cannot tolerate to carry through any responsibilities.
- Their thoughts have become so introspective that they **dwell on their misfortune.**
- They feel **resentful** that life has treated them so badly, wondering what they have done to deserve such hardship.
- They become wrapped up in self-pity, **grumble, moan or sulk** and when things go wrong, they find it hard to look at the bright side and forgive and forget.
- When adversity strikes, they turn it inwards upon themselves where if festers away creating a big chip on the shoulder and generating an attitude of **'poor old me, nobody cares.'**
- They **feel sorry for themselves** and find it hard to be cheerful because 'there is nothing to be cheerful about,' and can only see things from a negative angle.
- They forget that there is a positive side to every situation.

- These people take little interest in the affairs of others, and can be isolated, except to speak with **bitterness** and **unkindness** of their fortune and to decry their optimism and happiness.
- They are the unfortunate who do not hope or expect that anything good may come to them because they believe they are fated to suffer and that no one else experiences such pain, such difficulties, and such distress as them.
- They think **their prayers are never answered** and their efforts, **never rewarded.**
- Do not feel responsible for their **misfortune,** and are always **blaming circumstances** or others. Think fate gives no recognition to what they have put into life.
- Give up many things that they used to enjoy, resentfully withdrawing more and more from life. Make demands from life but are not prepared to give in return.
- They take without giving. They accept help of every kind as their right and with out gratitude.
- Accept help from others as a matter of course, though in the long run alienating any one who has tried to be helpful.
- They cannot realize that they are solely responsible for their own unhappy lives and that they have materialized these conditions from the substances of their strong negative thoughts.
- Stress the negative aspect of things, often appearing a wet blanket or spoil sport, morose, moody and touchy, trying to put a damper on the cheerful mood.
- Spiteful thoughts due to **bitterness, smoldering anger, unspoken feelings** but will not explode.
- Refuse in their mind to accept their own negativity with the result that nothing can change.

- They carry a **grudge** for years, **never try to solve their problems,** but remain polite with underground tension, they subtly criticize and put the other person down, that is their unspoken revenge.
- They do not only **harm themselves** but also poison the whole environment, committing a crime against the greater whole.
- Children feel **life has treated them unfairly,** find it **hard to forgive** and forget, feel resentful, when lightly scolded for some misdemeanor; they feel they do not deserve such a great punishment.
- Due to breaking their friendships, they are **sulky** and **resentful,** but the reason for their distress is not always apparent.

PHYSICAL SYMPTOMS DUE TO EMOTIONAL BLOCK

- Blood sugar imbalances (diabetes) are often the result of some bitterness related to the emotion or desiring nature.

PRACTICE

If the physical body does not keep flexible, it becomes stiff and contracted. The good health of the soul depends also on its ability to be yielding, flowing, and "for-giving." Negative feelings are dammed up and then become magnified and internalized, congesting the inner being.

Heals the soul condition of bitterness and resentment; it is for those who tend to "hold on" and become attached to negative emotions. Such persons often feel victimized by the circumstances of life – they feel that others are to blame for their misfortune; that life has been unfair to them; or they resent those who appear to have more status, prosperity, or felicity than themselves.

The aging process is especially difficult for Willow Types. At an energy level, such persons are unable to flow with the streaming of their lives.

THERAPEUTIC USES

It is interesting to note that Willow is the herbal precursor of aspirin, and is used particularly for such physical conditions.

Willow grew in damp, rheumy places so it treats rheumatic stiffness, aching in the muscles that accompany flu and other infections.

For fevers and chills, and digestive problems.

If you wash hair with this it removes dandruff.

All types of arthritis, especially with inflamed joints and gout, for cramps and inflammatory back pain and lumbago.

It was also used for its ability to bring down fevers, even in malaria.

Its astringent properties help to curb chronic diarrhea and dysentery.

It is used to stop the bleeding of wounds in the mouth and nose.

To stop vomiting due to drunkenness.

It helps to stay thin, sharp and full of vitality.

It helps in wind colic conditions, and dimness of sight and cataract, and clears the face and skin from spots and discoloring.

It can be used for heavy periods, and externally to treat cuts and wounds.

Willow can be made into gargles for sore throats, and mouthwashes for mouth ulcers and bleeding gums.

As a diuretic willow reduces fluid retention and helps eliminate toxins from the body via the urinary system.

Willow can be used for head colds. flu, fevers, and as a tonic to restore strength after illness. The willow is likely to be a good remedy for circulatory problems, because, like aspirin, it helps prevent rapid blood clotting.

Willow acts as a sexual sedative. It helps to clear congestion and pain in the ovarian and uterine area, and helps take away or lessen sexual desire, over stimulation, wet dreams and premature ejaculation.

Low-grade recurrent fevers, feeling of being over heated in the evenings.

POSITIVE QUALITIES

Brings about acceptance, forgiveness, and encourages one to take responsibility for one's life situation, flowing with life. Also helps those who sulk when told off, seek sympathy or try to make others feel guilty by bursting into tears.

TRANSFORMATION

Lifts the sufferer out of this hollowness or self-mortification so that he or she may adopt a more optimistic and positive approach to life.

62

YARROW
(The Flower of Invulnerability)

Botanical Name : *Achillea mileifolium*
Family Name : *Asteraceae (Sun flower family)*
English Name : Yarrow
Hindi Name : Biranjsipha

Group

Social influence.

Plant

A common wild plant with feathery leaves and white or pink flowers. Yarrow is a sacred plant to many cultures.

Yarrow is a member of the composite family, cousin to dandelion and daisy, and a perennial with aromatic leaves. It is found all over the globe in hedgerows, lanes and fields, preferring light sandy soils. Yarrow is one of the finest and most versatile healing plants, and respected since at least the time of the Ancient Greeks and Egyptians and also in China.

Note

Yarrow is planted as a border to repel ants, flies, beetles and it attracts all sorts of wasps and lady bugs. Planted near building foundations it is supposed to keep termites away.

The leaves, flowers and stems are all used for healing purposes. Cut the leaves from the stems and dry them separately. Because they are so fine you must dry the leaves quickly or they will discolour. Be sure that your drying room is warm enough (90-100 F). You can leave the flowers on the stems and hang the stems upside down in bunches to dry. Store the flowers separately and cut up the stems into small pieces and store them separately.

Key word

- Get impacted with people and weather.

Emotional Symptoms Due to Energy Block

- Extreme vulnerability to others and to the environment, easily depleted, overly absorbed by negative influences, psychic toxicity.
- Devitalized by city life, eating disorders, irritability, sensitive, stressed, self-vulnerability
- Those who easily get affected by their surroundings, and can be prone to many forms of environmental illness, allergies, or various psycho-somatic diseases.
- Such persons have an extraordinary capacity for healing, counseling, or teaching, because they are readily able to receive psychic information and to understand the pain and suffering of others. At the same time they are easily depleted, and are quite vulnerable to the thoughts or negative intentions of others.

- ❖ For negative influences such as radioactive fallout and thought forms from psychic attack or extreme **emotionalism.**
- ❖ For people who get affected from radiation.
- ❖ For exposure to nuclear radiation and other forms of **environmental stress** including radiation from X-rays, therapy and other invasive electromagnetic fields.
- ❖ When overall integrity of the energy field gets depleted.
- ❖ For those who feel too vulnerable and those who, through their professions, are confronted with the problems of others.
- ❖ For those who are easily effected and depleted by their surroundings and the influence of others and tend to be prone to environmental illnesses, allergies, psychosomatic problems.
- ❖ It helps to shield from out side influences and reduce leakage of energy and absorption of negative influences.

Physical Symptoms Due to Emotional Block

- ❖ Frequent addition to treatments during menopause.
- ❖ For venous hemorrhages and varicose veins which tend to occur in ruddy-complexioned people, after vigorous exercise or exertion, strains or injuries.
- ❖ It is particularly effective for children's eating disorders, immune disturbances and irritability.
- ❖ It helps in protecting the pregnancy.
- ❖ It is a strength giver and stress toner.

Practice

Yarrow is also helpful to protect against evil.

This remedy combines the remarkable light and fire processes of Yarrow plant with the strong formative forces of potentized sea salt. By strengthening the body with strong formative forces, which can meet the harmful attack of radiation,

This remedy is indicated not only for obvious exposure to nuclear fall-out, but also for the many ways in which nuclear radiation and other forms of aberrant and highly toxic energy infiltrates the modern world. Examples include video-display terminals, X-rays, radiation therapy, high-altitude radiation, and detection devices at airport terminals. It is an immensely important remedy; it stands as a counter-shield to the destructive forces, which threaten and plague human and planetary life, imparting powerful vitalizing and restorative properties.

As the soul becomes more spiritually open, it necessarily becomes more refined, sensitive, and absorbent.

HISTORY

Legend has used yarrow to staunch his soldiers' wounds during the Trojan War. For wound treatment, simply press fresh leaves and flower tops into cuts and crepes on the way to washing and bandaging them.

The Greek physician, writing in the 1st century AD referred to the healing properties of yarrow for battle wounds.

Throughout history until the First World War, yarrow has been used for treating wounds; hence its common name is soldiers' wound.

THERAPEUTIC USES

Yarrow has healing effects on mucous membranes, eases diarrhea, and improves thrombosis, blood clotting, arthritis, gout cramp, colic, digestion, inflammation, antiseptic, antispasmodic, fever, catarrh, sinusitis, hay fever, dust allergies, liver, ulcers, measles, colds, nosebleeds, abscesses, headache, gout, menopause, cellulite, acne, sunburn, smallpox, and chicken pox, early stages of fevers, especially with hot, dry skin. It induces sleep, and eases pain.

It helps in irregular menstrual bleeding, heavy and prolonged menstrual cramps, from puberty to menopause by working with the blood, circulation and the uterus, vaginal discharges, for pelvic infections and pelvic congestion. It helps to stem the flooding of heavy periods and to bring on delayed menstruation.

Yarrow is supportive for people undergoing radiotherapy and intestinal infections.

As a cream or compress for **bleeding piles** and **fistula, inflammation, ulcers,** and varicose veins.

In the bath to relieve aches and pains.

Yarrow is regarded as a good vulnerary and septic, due to its ability to stop bleeding, for wounds, cuts, gashes, punctures or abrasions.

For skin patches, as a lotion, to bathe with, and to use as a compress massage oil beneficial for rashes and skin ulcers.

Yarrow has also been used as an anesthetic.

Yarrow is applied to the gums or teeth to relieve toothache.

POSITIVE QUALITIES

Inner radiance and strength of aura, compassionate awareness, sensitivity, beneficent healing forces.

TRANSFORMATION

By 'astringing' the boundaries around a person and preventing their energies form 'bleeding' into their environment, it acts to strengthen and solidify the self, the essence, allowing and enhancing their ability to heal, teach, counsel or follow their chosen path.

63

ZINNIA
(The Flower of Smile)

Botanical Name : *Zinnia elegans*
Family Name : *Asteraceae*
English Name : Zinnia
Hindi Name : Zinnia

GROUP

Unhappy.

PLANT

This popular Mexican annual, flowers form early summer until late autumn. The single or double flowers appear in large heads that are crimson, orange, red violet, white or yellow.

KEY WORD

- No laughter in life.

EMOTIONAL SYMPTOMS DUE TO ENERGY BLOCK

- For over seriousness, dullness, lack of humor, overly somber, repressed inner child.
- For people who always **live in saddened state of mind,** are **morose, introvert** and have no laughter left in their lives. This condition also plays on the **emotion** of such people and manifests in the body.
- Such people tend to believe that laughter means being insincere to work.
- These people are **agitated, depressed, or hypersensitive** and have trouble communicating with children because they do not relate to their child-like nature.
- For **marital problems, parental image troubles,** and unfulfilled parental or maternal instincts.
- They create **tensions within** themselves as they strive for perfection and easily find fault with their own work.
- This remedy is clearly indicated for those who are **overly grave** and earnest, who take themselves and life too seriously, or who tend towards work holism or other forms of **unbalanced intensity.**
- They do not believe in the theory of **"Humor is uniquely human".**
- Other forms of life certainly experience joy and delight, but humor has to do with being able to step outside the Self, and not take the Self so seriously.
- They tend to work too hard and feel over burdened by responsibilities.

PHYSICAL SYMPTOMS DUE TO EMOTIONAL BLOCK

- Their nature gives rise to frequent headaches.

PRACTICE

The capacity to laugh at one's self, or to be "light-hearted," is quite literally a necessary balance to the somber heaviness or self-consciousness. Zinnia is a most wonderful remedy of this state of soul.

This essence especially helps the self to contact its inner child. Every child is born with the innate capacity to laugh and play, to enter into life with the full exuberance of the winged soul.

THERAPEUTIC USE

Blood purification, fever, malaria, headache, viral, bacterial, and degenerative diseases are mildly relieved by zinnia. The heart and abdominal chakras are stimulated.

POSITIVE QUALITIES

Cheerfulness and joy for those who are depressed, restless, hypersensitive and need to laugh. Zinnia flower essence brings the soul quality of humor to one's humanness, teaching that the soul who is good spirited is truly on a balanced spiritual path.

TRANSFORMATION

Zinnia restores humor by uplifting the person's outlook on life. It creates this effect by aligning the emotional body. This is partly the source of humor.

64

ASPARAGUS
(Plant for Ever)

Botanical Name : *Asparagus officinalis*
Common Name : *Sparrow grass*
Family : Asparagaceae
English Name : Asparagus
Hindi name : Shatavari

Plant

Rare in Britain, but found growing wild on the south west coast of England. Flowers are small, white in colour. Today it grows "wild" across many of the areas around the world where it is **grown for food.** Asparagus grows into a tall upright bush.

Keyword

- Tonic – rejuvenator.

SYMPTOMS

- Shatavari (this is an Indian word meaning 'a woman who has a hundred husbands') is the most important herb in Ayurvedic medicine for dealing with problems connected with women's fertility.
- The rhizome is a soothing tonic that acts mainly on the circulatory, digestive, respiratory and female reproductive organs.

PRACTICE

It acts as a **nerve tonic** for those with sedentary habits who suffer from symptoms of **gravels.** It has been found very beneficial in cases of **dropsy.**

THERAPEUTIC USES

- The virtues of Asparagus are well known as **diuretic, laxative,** cardiac and sedative.
- It is good to **clear the sight,** and holding it in the mouth eases **toothaches**.
- It helps those sinews that 'are shrunk by **cramps** and **convulsions**, and helps in **sciatica**. It is **antispasmodic**, **demulcent** and **refrigerant**.
- It is taken internally in the treatment of **infertility, loss of libido,** threatened **miscarriage, menopausal problems, hyperacidity, stomach ulcers** and **bronchial infections**. Externally it is used to treat **stiffness** in the **joints**.
- To treat **haemorrhage, piles, hoarseness** of voice, **cough, arthritis, poisoning,** diseases of **female genital tract, erysipelas, fever,** as aphrodisiac and as a **rejuvenator.**
- Asparagus is indicated in some general illnesses like **asthenia, anaemia, rheumatism, diabetes, brain complaints** as well as **renal Lithiasis**.

- ❖ Good for **kidney stones, nervous problems, female fertility, upset stomach, dyspepsia, promotes secretion of milk.**

POSITIVE QUALITIES

A person becomes active and takes challenges in life.

TRANSFORMATION

Habits can be taken care by analyzing them and live comfortably.

65

BANANA
(The Flower of Communication)

Botanical Name : *Musa Paradisiacal*

Family Name : *Musaceae*

English Name : Banana

Hindi Name : Kela

PLANT

This tropical plant grows to thirty feet, produces yellow flowers in clusters. There are many cultivated varieties of this popular fruit.

KEYWORD

- Tonic for bones.

SYMPTOMS

- For **moody** people.

- Banana essence **creates new bridges** so that one may easily find ways to communicate better with others.
- It treats the bone structure, including the dislocation of any bones, particularly in the **sacrum and spine.**
- It also strengthens the **bone marrow**, especially in its attachment to the teeth.
- Banana could be used in certain periodontal diseases in which there is a loss of support in the **bone level in the gum line.**
- The bone structure in the jaw is rejuvenated. It is used in **temporomandibular** [hinge joints like knee and elbow].
- Banana is a tonic, more than a cure, for blood sugar problems such as diabetes and **hypoglycemia**.
- It helps in weight problem when sugars get assimilated improperly into the system.
- Banana flower may increase the **progesterone hormone** and reduce the bleeding.
- While the essence **balances male and female sexuality**, it is more **applicable for the male.** The shape of the fruit symbolizes its relation to male sexuality.
- Great **tissue builder** and **energy provider**.

PRACTICE

The assimilation of **calcium, iron oxide, phosphorus, and zinc increase,** if there is a tendency for poor absorption and low body weight, take Banana essence with Geranium.

THERAPEUTIC USES

- Banana flower essence is good for acidity, diabetes, gastric ulcers, diarrhoea, hypertension, gout, hunger, nephritis, ulcerative colitis, genital-disorders, chronic cough, dyspepsia, constipation, joint pains, loss of blood, tuberculosis, urine problem, intestine, ulcers, nervous disorder, hysteria, dysentery, jaundice, wounds and cuts, inflamed kidneys and pain, hair loss, piles, menstruation, earache, sprained ankle, skin eruption, sudden pains, cramps, tension in back, neck, jaws, shoulders, rashes, skin irritation, stimulates liver activity, glandular disease, venereal disease, anaemia and disorders of the blood.

- It has thus been used as an adjunctive treatment for **jaundice** and some **hepatic** – related **ophthalmic** conditions.
- It helps to **increase weight** and **quenches the thirst** in cholera patients.
- Considered beneficial for **cancer** prevention and **heart diseases**.
- Used as a tonic for congestion of the **liver** and to prevent or cure scurvy.
- Also cures inflamed **colon** and diseases of the **rectum.**
- External treatment for **haemorrhoids** and other varicose conditions.

POSITIVE QUALITIES

Balanced mind will provide healthy body and strong bones.

TRANSFORMATION

Better communication with people.

66

BUR
(The Flower of Enlightenment)

Botanical Name	:	*Ficus Benghalensis*
Family Name	:	*Moraceae*
English Name	:	Banyan Tree
Hindi Name	:	Bargad

PLANT

It is a very large tree, with spreading branches, drooping down, leaves are rough, thick and broad. The fruits are green in colour, when ripe they are red. Fruits are not real, but contain innumerable minute flowers in them. Flowers bloom in spring and fruiting occurs during the monsoons. This tree survives for many years.

KEYWORD

- Tonic for religious quest.

SYMPTOMS

- ❖ This essence originated in the thought forms of children who saw that they wished a deeper **enlightened** state.
- ❖ A pattern is discovered in one's self, and that is what is explored and made deeper. Individuals may find that consciousness changes in ways they did not expect. Thus, it is wise to have an **open mind** when using this essence.
- ❖ This essence can promote states in which there is **greater expansion**, so one who may have never heard voices may go through a period in which they do hear voices. The essence should be continued during such states and the individual allowed deeper states of meditation to recognize that the voices are merely, released energy from many levels. These are often past lives that they contact on the way to greater enlightenment.
- ❖ The physical body is nourished in an energetic sense. Those fatigued but on a spiritual path should consider using the essence.

PRACTICE

It is cooling by nature.

In its original state this plant was used by people to stimulate beauty and friendship. They knew that eventually it would be used more extensively and would be developed with the process of enlightenment.

For beings that freely choose this, it is wise to use the energy of the plant not only as an essence, but also to be in its physical presence, as in reading a book about meditation while sitting beneath it. The test point is the sole of the foot.

Because it is intertwined with the energy of Buddha, the signature is not so obvious. It is inspiring in its appearance, but it is the association with this tree that is important. It is now intertwined with this thought form and will likely remain so for at least a thousand more years.

THERAPEUTIC USES

- Many **lung diseases** are assisted including lung **cancer,** diseases associated with smoking of any kind like **emphysema**, and **shortness of breath** such as with runners. When a person is constantly **fatigued,** there may be a misalignment of earth energy. The person may contact **colds** easily. A **paraplegic** will benefit from bur essence if he is also interested in spiritual awakening. Other diseases related to nervous disorders associated with the **spinal column, multiple sclerosis** will be eased, particularly when it affects the spinal column.
- **The latex of bur is applied on wounds, cracked soles, sinusitis, lymphadenitis, gonorrhoea, conjunctivitis, and also treats sagging breasts.**
- **Paralysis, urine problem** of gents where the energy and mettle of the body drains out. **Back pain**, **skin problems, worms**, and **vaginal problems**. [essence filled in cotton can be kept in, of ganga jal only]
- **Blood purifier. Leucorrhoea, hemorrhagic,** fertility Inflammatory, cooling, styptic, anodyne, depurative, arthritic, diarrhoea, **dysentery,** vomiting, burns, toothache, genital diseases, cough, diabetes, poly- urea.

POSITIVE QUALITIES

Imbalance gets balance when disharmony in a religious quest, not understanding some new age ideas, or inner harmony about one's purpose.

TRANSFORMATION

This order wants individuals to find enlightenment by choice.

67

CELERY
(Aromatic Flower)

Botanical Name : *Apium Graveolens*

Family Name : *Apiaceae*

English Name : Celery

Hindi Name : Shalari, Ajmod

Plant

Native to southern Europe and cultivated in Britain. Celery likes a cool to mild climate and does not enjoy the extremes of temperature. Its roots are shallow, so celery is sensitive to frost and drought.

Keyword

→ Tonic to soothe nerves

Therapeutic Uses

❖ Reduces **flatulence,** increases the secretion and **discharge of urine** and acts as an aphrodisiac, **laxative** and stimulant.

- It **strengthens the kidneys** and the **liver.**
- It is utilized as a **tonic** in combination with other herbs. Prevents **gall stones** and **stones in the kidney.**
- **Arthritis:** Celery is useful in the treatment of arthritis due to its high sodium content.
- **Also used in nervous affliction, blood disorders and respiratory disorders.**
- Celery is known to have **antispasmodic** properties and is useful in the treatment of **asthma, bronchitis, pleurisy and tuberculosis, indigestion, general debility, insomnia.**

POSITIVE QUALITIES

Mind becomes positive.

TRANSFORMATION

Practical approach in problems with time and life.

CORIANDER
(The Flower of Wind)

Botanical Name : *Coriandrum Sativum*

Family Name : *Umbelliferae*

English Name : Coriander

Hindi Name : Dhania

Plant

Indigenous to Southern Europe and found occasionally in Britain. In India flowering time is January to March. The colour of the flower is white. Coriander is a pungent herb, with a sweet, pleasant taste.

Keyword

→ Tonic for stomach

Symptoms

❖ **Poor circulation, lack of motivation, digestive problems, wind, neuralgia.**

- Coriander's **pain-relieving** properties make it suitable for **headaches**.
- It is warming, good for **muscular pain** and stiffness, arthritis, and rheumatism.
- Coriander is an effective stimulant and **tonic,** used to relieve **diarrhoea**, **flatulence, nausea, painful spasms,** and to stimulate appetite in cases of anorexia [loss of appetite].
- It is also a **nervous** stimulant, beneficial for apathy, nervous exhaustion and fatigue.
- It is useful for **haemorrhoids, poor circulation**, and fluid retention.
- Its energy is cooling and moisturizing.
- It has strong stimulant and alternative properties. Coriander acts as a diuretic and diaphoretic.
- Coriander stimulates the **plasma, blood** and **muscles.**
- Stimulant, aromatic and carminative.

PRACTICE

It is generally used with active purgatives as flavoring and to lessen their **griping tendencies**. Coriander water was formerly used for **windy colic**.

THERAPEUTIC USES

- Coriander alleviates **abdominal weakness**, such as **gas pains, vomiting, diarrhea** due to indigestion, **eye infection, urinary infection, cystitis, rashes**, **hives, burns, colic pains, vomiting, respiratory problems**.
- It eases **allergies, asthma, cough** and hay fever.
- It purifies the blood, decongests the **liver**, and reduces heat and fever in the body.

65. Banana

66. Bur

67. Celery

68. Coriander

69. Gainda

70. Grape Fruit

71. Gulmohar

72. Kadam

- As an anti-inflammatory, coriander benefits **arthritis**.
- Coriander is typically an ingredient in eyewashes for **blindness**, and has been indicated as a remedy for measles. Allays thirst, is a brain and heart tonic.

POSITIVE QUALITIES

It can control the emotions.

TRANSFORMATION

The emotions get balanced, so these people are able to take right decisions.

69

GAINDA
(Flower of Tradition)

Botanical Name	:	*Tagetes erecta*
Family Name	:	*Asteraceae*
English Name	:	Indian Marigold
Hindi Name	:	Gainda

PLANT

Gainda is among the very popular flowers commonly found in India and other countries. It can be easily cultivated, is widely adaptable to varying soils and climatic conditions and has a good flowering duration. This bushy plant with around 20 to 30 species has a long flowering period and the colours range from orange, yellow, and gold, cream to apricot. They are used in making garlands. Make excellent beds and pot decorations. ***Gainda are not fussy, they will adapt to most garden soils.***

KEYWORD

→ **Tonic for degeneration.**

THERAPEUTIC USES

- The Gainda has been used in traditional medicine to treat everything from **menstrual** disorders to **eczema**, though it's most important use is in **treating muscular degeneration of the eye.**
- It has a wide range of uses, from soothing **indigestion**, and **stomach cramps** to relieving **insomnia** and **cancer** diseases.
- Is an **antibiotic, cathartic, diuretic, emetic, expectorant, poultice, and tonic.** It is used in treating **joint pains, burns, scalds**, and as a **warts** remover with juice of the leaf.

NOTE

Today, with modern medical science, doctors believe that Gainda has some miracle in it, because Gainda can work on prevention of AIDS, diabetes and cancer.

POSITIVE QUALITIES

Can adjust with different nature of people.

TRANSFORMATION

Adaptability gives them good health.

70

GRAPE FRUIT
(Flower of Clear Thought)

Botanical Name	:	*Citrus Paradisi*
Family Name	:	*Rutaceae*
English Name	:	Grapefruit
Hindi Name	:	Chakutra

Plant

This tall fruit tree has been recognized as a distinct species since 1830. The large white or creamy white flowers appear alone or in clusters on the leaf axils.

Keyword

→ Tonic for nerve stress.

Symptoms

❖ It has a regenerative effect on the body manifesting in clearer thoughts and the release of **tension stored in the temples,**

head and jaw bone. Although grapefruit releases **stress** in the skeletal and **muscular systems**, it is associated neither with specific aspects of stressing the system nor with specific emotional states. It merely affects the **autonomic nervous system** in the area relating to and controlling the **jaw line**.

- This is an excellent remedy for **headaches.**
- It acts as a mild **tonic** to the meridians, and the **pineal gland** is stimulated.
- It also stimulates a lustrous look in the hair because more blood is drawn into that region, which keeps the **scalp in better** condition.
- Manipulating the **cranial plates** usually balances the entire structure releases tension in the face that contributes to **aging**, so you might call this essence a liquid **face-lift.**
- When someone massages your muscles, you might feel more **relaxed,** but this does not necessarily release stress from the body. Stress in the muscles often comes from the mental body and its association with the **muscular system.** An aggravated mental body often creates muscular tension. On the other hand, tensions can be stored in the muscles that have absolutely nothing to do with mental tension.
- If you fought with someone there might be some fear, but the aches in your muscles would be from the direct physical contact. The mental body is aligned with the rest of the system.
- **Healers treating the skeletal** or muscular systems would find this a more effective remedy than would practitioners trying to eliminate psychological stress.

PRACTICE

It strengthens the physical body and many aspects of re-growth that makes it easier for sunlight energy to be transferred to people. It is often wise to prescribe grapefruit essence with another remedy that will specifically relieve tensions stored in the mental body. Grapefruit has, at best, only a mild direct affect on the mental body.

THERAPEUTIC USES

- For **insomnia**, as a **cardiac tonic**, stimulates the **digestive tract**, aids **gas** and is also good for curing **malaria, anti-fungal** remedy.
- Diuretic properties helpful with water retention and **liver** and **gall bladder** conditions.
- Rubbed on the skin, grapefruit is beneficial in treating **acne** and oily skin.
- For **urinary infections**, effective in **lowering serum cholesterol**.
- Healing of an **injury** from a **fall** will be assisted for most people. This applies particularly to the **neck** and **head** region, as well as the **bones** of the **spine** and **pelvis**.

POSITIVE QUALITIES

This is ultimately to provide for mankind a greater sense of purpose and strength.

TRANSFORMATION

In a way they share certain inner peacefulness and resourcefulness with mankind.

71

GULMOHAR
(Red Hot Flower)

Botanical Name	:	*Delonix regia*
Family Name	:	*Fabaceae*
English Name	:	Flame Tree
Hindi Name	:	Gulmohar

PLANT

It is a large deciduous tree, native of Madagascar and reaching a height of 12-20 m with spreading branches, umbrella shaped crown and greyish bark. Flowers are 5 cm wide, scarlet in colour with a mild scout.

KEYWORD

- Tonic for sexual violence

SYMPTOMS

- For those who live in the world of fantasy and day -dreaming.

- For those who want to run away from the challenges of life and are escapists.

PRACTICE

Spiritual healing for those who have committed **acts of sex related violence** in the past lives.

POSITIVE QUALITIES

Restores deep peace and harmony in present life, letting the sexual energy flow so love making becomes fulfilling once more.

TRANSFORMATION

This remedy brings people down to earth gently. They start facing reality and responsibilities.

72

KADAM
(Flower of Heart)

Botanical Name	:	*Neolamarckia cadamba*
Family Name	:	*Rubiaceae*
English Name	:	Kaim
Hindi Name	:	Kadam

PLANT

The plant's origin is in India. A large tree its leaves opposite and simple, flowers fragrant occurring in globular heads- 3-4 cm in dia, pulpy, edible, taste-bitter.

KEYWORD

- Tonic for heart.

THERAPEUTIC USES

- **Tonic, astringent, stomach ache, digestion, wound healing. Snake bites, cardiac** problems, **anti- depressant**

effect on spinal reflex. Is hypertensive, anti-pyretic**, anti-diuretic, anti-bacterial, anti-abortion**, **improves complexion**.

- ❖ It Is useful in **gases, colic** and **fever**, internal and external **hemorrhages**, flatulence, dyspepsia, **inflammation, skin diseases, leprosy, erysipelas**. Decreases cholesterol, phospholipids, triglycerides.

NOTE

- ❖ For eyes, spray the essence on the **eyelids.**
- ❖ For mouth—**gargle** 2 or 3 times

POSITIVE QUALITIES

They are able to face the situation.

TRANSFORMATION

In a difficult situation, they think of logic instead of being emotional.

73. Loofah

74. Mogra

75. Oregano

76. Papaya

77. Passion Flower

78. Peach

79. Portulaca

80. Saunf

81. White Poppy

73

LUFFA
(The Flower of Cleansing Energies)

Botanical Name : *Luffa Acutangula*
Family Name : *Cucurbitaceae*
English Name : Sponge Gourd
Hindi Name : Torai [Dhari Wali]

Plant

Sponge Gourd is a rampant, fast growing annual vine that produces pretty yellow flowers and a popular vegetable and fruit that is edible when immature and used as a back scrubber or sponge when fully mature. The fruits are green, up to 24 inches long and 3 inches diameter; they are cylindrical and smooth, and shaped like a club, slighter wider on one end. Small fruits look like okra or little cucumbers. On older fruits, the outer skin eventually dries and turns brown and papery

KEYWORD

→ Tonic for skin

SYMPTOMS

- Luffa primarily **rejuvenates the skin tissues** sensitivity, not only on the cellular level but also on the physical level.

  .t affects the physical body, closely interacts with the skin. By strengthening the body, the life force is better able to penetrate the pores of the skin.
- These people are **claustrophobic** individuals; they feel difficulty in breathing not in the literal sense but they feel uneasy.
- They are undisciplined people who feel no rules are to be followed.
- They are **hyperactive people**, and **hyperkinetic children**.
- Skin defines the space of the physical body; thus, people who are too introverted or extroverted can be helped by Luffa.

PRACTICE

"With Luffa the point is to allow increased interchange through subtler dimensions so that people will understand the intertwining nature of cleansing and **healing energies** with those of inspirational energies. This will be shared throughout many species, including plants, animals, and mankind."

Luffa aids in assimilating vitamin C, E, and all the B vitamins. This is an excellent remedy to use externally on the skin.

THERAPEUTIC USES

- **Heart tonic, Stomach ache**, Carminative, **wound healing**, Antidote, **Diuretic**.

- Used in—**Cough,** Bilious, **Anaemia, Liver diseases, Leprosy, Piles, Oedema**, **Bowel complaints, Jaundice, Abdominal lump, Anorexia, Asthma, Fever, Poly urea, Spleen enlargement. For rheumatism, backache, internal haemorrhage, chest pains, expectorant, galactagogue** and are useful in **fever, syphilis, tumours, bronchitis.**
- Luffa is a good remedy to use for any **skin disorder**, eliminates toxicity, particularly **eczema, ulceration**, **fungus** and **allergies.**
- The dried fruit fibres are used as **abrasive sponges** in **skin care,** to remove **dead skin** and to stimulate the **circulation.**

POSITIVE QUALITIES

The skin and body are given breathing space.

TRANSFORMATION

Person starts looking for a brighter future and becomes energetic.

74

MOGRA
(Innocent Flower of Vishnu)

Botanical Name : *Jasminum Sambac*
Family Name : *Oleaceae*
English Name : Belle of India
Hindi Name : Madan mogra
Common Name : Arabian Jasmine 'Belle of India',

PLANT

A shrub with white scented flowers. In India, the Mogra flower has a great significance in religion, and is used for making perfumes and medicine. The flower is associated with innocent purity, and is considered a favourite flower of Lord Vishnu. Garlands of Mogra are very common offerings to the Gods.

KEYWORD

→ Tonic for feeding mothers

THERAPEUTIC USES

- Apply the essence on the breast to **stop the milk** post feeding and to make them **firm.**
- Aroma therapists use Mogra as a **healing and calming influence.** It is used in decoctions for relieving **sore eyes**.
- It is **cooling,** a **wound healer, an anti-inflammatory,** and a **uterus stimulant.**
- Used in stomach **ache, ulcers, ophthalmic, breast abscess**, and useful for **ears, nose** and **mouth.**
- Mogra is also well respected for its medicinal properties.

POSITIVE QUALITIES

Mind becomes relaxed.

TRANSFORMATION

Mind starts thinking on the right path and takes the correct decisions.

75

OREGANO
(Flower of Spices)

Botanical Name : *Origanum Vulgare*
Family Name : *Lamiaceae*
English Name : Oregano
Hindi Name : Sathra

PLANT

Oregano is a spicy, Mediterranean, perennial herb, particularly common in Greek and Italian cuisines. It has hairy leaves and bracts, and white flowers. It is the leaves that are used in cooking, and the dried herb is often more flavorful than the fresh, aromatic, warm and slightly bitter.

KEYWORD

- → Tonic as a pain reliever

THERAPEUTIC USES

- Useful for **bronchitis, viral infections, fungal infections, thrush, rheumatism**, **arthritis, asthma**, and **indigestion, expe*ctorant, tonic***.
- Oregano has been used as a culinary and medicinal herb for thousands of years. It has a beneficial effect upon the **digestive and respiratory systems.**
- The plant is taken internally in the treatment of **colds, influenza, stomach upsets** and **painful menstruation**.
- Frequently relieves the pain of **toothache, swelling, itching, and sores**. Also good for **tired joints and muscles, gas bloating, coughs, urinary problems, headaches**, and **swollen glands** and to induce and **regulate a woman's menstrual cycle**. Others swear that it can cure **fevers, diarrhoea, vomiting, and jaundice.**
- **Cures fungus, yeast, parasites, bacteria** and gives full-strength to kill off **skin infections** which proliferate because **fungi thrive on dead skin cells.** Other skin conditions that benefit from **applying oil of oregano include eczema, ringworm, athlete's foot and psoriasis.**

POSITIVE QUALITIES

To gel with body and relax the muscles

TRANSFORMATION

It strengthens the mind to understand the body problems.

76

PAPAYA
(Flower of the Mind)

Botanical Name	:	*Carica Papaya*
Family Name	:	*Caricaceae*
English Name	:	Papaya/Pawpaw
Hindi Name	:	Papita

PLANT

This tropical fruit tree produces small yellow male, female, and hermaphrodite flowers. The flowers are funnel shaped with five separate petals. Slight differences in the clinical effects of using the male, female, and hermaphrodite essences will be described. Later a digestive enzyme, apian, is extracted from the fruit.

KEYWORD

- Tonic for the married couple

SYMPTOMS

- When the person is not able to **focus his mind** on the higher Self.
- For married people when they as a **couple have no clarity** and consciousness between themselves as individuals and as man and wife.
- It resolves an identity **crisis people have about their sexuality**. This includes the problems society creates concerning **homosexuality and lesbianism.**
- Papaya helps such individuals to decide if one sex should dominate emotionally, mentally, and perhaps even anatomically.
- **Suppressed emotions** and **tensions** are gradually brought to the surface to be examined and resolved.
- For those who **do not wish to claim responsibility for their own health when** they feel 'burnt out' from working for others' health, welfare and safety.
- For those who are **overly concerned about others**.
- Sensitivity in the entire physical body increases. With **hypnosis** and perhaps creative visualizations and meditation, different parts of the body become more or less sensitive. By focusing the individual's consciousness on specific parts of the body, **pain can be eased** or stopped.
- There is a **slight expansion of the pineal** and **pituitary glands'** activities, but this is more a by-product of papaya's influence on the subtle bodies rather than the direct effect of the essence. It also alleviates problems associated with **mixed-brain dominance**.

PRACTICE

It was originally developed in olden times to aid certain enzymatic and digestive processes to assimilate the life force into the colon.

The development of the stomach and the eating of meat are relatively recent in the history of humanity.

It increases memory retention and assimilation of information obtained on the higher planes, integrating it into daily life. **Clairvoyant vision, telepathic ability,** and most psychic skills improve.

Some would consider papaya an aphrodisiac**.** The **breasts can slightly expand** and become more sensitive, and other slight adjustments can take place such as in the **shape of the pelvis.** The **male gets more fertile and the tip of the penis may get more sensitive**.

Therapeutic Uses

- ❖ Used in haemorrhagic diseases, piles, latex useful in spleen, anathematic, liver enlargement, ringworms, diarrhoea, and cardiac diseases.
- ❖ Various hormones are activated, including those associated with sexuality.

Positive Qualities

Papaya alleviates tensions in the dream state. This cleansing of tensions in the subconscious mind also alleviates tensions from the physical body.

Transformation

Ultimately, papaya will bring a greater sense of gentleness and assimilation in the understanding of basic spiritual principles in order to build upon such principles so that mankind as a whole will understand them.

77

PASSION FLOWER
(Flower of Happiness)

Botanical Name	:	*Passiflora Incarnata Passiflora Caerulea (Blue Flower)*
Family	:	*Passifloraceae*
English Name	:	Passion Flower
Hindi Name	:	Jhumkalata

PLANT

A native of Virginia in the United States. The Passion Flowers are so named from the supposed resemblance of the finely-cut corona in the centre of the blossoms to the Crown of Thorns and the other parts of the flower to the instruments of the Passion of Our Lord.

KEYWORD

- Tonic for happiness

SYMPTOMS

- The importance of following a path of love and anxiety.
- Listen to your inherent goodness, doing no harm to others, allowing everyone perfect freedom to follow their path, as they must allow you perfect freedom to follow yours.
- If you feel disapproval from others you should trust your intuition to make your own way.
- The greatest challenge lies in winning freedom from your closest family members, but, at no point should they be seen as enemies, rather as worthy companions in the game of life, who are offering you the opportunity to become strong.
- Do not be afraid, plunge into experiences, and remember there is no right or wrong. It is all relative to the circumstances

THERAPEUTIC USES

- Promise in fighting **Parkinson's disease, Cancer, HIV, Leukaemia**, and more. Also used in the treatment of **women's complaints**.
- For happiness from inside It is non –addictive. The drug is known to be a depressant to the motor side of the spinal cord, slightly reducing arterial pressure, though affecting circulation but little, while increasing the rate of respiration.
- Passionflower is used as an alternative medicine in the treatment of insomnia, **nervous tension, irritability, neuralgia, irritable bowel syndrome, premenstrual tension and vaginal discharges.**
- **Sedative,** slightly **reduces blood pressure** and increases **respiratory** rate.
- It is of great service in **epilepsy.**

- Relieves pain, **anxiety, depression, inflammation, convulsions**, mildly sedative, tranquilizes, kills germs, enhances libido, hysteria, alcoholism, hyperactivity in children, **rapid heartbeat, headaches, colic in infants, diarrhoea, hypertension, asthma, whooping cough, bronchitis and other tough coughs, for urinary infections and as a mild diuretic.**

NOTE

- It is non –addictive. The drug is known to be a depressant to the motor side of the spinal cord, slightly reducing arterial pressure, though affecting circulation a little, while increasing the rate of respiration.

POSITIVE QUALITIES

Found happiness to be the key, and the gauge by which to measure how closely your life resonates with your soul's blue print.

TRANSFORMATION

The voice guides you via desires, intuitions, ideals, likes and dislikes and can lead you through all of life's challenges as long as it is listened to.

78

PEACH
(Flower of Health)

Botanical Name : *Prunus persica*

Family Name : *Rosaceae*

English Name : Peach

Hindi Name : Adoo

PLANT

Cultivated in Asia for centuries and introduced in Europe from Persia. While originally from China, this fruit tree is now grown in many parts of the world. Soft, pink flowers appear in the spring. In some cultures, peach is used for respiratory and digestive problems.

KEYWORD

- Tonic as a healer

SYMPTOMS

- When people are in **depression.**
- For **moody** people.
- Peach **activates the body fluid,** aligning them with all the subtle bodies, particularly the **mental, emotional, and soul bodies**. It brings the **harmonics of these bodies into the physical body**, so that emotional or mental diseases that would today be considered stress related can be alleviated.
- A catalyst essence for speeding up all healing processes, including **grief.**

PRACTICE

This is a universal amplifier for all forms of healing. It can reduce by twenty five to fifty percent the time that would usually be needed for healing to take place. While peach can accomplish this alone, it is an excellent catalyst to use in combination with other remedies.

Peach strengthens the meridians if there is a tendency for poor absorption and low body weight, take peach essence with Geranium.

THERAPEUTIC USES

- **Diuretic:** It stimulates **urine** elimination, useful in illnesses like: **obesity**, arterial **hypertension, dropsy (accumulation of liquids in the body with swelling of tissues), oedemas, kidney pain** (nephritis), renal calculations, renal inadequacy and inflammation of urinary bladder (cystitis), etc.
- **External use:** Analgesic- relieves the pains produced by blows, **twists, sprains, bruises, sedative, expectorant and helps in jaundice cases.**

  Psycho-structural diseases including **slipped discs and hypersensitivity** to the sun, such as various forms of **lupus**, can be efficiently treated with this essence. Body builders could cut back on lifting weights without losing muscle tone. Chiropractors, osteopaths, massage technicians, and people accustomed to doing constant exercises will especially benefit from peach.

- ❖ Some balancing of metabolism will be noted. It helps in **chronic fatigue** syndrome, the **Epstein - Barr virus**. There will be some **easing of difficult mood swings** and a tendency towards **depression, hardening of the arteries**, **mistral valve prolapsed,** and heart arrhythmia will be correct.

Positive Qualities

Ultimately, this plant will provide a greater sense of combined force and gentleness for all people. It also allows this inner strength to be given greater direction in groups, so that a genuine understanding of purpose among many species will result.

Transformation

This essence enhances a sense of joy, greater lightness, and ease in sleep. There is a general healing tendency.

79

PORTULACA
(Flower to Relax the Mind)

Botanical Name : *Portulaca oleracea*
Family Name : *Portulacaceae*
English Name : Portulaca
Hindi Name : Lunia

PLANT

Portulaca belongs to North America. It has smooth, reddish, mostly prostrate stems and alternate leaves clustered at stem joints and ends. The deep pink flowers have five regular parts and are up to 6 mm wide.

KEYWORD

→ Tonic to remove stress

SYMPTOMS

Exhaustion and stress at work place and depression.

PRACTICE

Known as *"Sanhti or Punarva"* in North India it is known to act as a **liver tonic.**

Tonic for exhaustion, stress and depression.

THERAPEUTIC USES

- Used in diseases of the liver, **heart attacks** and strengthening the **immune system,** coughs, sores, burns, skin diseases and insect stings [including caterpillar stings], **stomach aches, headaches and earaches**.
- Remedy **for constipation, inflammation, urinary disease**, and v*ermifuge.*
- The plant is an anti-bacterial, anti-scorbutic, depurative, diuretic and febrifuge.
- It affects **blood pressure, clotting**, prevents inflammation, **lowers cholesterol** (LDL), prevents certain cancers and controls coronary spasms. Has effects **on the brain** and may aid in such conditions as **depression, bipolar disorder, Alzheimer's disease,** autism, schizophrenia, attention deficit disorder, hyperactivity and **migraines**.
- Weak digestion, boils, sores, bee stings.

POSITIVE QUALITIES

It works as punarva in the mind and body

TRANSFORMATION

The mind is stress free and relaxed at work time.

80

SAUNF
(Cooling Flower)

Botanical Name	:	*Foeniculum Vulgare Mill*
Family Name	:	*Gilbert Umbelliferae*
English Name	:	*Fennel Fruit*
Hindi Name	:	*Saunf*

Plant

A large annual herb, innately compound leaves, flowers yellow in compound umbels.

Keyword

- Tonic for brain

Therapeutic Uses

- **Fever, urine- inflammation, thirst, dysentery, diarrhoea, cholera, colic, spleen, anathematic, analgesic, brain**

tonic, anti-acid, flatulence, cough, asthma, kidney disease, flavouring agent, Burning in urine gets better, good for **uterine diseases** also.

- Saunf **increases the milk** of the feeding mother and also helps the child in the womb.
- Children stomach ache, eyesight, glaucoma, hypertension.

POSITIVE QUALITIES

Cooling and relaxing

TRANSFORMATION

It brings harmony in the body and mind.

81

WHITE POPPY
(Flower of Dreams)

Botanical Name : *Papaver somniferum*

Family Name : *Papaveraceae*

English Name : White poppy

Hindi Name :

PLANT

The plant is an erect, herbaceous annual, varying much in the colour of its flowers, as well as in the shape of the fruit and colour of the seeds. The flowers vary in colour from pure white to reddish purple. In the wild plant, they are pale lilac with a purple spot at the base of each petal.

KEYWORD

- Tonic to calm.

THERAPEUTIC USES

- It is the best possible hypnotic and sedative drug, frequently used to relieve pain and **calm excitement**. It has also been used as an **astringent, expectorant, diaphoretic, anti-spasmodic, anodyne, diarrhoea, dysentery** and some forms of cough. Applied externally it provides **quick pain relief**. Also useful in **pleurisy** and **erysipelas.**

NOTE

- Mixture can be made and used as a gargle.

POSITIVE QUALITIES

Mind gets relaxed and one starts to take positive steps.

TRANSFORMATION

Anxiety gets better and starts living in the present.

INDIAN RESCUE REMEDY

Indian rescue remedy has a calming and stabilizing effect on the emotions during a crisis. However rescue remedy cannot replace medical treatment, it only helps to prevent or quickly overcome the energy trauma that otherwise would have serious physical consequences.

The energy trauma includes variety of emotional and psychological disturbances like fear, panic, severe mental stress, tension and shock. Under these conditions the subtle elements in our body, have the tendency to withdraw from the physical body and which is thus not able to initiate the self-healing processes.

I Rescue remedy prevents the disintegration of the energy system, quickly restoring it to normal. The healing process is then able to commence immediately.

The Components of I Rescue Remedy

Ashoka : for trauma, both mental and physical.

Bottle Brush : For terror, panic, hysteria and great fear.

Periwinkle : For impatience, irritability, and agitation with stress.

Poppy Red : For unconsciousness, faintness and out of body sensations.

Peepal : For fear of loosing control, goose flesh.

The stock bottle of I Rescue Remedy contains a mix of all the above five flowers.

SYMPTOMS

- I Rescue Remedy is specially designed to help and balance life's ups and down.
- To get rid of the impact, which has happened, or is presently happening.
- Its gentle action assists the return to a positive outlook, when comfort and reassurance are needed.
- For those attracting negativity from others, feeling undefined fears.
- For 'psychic attack' and also loss of memory, offer's protection from negative thoughts, cultivates self-confidence and ability to feel comfortable with any one.
- I Rescue Remedy is needed before a driving test, for fear of traveling, exams, flight or when you simply need a little help to cool anxiety or irritation.
- I Rescue Remedy treats the individual, not the disease or symptoms, and it encourages the body's own potential to look after itself by helping restore a more positive outlook and is also given for immediate respite from trauma.
- It should be taken when a person feels in need of rescue, is unsettled, or is not quiet in step with him or her self. This may be after an argument, a trying event like divorce or

separation, or any circumstances which has demanded supreme nervous effort.

- ❖ I Rescue must be taken before salvage and restoration.
- ❖ I Rescue remedy speeds recovery after surgery.
- ❖ It is for all emergencies. Carry a small bottle with you at all times.

External Help

- ❖ Use I Rescue cream after sun burn, cuts, bruises, or damage from accident.

  I Rescue can be added to any skin wash, douche, or compress if some element of rescue is needed.

Note

I Rescue remedy helps not only the victims but also the bystanders and those who give assistance. The victim will unconsciously derive considerable reassurance from the feeling that those around him are calm, collected and confident. This will assist the process of recovery.

I Rescue Remedy is reported to have a positive calming and stabilizing effect in a broad range of stressful situations like nervousness, anxiety, and the stress arising from bereavement, great fright, hysteria, anguish and desperation.

I Rescue Remedy can be taken directly from the stock bottle or can be applied in the case of unconsciousness on the head, temple, behind the ears and on the lips, on the wrists.

The cream can be applied by smoothing gently into the effected area, or by applying on a piece of gauze to wounds.

I Rescue Remedy should not become a form of routine medication. It is indicated as first aid in greater or lesser emotional emergencies, but certainly not to make up for a lifestyle that threatens to destroy the personality through a lack of common sense.

PHYSICAL REPERTORY

HOW TO USE THE REPERTORY

These indications for the use of the remedies should be studied together with the book "Flowers that Heal". There is no hard and fast rule in treating the patients with these remedies, as each patient must be regarded as an individual, to be helped with his personal and particular circumstances with his moods. However, please remember – read– 'state of mind' (given in the book), then judge and give the essence.

The repertory is just an aid in prescribing the remedy, but the method is the same – understanding the nature of the person. As stated earlier – the same disease has different effects on different people; it is the 'effects' that need treatment – they are the guide to the real cause. For example – a patient has seen an accident, and after that accident scene he develops asthma. Here, asthma is the disease of which the cause is shock, so first he is to be given the remedy for shock, and see the improvement before proceeding further.

PHYSICAL REPERTORY

Abdominal pain : Ashwagandha, Basil, Bougainvillea, Chamomile, Curry leaf, Ginger, Hibiscus, Loofah, Mustard, Pine, Water melon.

Abortion : Lemon.

Abscess : Aloe vera, Drumstick, Eucalyptus, Geranium, Kachnar, Pansy, Rose red, Yarrow.

Absorption : Calendula, Lemon.

Accidents : Amaltas, Bottle brush, Ginger.

Aches : Bougainvillea, California poppy, Ginger, Mustard, Willow, Yarrow.

Acid : Aloe vera.

Acidity : Aloe vera, Basil, Banana, Chamomile, Curry leaf, Champa, Coriander, Drumstick, Garlic, Ginger, Gooseberry, Holly hock, Jasmine, Lemon, Mulberry, Neem, Peepal, Rose red, Saunf, Tamarind.

Acne : Aloe vera, Basil, Banana, Bottle brush, Calendula, Coriander, Geranium, Grape fruit, Geranium, Holly hock, Lemon, Ox eye daisy, Onion, Peppermint, Radish, Salvia, Yarrow.

Addictions : Amaltas, Basil, Bottle brush, California poppy, Canna, Chamomile, Fever few, Ginger, Holly hock, Kachnar, Morning glory, Mustard, Peppermint, Petunia, Pine, Salvia.

Adolescence : Bottle brush, Peppermint, Walnut, Yarrow.

Adrenal glands : Bottle brush, Chamomile, Pansy.

Ageing : Ashoka, Ashwagandha, Garlic, Gooseberry, Grape fruit, Hibiscus, Jasmine, Marjoram, Mustard, Peepal, Petunia, Rose red.

Aids : Aloe vera, Ashoka, Ashwagandha, Bottle brush, Calendula, Garlic, Hibiscus, Pansy, Tuberose.

Alcoholic : Ashoka, Ashwagandha, Bottle brush, California poppy, Fever few, Ginger, Morning glory, Mustard, Nasturtium, Passion flower, Petunia, Salvia.

Allergies : Aloe vera, Balsam, Banana, Chamomile, Corn, Fever few, Garlic, Loofah, Mulberry, Onion, Poppy red, Pine, Periwinkle, Rangoon creeper, Rose red, Salvia, Yarrow, Snapdragon, Tuberose, I Rescue cream.

Alzheimer's disease : Portulaca.

Amoebiasis : Calendula, Lemon, Rose red, Tuberose, Yarrow.

Anaemia : Ashoka, Ashwagandha, Asparagus, Balsam, Banana, Basil, Champa, Gooseberry, Jasmine, Loofah, Mulberry, Nasturtium, Pansy, Pomegranate, Rose red, Sunflower, Yarrow.

Analgesic : Amaltas, Ashwagandha, Hibiscus.

Anathematic : Ashoka, Banana, Bur, Lemon, Pomegranate.

Aneurysms : Papaya.

Ankle : Banana.

Anorexia : Aloe vera.

Anti-analgesic : Ashwagandha.

Anti-bacterial : Ashoka, Ashwagandha, Basil, Calendula, Gainda, Garlic, Kadam, Mustard, Oregano, Portulaca.

Anti-biotic : Garlic, onion.

Anti-dyspeptic : Ashoka.

Anti-oxidant : Oregano.

Anti-parasitic : Garlic.

Anti-scorbutic : Portulaca, Radish.

Anti-septic : Asparagus, Basil, Calendula, Drumstick, Eucalyptus, Geranium, Kachnar, Lemon, Mustard, Oregano, Peppermint, Pine, Portulaca, Rose red, Yarrow.

Anus : Bottle brush, Curry leaf, Pomegranate.

Anxiety : Amaltas, Balsam, Bottle brush, Bougainvillea, California poppy, Chamomile, Curry leaf, Garlic, Geranium, Marjoram, Pansy, Passion Flower, Petunia, Peepal.

Aphrodisiac : Asparagus, Ginger, Jasmine, Nasturtium, Pomegranate, Petunia.

Appetite loss : Aloe vera, Ashwagandha, Basil, Champa, Coriander, Fever few, Ginger, Gooseberry, Lemon, Marjoram, Mulberry, Mustard, Nasturtium, Peppermint, Pomegranate, Rose red.

Appetiser : Lemon, Pomegranate.

Apnoea : California poppy, Eucalyptus, Jasmine, Morning glory, Poppy red.

Arteriosclerosis : Bottle brush, Garlic, Him water, Pansy.

Arthritis : Asparagus, Basil, Bur, Calendula, Celery, Coriander, Drumstick, Fever few, Garlic, Geranium, Ginger, Harshringar, Him water, Mulberry, Mustard, Oregano, Ox eye daisy, Peppermint, Snapdragon, Water melon, Willow, Yarrow.

Arthritis Osteo : Ashwagandha, Basil, Curry leaf, Drumstick, Eucalyptus, Feverfew, French marigold, Gooseberry, Harshringar, Kachanar, Lemon, Loofah, Marjoram, Mulberry, Mustard, Neem, Onion, Ox eye daisy, Pansy, Peepal, Pine, Pomegranate, Sun flower, Willow, Walnut.

Asthenia : Asparagus.

Asthma : Ashoka, Ashwagandha, Basil, Bottle brush, California poppy, Celery, Chamomile, Curry leaf, Drumstick, Eucalyptus, Feverfew, Garlic, Ginger, Gooseberry, Harshringar, Him water, Hibiscus, Jasmine, Kachanar, Lemon, Loofah, Morning glory, Mulberry, Mustard, Onion, Oregano, Ox eye daisy, Pansy, Passion flower, Peepal, Pine, Peppermint, Pomegranate, Rose red, Sunflower, Walnut, Yarrow, I Rescue.

Astringent : Aloe vera, Ashoka, Calendula, Champa, Geranium, Harshringar, Jasmine, Kachanar, Kadam, Lemon, Neem, Ox eye daisy, Passion flower, Pear, Pomegranate, Rose red, Walnut, Willow, White poppy.

BABIES, KIDS AND CHILDREN

Babies **for pain :** Calendula.

Babies non addictive for calming **restless, anxiety, tension, insomnia –** Chamomile.

Absent minded and inattentive for exams : French marigold, Neem.

Adolescents : ashamed of changes : Basil, Bottle brush, Salvia.

Anxiety, fear, moody, changeable, tense, angry : Bottle brush.

Kids want **bedroom door open :** Peepal.

Bedwetting : Fever few, Garlic, Petunia, Pine, Rose red, Salvia, Willow.

Before exams : Neem and I Rescue.

Boarding school : Bottle brush.

Kids who **bully** playmates : Mulberry, Onion, Petunia, Sunflower.

Constipation and diarrhoea : Chamomile.

Colicky baby : Chamomile, Passion flower.

Kids torn between **divorced parents :** Ashoka.

Discouraged school kids : Holly hock.

Drowsy and apathetic : Poppy red.

Excessive energy and inability to rest : Aloe vera.

Fever : Chamomile.

Fear of teacher : Garlic.

First day at school : Bottle brush, Corn, Garlic, Morning glory.

Good for babies : Amaltas.

Grinding lower jaws : Canna.

Growth : Onion.

Homesickness : Morning glory.

Hyperactive kids who do not want to go to bed at night **:** Aloe vera.

For **maltreated** kids **:** Peepal, Rose.

Moodiness, rebelliousness in the first born when second child is born **:** Chamomile, Mulberry, Petunia.

Nervous, despondent over minor setbacks in class, do not want to go to school **:** Holly hock.

Never still, wakefulness **:** Periwinkle.

Nightmares, wake up panic-stricken, afraid to go back to sleep **:** Bottle brush.

For the **newborns trauma :** Bottle brush, Ginger.

Orphans : Morning glory.

Look like basement kids with **pale, waxy, yellowy faces** and dark shadows under their eyes **:** Ashoka, Rose red.

Pain relieve : Chamomile.

Panic in the dark for no reason **:** Peepal.

Can't keep up with their peers : French marigold.

Sleep walking or talking **:** Peepal.

Stutter or stammer : Snapdragon.

Temper tantrums : Fever few.

Teething : Ashwagandha, Balsam, Bottle brush, Calendula, Chamomile, Holly hock, Pine, Walnut.

Teething babies to cool their inflamed gums : Holly hock.

Terrified of exams **:** Bottle brush.

Throw on the ground and hit their head on the wall **:** Fever few, Petunia.

Timid, shy, clinging : Garlic, Rose, Tamarind.

Tooth pain : rub Chamomile on cheek.

Tortured by schoolwork : California poppy.

Tumour : Periwinkle.

Worry about schoolwork **:** Bottle brush.

Back pain : Aloe vera, Amaltas, Ashwagandha, Basil, Bur, Calendula, California poppy, Champa, Ginger, Kachnar, Lemon, Loofah, Mustard, Periwinkle, Pine, Sunflower, Willow.

Bacteria : Aloe vera, Ashwagandha, Champa, Mustard.

Bad breath : Basil, Pomegranate.

Baldness : Banana, Corn, Gooseberry, Hibiscus, Lemon, Lotus, Nasturtium, Pomegranate, Tuberose, Walnut.

Bed wetting : Ashwagandha, Corn, Fever few, French marigold, Garlic, Ginger, Pansy, Petunia, Pine, Poppy red, Rose red, Salvia, Sweetpea, Walnut, Willow.

Bells Palsy : Garlic, Snapdragon.

Bee sting : Holly hock.

Beauty : Lemon, Radish.

Bile : Calendula, Peppermint.

Biliousness : Amaltas, Lotus, Onion.

Birthmarks : Salvia.

Bites Venomous : Fever few, Peepal.

Black heads : Coriander, Radish.

Bladder : Basil, California poppy, Chamomile, Corn, Ginger, Gooseberry, Holly hock, Nasturtium, Pine, Pomegranate, Rose red, Water melon.

Bleeding : Ashoka, Calendula, Garlic, Geranium, Gooseberry, Jasmine, Lotus, Ox eye daisy, Pomegranate, Rose red.

Blinding : Petunia.

Blisters : Ashwagandha, Geranium.

Blood circulation : Aloe vera, Amaltas, Ashwagandha, Asparagus, Calendula, California poppy, Champa, Coriander, Cosmos, Eucalyptus, Garlic, Geranium, Ginger, Gooseberry, Harshringar, Kachanar, Lemon, Lotus, Marjoram, Morning glory, Mustard, Onion, Peppermint, Petunia, Pine, Poppy red, Radish, Rose red, Tuberose, Walnut, Willow, Yarrow.

Blood cleanser : Aloe vera, Ashwagandha, Bur, Bottle brush, Champa, Curry leaf, Kachnar, Lemon, Mulberry, Nasturtium, Neem, Pansy, Pomegranate, Tuberose, White rose, Zinnia.

Blood disorder : Balsam, Banana, Basil, Bottle brush, Celery, Garlic, Pansy, Peepal, Rose red, Water melon.

Blood thinner : Calendula, Garlic, Ginger, Harshringar, Onion, Pansy, Willow, Yarrow.

Blood pressure high : Ashoka, California poppy, Curry leaf, Garlic, Gooseberry, Him water, Lemon, Marjoram, Mulberry, Onion, Pansy, Portulaca, Tuberose.

Blood Pressure low : Ashwagandha, Him water, Marjoram, Petunia, Periwinkle.

Body smell : Geranium.

Body stiffness : Amaltas, Bougainvillea, Curry leaf, Drum stick, Eucalyptus, Ginger, Hibiscus, Salvia.

Boils : Aloe vera, Ashwagandha, Calendula, Canna, Champa, Chamomile, Eucalyptus, Fever few, Geranium, Holly hock, Hibiscus, Neem, Ox eye daisy, Peepal.

Booster : Lotus.

Bone : Banana, Ginger, Gooseberry, Jasmine, Mulberry, Radish.

Bowel disorder : Aloe vera, Calendula, Kachnar, Loofah, Morning glory, Nasturtium.

Brain : Asparagus, Corn, French marigold, Gooseberry, Hibiscus, Jasmine, Lemon, Marjoram, Pansy, Periwinkle, Petunia, Pomegranate, Poppy red, Portulaca, Snapdragon, Sweetpea, Saunf.

Breast problems : Aloe vera, Ashwagandha, Basil, Bottle brush, Bur, Calendula, Chamomile, Geranium, Holly hock, Mogra, Ox eye daisy, Papaya, Peepal, Saunf, Walnut, I Rescue in water.

Breathe bad : Peppermint.

Breathing difficulty : Ashwagandha, Balsam, Bougainvillea, Bottle brush, Bur, California poppy, Champa, Drumstick, Eucalyptus, Fever few, Garlic, Ginger, Kachnar, Nasturtium, Peepal, Pine, Radish, Snapdragon, Tuberose, I Rescue.

Brittle hair : Aloe vera.

Bronchial Asthma : Garlic, Ginger, Rose red.

Bronchitis : Ashwagandha, Asparagus, Banana, Basil, Celery, Chamomile, Cosmos, Drumstick, Eucalyptus, Garlic, Ginger, Gooseberry, Loofah, Mustard, Nasturtium, Onion, Oregano, Ox eye daisy, Pansy, Peach, Peepal, Peppermint, Pine, Rose red, Snapdragon, Sun flower, Water melon.

Bruises : Calendula, Curry leaf, Holly hock, Jasmine, Marjoram, Ox eye daisy, Onion, Pansy, Petunia, Sunflower, Yarrow.

Bulimia [for pcople eat in depression and vomit] **:** Bougainvillea, Fever few, French marigold, Pine, Petunia, Rose red, Salvia.

Bulimia [This disorder is also marked by fear of weight gain] **:** Fever few, French marigold, Petunia, Rose red, Salvia.

Burns minor : Aloe vera, Chamomile, Curry leaf, Coriander, Gainda, Geranium, Holly hock, Portulaca.

Burning sensation : Ashoka, Champa, Hibiscus, Holly hock, Lemon, Lotus, Mulberry, Neem, Pomegranate, Tuberose.

Bursitis : Calendula, Holly, Jasmine, Mulberry, Willow.

Cancer : Aloe vera, Ashoka, Banana, Calendula, Corn, Drumstick, Gainda, Garlic, Onion, Passion flower, Periwinkle, Pine, Poppy red, Portulaca, Salvia, Snapdragon, I Rescue.

Candidiasis : Aloe vera, Garlic.

Carbuncle : Ashwagandha, Drum stick, Holly hock.

Cardiac : Ashoka, Drumstick, Grapefruit, Kadam, Periwinkle, Papaya.

Cardiovascular system : Ashoka, Ashwagandha, Asparagus, Drumstick, Gooseberry, Hibiscus, Mustard, Pomegranate, Sweetpea.

Catarrh : Basil, Bougainvillea, Calendula, Eucalyptus, Feverfew, Garlic, Ginger, Geranium, Harshringar, Hibiscus, Jasmine, Marjoram, Mustard, Nasturtium, Ox eye daisy, Pansy, Pine, Yarrow.

Carbuncle : Ashwagandha, Drum stick, Holly hock.

Cartilage : Jasmine.

Cellulite : Bottle brush, Geranium, Yarrow.

Cervical : Aloe vera, Ashwagandha, Bougainvillea, California poppy, Fever few, Ginger, Him water, Mulberry, Nasturtium, Pansy, Periwinkle, Petunia, Radish, Willow, I Rescue.

Cervix : Increases the blood flow : **Sweetpea.**

Chest : Ginger, Loofah, Nasturtium, Pine, Pomegranate, Poppy red.

Chest infections : Basil, Eucalyptus, Ginger, Holly hock, Mustard, Onion, Poppy red.

Chicken Pox : Calendula, Eucalyptus, Neem, Yarrow.

Chilblains : Calendula, Chamomile, Champa, Eucalyptus, Garlic, Geranium, Marjoram, Mustard, Onion, Walnut, Yarrow.

Childbirth : Ashwagandha, Amaltas, Calendula, Chamomile, Cosmos, Garlic, Ginger, Holly hock, Jasmine, Onion, Peepal, Periwinkle, Pomegranate, Radish, Rose red, Water melon, Walnut, I Rescue.

CHILDREN

Asthma : [Chamomile oil – chest].

Bed wetting : Corn, [Pansy – dreams].

Children do not survive after birth : Peepal.

Children disturb dreams : Ashwagandha, Calendula, Pansy, Willow, I Rescue.

Cholera infants : Poppy red.

Colic [particularly in babies] : Chamomile.

C[illegible] : Chamomile.

Constipation : Chamomile, Pomegranate, [Periwinkle – **mild**].

Cough : Poppy red.

Diarrhoea : Chamomile.

Dropsy : Chamomile.

Ear pain : [Chamomile – **cold, flu** – rub oil on side of ears].

Eczema : [Chamomile oil – **burning, itching, thick skin**].

Fevers : Chamomile.

Fevers and infections : Calendula.

Good essence for – children : Amaltas, Petunia.

Good for growing – children : White rose.

Good for hyperactive – children : Loofah, Passion flower.

Gums Inflamed : Holly hock.

Hysteria : [Chamomile oil **: rub on temples].**

Mucus : Peepal.

Nausea : Peepal.

Skin : [Chamomile **: patches on face, head, neck, elbow, knee:** massage oil].

Swelling : [Chamomile oil : massage on **legs, hands, below knees**]

Teething : Holly hock, Chamomile.

Teething babies to cool their inflamed gums : Holly hock.

Tumour paediatric : Periwinkle.

Thirst : Peepal.

Urticaria : Chamomile.

Vomiting : Peepal.

Weak health : Peach.

Wet dreams : Willow.

Whooping cough : Ginger.

Chilli : Ginger, Willow.

Choking : Bottle brush, Eucalyptus, Ginger, Kachanar, Rock Rose.

Cholera : Banana, Eucalyptus, Garlic, Ginger, Lemon, Peppermint, Poppy red.

Cholesterol : Banana, Coriander, Garlic, Ginger, Gooseberry, Grape fruit, Hibiscus, Him water, Lemon, Lotus, Onion, Portulaca, Sunflower.

Cleanser : Lemon, Pansy.

Clitoris : Sweetpea.

Cold : Aloe vera, Basil, Bougainvillea, Bur, Calendula, Chamomile, Eucalyptus, Fever few, Garlic, Ginger, Harshringar, Hibiscus, Jasmine, Lemon, Loofah, Mustard, Nasturtium, Onion, Oregano, Pansy, Peepal, Peppermint, Pine, Radish, Rose red, Sunflower, Tamarind, Willow, Yarrow

Colic : Ashoka, Ashwagandha, Basil, California poppy, Calendula, Chamomile, Eucalyptus, Gooseberry, Ginger, Kadam, Marjoram, Mustard, Onion, Oregano, Peach, Peppermint, Portulaca, Saunf, Walnut, Yarrow, I Rescue.

Colitis : Aloe vera, Ashoka, Banana, Bottle brush, Calendula, Canna, California poppy, Champa, Chamomile, Cosmos, Coriander, Garlic, Geranium, Ginger, Jasmine, Kachnar, Morning glory, Mulberry, Mustard, Papaya, Poppy red, Willow.

Complexion : Ashoka, Basil, Gooseberry, Kadam.

Congestion : Aloe vera, Basil, Calendula, Eucalyptus, Fever few, Garlic, Ginger, Geranium, Jasmine, Pine.

Conjunctivitis : Aloe vera, Bur, Calendula, Coriander, Marjoram, Pomegranate, Rose red.

Constipation : Aloe vera, Amaltas, Ashwagandha, Basil, Banana, Bottle brush, California poppy, Chamomile, Champa, Curry leaf, Drumstick, Garlic, Ginger, Gooseberry, Harshringar, Hibiscus, Kachanar, Lemon, Lotus, Marjoram, Mustard, Peepal, Periwinkle, Poppy red, Portulaca, Radish, Rose red, Salvia, Tamarind, Water melon, Willow.

Contraceptive : Hibiscus.

Convalescence : Willow.

Convulsions : Asparagus, Chamomile, Coriander, Feverfew, Garlic, Ginger, Gooseberry, Holly hock, Marjoram, Mulberry, Passion flower, Rose red.

Cooling : Aloe vera, Asparagus, Bur, Gooseberry, Hibiscus, Holly hock, Lotus, Mogra, Peepal, Pansy, Rangoon creeper.

Cores : Lemon.

Coronary heart disease : Poppy red.

Cosmetic : Ashoka, Basil, Grape fruit, Gooseberry, Harshringar, Kadam, Radish.

Cough : Aloe vera, Ashwagandha, Asparagus, Banana, Basil, Bur, Bottle brush, Chamomile, Champa, Drumstick, Feverfew, Garlic, Gooseberry, Harshringar, Hibiscus, Holly hock, Kachanar, Lemon, Loofah, Marjoram, Mustard, Mulberry, Neem, Onion, Oregano, Ox eye Daisy, Pansy, Pine, Poppy red, Pomegranate, Portulaca, Radish, Rose red, Sunflower, I Rescue.

Cough chronic : Ginger, Holly hock, Salvia, Tamarind, Tuberose, Walnut.

Cradle cap : Bottle brush, Calendula, Pansy, I Rescue Cream.

Cracked and Chapped : Rose red, Mustard.

Crack soles : Bur.

Cramps : Asparagus, Banana, Balsam, Basil, Bottle brush, Calendula, Chamomile, Ginger, Garlic, Jasmine, Marjoram, Periwinkle, Peppermint, Pine, Willow, Yarrow.

Cranial plates : Grape fruit, Snapdragon.

Cries in sleep : Chamomile.

Croup : Eucalyptus, Pansy.

Cuts : Aloe vera, Banana, Calendula, Chamomile, Coriander, Geranium, Ox eye daisy, Peppermint, Willow, Yarrow.

Cysts : Garlic, Pomegranate, Sweetpea.

Cystitis [inflammation of the urinary bladder] **:** Bottle brush, Calendula, Chamomile, Corn, Eucalyptus, Garlic, Holly hock, Jasmine, Nasturtium, Pansy, Pine, Pomegranate, Sweetpea.

Dampness : Calendula.

Dandruff : Lemon, Harshringar.

Day dreamer : Corn, Neem, Poppy red, Sweetpea.

Deafness : Calendula, Peepal.

Decongestant : Eucalyptus, Fever few.

Degenerative disease : French marigold, Peach, Zinnia.

Delirium : Chamomile, Fever few.

Delusion : Lotus, Peepal.

Demulcent : Aloe vera, Asparagus, Banana, Hibiscus, Pansy, Pine.

Deplete : Nasturtium.

Depression : Ashoka, Basil, Bottle brush, Canna, Champa, Chamomile, Fever few, French marigold, Geranium, Ginger, Hibiscus,

Holly hock, Jasmine, Kadam, Marjoram, Morning glory, Mustard, Passion flower, Peach, Peppermint, Petunia, Pine, Portulaca, Rose red, Salvia, Sweetpea, Tuberose, Walnut, Water melon, Willow, Zinnia.

Depurative : Bur.

Detergent : Walnut.

Diabetes : Aloe vera, Asparagus, Ashwagandha, Banana, Bougainvillea, Curry leaf, French marigold, Gainda, Garlic, Geranium, Gooseberry, Harshringar, Hibiscus, Kachanar, Lotus, Mustard, Neem, Onion, Peepal, Periwinkle, Poppy red, Radish, Rose red.

Diaphoretic : Peppermint, White poppy.

Diaper rash : Geranium.

Diarrhoea : Ashoka, Balsam, Banana, Basil, Bur, Calendula, Chamomile, Curry leaf, Eucalyptus, Fever few, Garlic, Geranium, Ginger, Gooseberry, Hibiscus, Kachanar, Lemon, Lotus, Marjoram, Oregano, Ox eye daisy, Papaya, Passion flower, Pear, Peppermint, Pomegranate, Rangoon creeper, Rose red, Walnut, Willow, White poppy, Yarrow.

Diphtheria : Mulberry, Peepal.

Disease : Ashoka.

Dysuria : Ashoka.

Diuretic : Ashoka, Ashwagandha, Asparagus, Calendula, Celery, Gainda, Garlic, Geranium, Ginger, Gooseberry, Grape fruit, Harshringar, Hibiscus, Holly hock, Kadam, Lemon, Loofah, Lotus, Mustard, Onion, Ox eye daisy, Pansy, Papaya, Passion flower, Peach, Pine, Portulaca, Radish, Rose red, Saunf, Willow.

Dizziness : Ashoka, Ginger.

Douche : Calendula.

Douche for vaginal infections : Chamomile.

Dreams terror : Aloe vera, Amaltas, Basil, Bottle brush, Morning glory, Peepal, Pansy.

Dropsy : Asparagus, Marjoram, Onion, Peach.

Drug abuse : Morning glory.

Dryness : Aloe vera, Jasmine, Lemon, Mustard, Radish, Rose red, Zinnia.

Dyscrasia : Banana.

Dysentery : Ashoka, Asparagus, Banana, Bur, Calendula, Curry leaf, Eucalyptus, Garlic, Ginger, Gooseberry, Harshringar, Kachanar, Loofah, Lotus, Pomegranate, Rose red, Saunf, Sun flower, Willow, White poppy.

Dysmenorrhoea : Him water.

Dyspepsia : Banana, Eucalyptus, Ginger, Kadam, Lemon, Marjoram, Peppermint.

Ear : Aloe vera, Bottle brush, Calendula, California poppy, Champa, Chamomile, Eucalyptus, Fever few, French marigold, Garlic, Holly hock, Loofah, Mogra, Mulberry, Neem, Onion, Oregano, Ox eye daisy, Pansy, Peepal, Pine, Portulaca, Rose red, Snapdragon, Tuberose, Walnut.

Eating disorder : Chamomile, Geranium, Ginger, Morning glory Snapdragon.

Eczema : Aloe vera, Basil, Bottle brush, Calendula, Chamomile, Champa, Gainda, Geranium, Holly hock, Loofah, Mulberry, Oregano, Pansy, Pine, Walnut.

Edema : Ashoka, Ashwagandha, Banana, Chamomile, Drumstick, Gooseberry, Kachanar, Loofah, Peach.

Elbow : Bottle brush.

Enteritis : Calendula, Rose red.

Emergency : Balsam, Pomegranate.

Emetic : Gainda, Loofah, Mustard, Passion flower.

Emotions : Balsam, Eucalyptus, Garlic, Jasmine, Lemon, Lotus, Marjoram, Nasturtium, Onion, Periwinkle.

Energy : Banana, Corn, Mulberry.

Energiser : Lemon, Lotus, Mustard.

Enteritis : Rose red.

Epilepsy : Drumstick, Mulberry, Onion, Passion flower, Peppermint.

Epstein Barr : Bottle brush, Eucalyptus, Ginger, Gooseberry, Hibiscus, Peach.

Erysipelas : Asparagus, Kadam.

Esteem : Bougainvillea, California poppy, Cosmos, Jasmine.

Estrogenic effect : Calendula.

Evil influences : Calendula.

Exhaustion : Aloe vera, Banana, Basil, Bur, Canna, Coriander, Eucalyptus, Ginger, Gooseberry, Hibiscus, Mogra, Nasturtium, Peppermint, Periwinkle, Peach, Pine, Pomegranate, Portulaca, Radish.

Expectorant : Amaltas, Basil, Drumstick, Eucalyptus, Gainda, Garlic, Ginger, Harshringar, Holly hock, Kachanar, Loofah, Onion, Oregano, Pansy, Peppermint, Pine, Poppy red, Sun flower, White poppy.

Excess hunger : Peepal.

Eye problems : Aloe vera, Asparagus, Ashwagandha, Basil, Canna, California poppy, Calendula, Chamomile, Champa, Coriander, Curry leaf, Drumstick, Gainda, Ginger, Gooseberry, Jasmine, Kachnar, Kadam, Lemon, Marjoram, Morning glory, Mogra, Nasturtium, Neem, Onion, Ox eye daisy, Pomegranate, Rose, Salvia, Walnut, White rose, Willow.

Eye strained : Aloe vera, California poppy, Peepal, I Rescue cream.

Glaucoma : Aloe vera, Chamomile, California poppy, Mulberry, Nasturtium, Radish, Salvia, Willow, Yarrow.

Eye eczema : Aloe juice, Calendula, Geranium, Pansy.

Eye sight poor : Garlic, Ginger, Jasmine, Kachnar, Lemon, Morning glory, Ox eye daisy, Peepal, Poppy red, Pomegranate.

Face : Snapdragon, Willow.

Facial tissue muscles : Amaltas, Basil, Snapdragon.

Failure : Ashoka, Jasmine.

Fainting : Ashwagandha, Basil.

Faith : Ashoka, Basil, Morning glory.

Fat metabolism : Aloe vera.

Fatigue : Aloe vera, Basil, Bur, Morning glory, Peppermint, Rose red.

Fatty tissue : Aloe vera, Kachnar, Sunflower.

Fear : Balsam, Basil, Bottle brush, Bougainvillea, Lotus, Mulberry, Ox eye daisy, Peepal.

Feet : Bottle brush, Lemon.

Fertility : Ashoka, Asparagus, Ashwagandha, Calendula, Canna, Jasmine, Kachnar, Pomegranate, Poppy red, Radish, Rose red, Water melon, Yarrow.

Fever : Aloe vera, Ashwagandha, Amaltas, Asparagus, Basil, Bougainvillea, Calendula, Chamomile, Curry leaf, Eucalyptus, Fever few, Garlic, Ginger, Harshringar, Hibiscus, Kadam, Lemon, Lotus, Marjoram, Mustard, Mulberry, Neem, Onion, Oregano, Pansy, Passion flower, Peppermint, Pomegranate, Pine, Rangoon creeper, Rose red, Water melon, Willow, Yarrow, Zinnia.

Fibrosis : Calendula.

Fissures : Aloe vera.

Fistula : Periwinkle, Yarrow.

Flatulence : Celery, Chamomile, Coriander, Curry leaf, Drumstick, Garlic, Ginger, Gooseberry, Kadam, Marjoram, Onion, Peppermint, Pomegranate, Radish.

Fleas : Pine.

Flu : Basil, Bottle brush, Calendula, Coriander, Eucalyptus, Garlic, Ginger, Mustard, Pansy, Peppermint, Pine, Rose red, Sunflower, Willow, Yarrow.

Fluid retention : Celery, Chamomile, Coriander, Garlic, Geranium, Pansy, Pine, Rose red, Willow.

Food poisoning : Ashwagandha, Onion, I Rescue.

Fractures : Jasmine.

Fungus feet : Ashwagandha, Bottle brush, I Rescue.

Fungal infection- Ashoka, Ashwagandha, Banana, Basil, Bur, Calendula, Coriander, Drumstick, Garlic, Grape fruit, Hibiscus, Loofah, Oregano.

Gall bladder : Calendula, California poppy, Chamomile, Champa, Harshringar, Peppermint, Rose red, Mulberry, Nasturtium.

Gallstones : Calendula, California poppy, Celery, Champa, Holly hock, Mulberry, Peepal, Peppermint, Radish, Rose red, Willow.

Gangrene : Garlic.

Gasses : Aloe vera, Ashoka, Ashwagandha, Amaltas, Basil, Balsam, Celery, Coriander, Drumstick, Eucalyptus, Ginger, Grape fruit, Kadam, Lemon, Mustard, Neem, Onion, Oregano, Peach, Peppermint, Pomegranate, Walnut, Willow, Yarrow.

Gastro-enteritis : Ashoka, California poppy, Canna, Chamomile, Champa, Cosmos, Geranium, Ginger, Jasmine, Kachnar, Morning glory, Mulberry, Mustard, Radish, Willow.

Gastro-intestinal disorder : Banana.

Genetic : Banana, Corn, French marigold, Lotus, Sunflower.

Genital disorder : Banana, Bur.

Giddiness : Ashwagandha, Lemon, Lotus, Peppermint.

Glands pituitary : French marigold.

Glands swollen : Banana, Willow.

Glandular : Balsam, Banana, Calendula, Grape fruit, Kachanar, Pansy.

Gloomy look : Jasmine, Mustard.

Goose flushes : Balsam, Peepal.

Goitre : Kachnar.

Gonorrhoea : Hibiscus, Kachanar, Peepal, Sweetpea.

Gout : Aloe vera, Ashwagandha, Basil, Banana, Calendula, California poppy, Chamomile, Champa, Eucalyptus, Garlic, Ginger, Marjoram Mustard, Neem, Ox eye daisy, Pansy, Pine, Willow, Yarrow.

Grazes : Calendula, Geranium.

Gravel : Nasturtium, Onion, Radish.

Grinding teeth : Morning glory, Snapdragon.

Groins : Calendula.

Gums : Aloe vera, Banana, Bur, Calendula, Chamomile, Holly hock, Lemon, Onion, Pomegranate, Walnut, Willow, Yarrow.

Jaws pain : Banana, Basil, Holly hock, Periwinkle, Snapdragon, Tuberose.

Gut lining : Aloe vera.

Haematuria : Kachnar.

Haemoglobin : Eucalyptus.

Haemorrhage : Ashoka, Asparagus, Kadam, Lemon, Loofah, Papaya, Yarrow.

Haemorrhoids : [piles] Aloe vera, Bottlebrush, Calendula, Coriander, Curry leaf, Feverfew, Geranium, Nasturtium, Periwinkle, Yarrow.

Hair problem : Aloe vera, Banana, Corn, Chamomile, Curry leaf, Ginger, Gooseberry, Hibiscus, Lemon, Onion, Peach, Tuberose, Walnut.

Hangover : Ginger.

Harmony : Ashoka, Bur, California poppy, Garlic, Lotus, Mulberry, Nasturtium.

Hay fever : Bougainvillea, Fever few, Garlic, Marjoram, Mustard, Onion, Pine, Rose red, Yarrow.

Head colds : Basil.

Headache : Basil, Bougainvillea, Canna, California poppy, Calendula, Chamomile, Eucalyptus, Fever few, Garlic, Grape fruit, Gooseberry, Jasmine, Lemon, Marjoram, Mustard, Nasturtium, Peepal, Peppermint, Petunia, Pine, Rose red, Sunflower, Tuberose, Yarrow, Zinnia.

Healing : Aloe vera, Garlic, Onion.

Hearing : Bottle brush, California poppy.

Heart : Amaltas, Ashwagandha, Basil, California poppy, Chamomile, Cosmos, Garlic, Hibiscus, Him water, Kadam, Kachnar, Lemon, Lotus, Mustard, Mulberry, Neem, Onion, Ox eye daisy, Pansy, Passion flower, Peach, Pomegranate, Poppy red, Portulaca, Radish, Rose, Walnut.

Heat : Aloe vera, Banana, Bottle brush, Fever few, Hibiscus, Holly hock, Kachnar, Mulberry, Neem, Onion, Ox eye daisy, Peppermint, Rose red, Sunflower, Willow.

Hepatic : Banana.

Hepatitis : Calendula, Pansy.

Herpes : Calendula, Eucalyptus, Pansy, Walnut.

Hiccups : Balsam, Drumstick, Lemon, Mustard, Neem, Onion.

Hormones : Banana, Fever few, Papaya, Sweetpea.

Horse voice : Asparagus, Fever few, Gooseberry, Papaya, Peach, Sweetpea.

Hot : Aloe vera.

Hot flushes : Periwinkle.

Hunch back : Champa.

Hunger pangs : Nasturtium, Periwinkle, Rose red.

Hygienic : Peepal.

Hyper acidity : Asparagus, Calendula, Curry leaf, Gooseberry, Neem, Portulaca, Rose red.

Hyper active : Aloe vera, Canna, Chamomile, Loofah, Nasturtium, Petunia.

Hypertension : Aloe vera, Ashoka, California poppy, Canna, Champa, Cosmos, Drum stick, Fever few, Kachnar, Mulberry, Nasturtium, Onion, Passion flower, Peach, Periwinkle, Petunia, Rose red, Sunflower, Water melon, Willow.

Hysteria : Banana, Basil, Bottle brush, Bougainvillea, California poppy, Celery, Corn, Drumstick, Chamomile, Cosmos, Feverfew, French Marigold, Marjoram, Mulberry, Passion flower, Peppermint, Petunia, Pomegranate, Radish, Rose red, Salvia, Tamarind, Zinnia.

Hysterectomy : Garlic, Ginger, Hibiscus, Pine, Salvia.

Ice cold : Bottle brush.

Immune system : Ashwagandha, Garlic, Ginger, Morning glory, Portulaca, Rose red.

Impetigo : Pansy, Peppermint.

Impotence : Ashwagandha, Banana, Calendula, Ginger, Onion, Peepal, Rose red, Tuberose.

Indigestion : Aloe vera, Amaltas, Ashoka, Ashwagandha, Asparagus, Banana, Basil, Calendula, Chamomile, Coriander, Curry leaf, Eucalyptus, Fever few, Gainda, Garlic, Ginger, Gooseberry, Grape fruit, Hibiscus, Holly hock, Kachnar, Kadam, Lemon, Marjoram, Mustard, Nasturtium, Onion, Oregano, Periwinkle, Papaya, Peepal, Peppermint, Pomegranate, Pine, Radish, Rose red, Walnut, Water melon, White rose, Yarrow.

Infection : Aloe vera, Ashwagandha, Basil, Calendula, Champa, Eucalyptus, Garlic, Geranium, Ginger, Gooseberry, Holly hock, Jasmine, Nasturtium, Peppermint, Pomegranate, Rose red, Salvia, Willow.

Infertility : Asparagus, Marjoram, Pomegranate, Water melon.

Inflammation : Aloe vera, Amaltas, Ashoka, Ashwagandha, Bottle brush, Bur, Calendula, Chamomile, Champa, Corn, Drumstick, Eucalyptus, Fever few, Geranium, Jasmine, Kachanar, Kadam, Hibiscus, Holly hock, Mogra, Morning glory, Neem, Onion, Ox eye daisy, Pansy, Pine, Rose red, Snapdragon, Walnut, Yarrow.

Influenza : Basil, Calendula, Eucalyptus, Jasmine, Lemon, Nasturtium, Pansy, Peppermint, Sun flower.

Injection : lemon **: rub on arm after.**

Injury : Calendula, Grape fruit, Marjoram.

Illness : Basil, Bottle brush, Champa.

Insect bites : Aloe vera, Basil, Calendula, Champa, Chamomile, Curry leaf, Eucalyptus, Fever few, Garlic, Geranium, Holly hock, Jasmine, Neem, Onion, Peepal, Portulaca, Radish, Tamarind.

Insomnia : Aloe vera, Ashwagandha, Balsam, Banana, Basil, California poppy, Canna, Celery, Chamomile, Champa, Fever few, Gainda, Garlic, Geranium, Ginger, Grape fruit, Him water, Lemon, Marjoram, Morning glory, Mustard, Onion, Passion flower, Peepal, Peppermint, Periwinkle, Petunia, Poppy red, Rose red, Sunflower, Yarrow.

Intellect : Nasturtium, Peepal.

Intestines: Aloe vera, Ashwagandha, Banana, Calendula, Champa, Eucalyptus, Garlic, Ginger, Holly hock, Kachnar, Marjoram, Peppermint, Pomegranate, Rose red, Marjoram, Onion, Pomegranate, Yarrow, Basil, Banana, Pomegranate.

Intermittent fever : Drumstick.

Iron : Eucalyptus.

Irritability : Aloe vera, Amaltas, Calendula, Chamomile, Ginger, Holly hock, Marjoram, Morning glory, Mulberry, Passion flower, Snapdragon, Fever few, Gooseberry, Rose red, Mustard.

Irritable bowel syndrome : Aloe vera, Banana, Chamomile, Geranium, Ginger, Kachnar, Marjoram, Passion flower, Peppermint, Radish, Yarrow.

Itchy dry skin and rashes : Aloe vera, Chamomile, Champa, Drum stick, Mulberry, Peepal, Peppermint.

Itching : Amaltas, Champa, Drumstick, Lemon, Mulberry, Oregano, Radish, Ashwagandha, Calendula, Onion, Pansy, Peppermint, Pomegranate.

Ivy : Aloe vera.

Jaundice : Aloe vera, Banana, Calendula, Champa, Eucalyptus, Garlic, Ginger, Lemon, Loofah, Neem, Onion, Oregano, Peach, Periwinkle, Pomegranate, Radish, Rose, Tamarind, Banana, Snapdragon, White rose.

Jet lag : Bottle brush.

Jitters : Morning glory, Onion.

Joint pains : Chamomile, Ginger, Mulberry, Mustard, Pine, Willow, Yarrow, Aloe vera, Asparagus, Eucalyptus, Him Water, Ashwagandha, Banana, Gainda, Holly hock, Lemon, Marjoram, Oregano, Walnut, Garlic, Water melon, Jasmine, Pansy.

Kidney : Drum stick, Ginger, Pansy, Pear, Pomegranate, Aloe vera, Basil, Corn, Aswagandha, Banana, Bottle brush, Ginger, Rose red,

Water melon, Curry leaf, Peach, Celery, Lemon, Nasturtium, Pine, Ox eye daisy.

Kidney and bladder stones : Eucalyptus, Geranium, Ginger, Rose red, Snapdragon, Watermelon.

Kidney tonic : Ashwagandha, Basil, Bottle brush, Garlic, Geranium, Ginger, Nasturtium, Pansy.

Knee : Banana, Jasmine.

Labour pain : Aloe vera, Ashwagandha, Hibiscus, Periwinkle, I Rescue.

Laryngitis : Eucalyptus, Lemon, Mulberry, Snapdragon, Sunflower, Onion.

Larynx : Snapdragon.

Laxative : Asparagus, Banana, Celery, Harshringar, Loofah, Mulberry, Mustard, Aloe vera, Harshringar, Walnut, Water melon, Hibiscus, Kachnar.

Leprosy- Basil, Champa, Coriander, Drumstick, Kachnar, Kadam, Loofah, Neem, Peepal.

Lethargy : Calendula, Ginger, Mustard, Poppy red, Aloe vera, Corn, Peppermint.

Leucoderma : Ashoka, Ashwagandha, Curry leaf, Marjoram, Tamarind.

Leucorrhoea : Ashoka, Ashwagandha, Bur, Calendula, Champa, Hibiscus, Pomegranate, Tamarind, Yarrow, Gooseberry, Jasmine.

Leukaemia : Aloe vera, Corn, Harshringar, Pansy, Papaya, Passion flower, Periwinkle.

Lethargy : Calendula, Mustard, Poppy red.

Libido : Asparagus, Passion flower.

Lice : Lemon, Pine.

Life threatening disease : Peepal.

Lips : Snapdragon.

Lisping : Lemon.

Listening problem : French marigold.

Liver : Basil, Celery, Champa, Holly hock, Lemon, Loofah, Morning glory, Mustard, Peepal, Walnut, Yarrow, Aloe vera, Ashwagandha, Balsam, Chamomile, Geranium, Peppermint, Portulaca, Rose red, Tamarind, Banana, Calendula, Coriander Drumstick Fever few, Eucalyptus, Garlic, Gooseberry, Jasmine, Kachnar, Lotus, Nasturtium, Neem, Onion, Periwinkle, Papaya, Pomegranate.

Longevity : Lotus, Papaya, Peepal.

Loss of Appetite : Champa, Coriander, Gooseberry, Lemon, Pomegranate.

Low body weight and weakness : Ashwagandha.

Loss of libido : Asparagus.

Lumbago : Mustard, Willow.

Low resistance : Amaltas.

Low spirits : Fever few.

Low vitality : Amaltas.

Lumbar pain : Mustard, Pine.

Lumps : Champa, Salvia, Sweetpea.

Lumbago : Mustard, Willow.

Lunacy : see brain.

Lung congestion : Bur, Coriander, Cosmos, Curry leaf, Eucalyptus, Garlic, Ginger, Jasmine, Onion, Pine, Rose red, Watermelon, I Rescue.

Lupus : Peach.

Lymph glands : Calendula, Eucalyptus, Geranium.

Lymphadenitis : Bur.

Lymphoma : see lumps.

Madness : Mulberry, Pomegranate, Rose red, Walnut, Water melon.

Maiming sickness : Pomegranate.

Maintains stamina : Morning glory.

Malaise : Eucalyptus.

Mal absorption : Banana, Basil, Pansy, Rose red, Yarrow, Champa, Coriander, Corn, Fever few, French marigold, Geranium, Hollyhock, Jasmine, Lotus, Peepal, Rangoon creeper.

Malaria : Aloe vera, Basil, Calendula, Champa, Eucalyptus, Fever few, Grape fruit, Ginger, Lemon, Peepal, Sun flower, Willow, Zinnia.

Malnutrition : Rangoon creeper.

Mastitis : Geranium.

Marital problems : Honeysuckle, Jasmine, Papaya, Poppy red. Basil, Zinnia.

Measles : Basil, Champa, Eucalyptus, Fever few, Marjoram, Neem, Rose red, Salvia, Yarrow, I Rescue, Calendula.

Meditation : California poppy, Harshringar, Papaya, Petunia, Lotus, Nasturtium, Neem.

Meningitis : Ashoka, Bottlebrush, Ginger, Mulberry, I Rescue.

Menopause : Ashwagandha, Asparagus, Bottle brush, Calendula, California poppy, Chamomile, Fever few, Ginger, Geranium, Hibiscus, Holly hock, Lotus, Morning glory, Mustard, Nasturtium, Periwinkle, Radish, Tamarind, Yarrow, Ashoka, Walnut.

Menorrhoea : Ashoka, Banana, Bur, Harshringar, Him water, Kachnar.

Mental : Mulberry, Fever few, Jasmine, Kachnar, Snapdragon, Mustard, Nasturtium, Neem, Onion, Ox eye daisy, Peepal, Peppermint, Radish.

Mental lead – to remove from body : Garlic, Onion.

Mentally imbalance : Ashwagandha, Peppermint, Kachnar, Snapdragon, Ox eye daisy, Pear.

Menstrual cramp : [see pms] Ginger, Jasmine, Peppermint, Geranium, Jasmine, Ox eye daisy, Willow, Kachnar, Rose red, Yarrow.

Metabolism : Cosmos, Kachnar, Nasturtium, Peppermint.

Menstruation : Calendula, Jasmine, Ginger, Onion.

Metabolism : Calendula, Cosmos, Kachnar, Nasturtium, Peppermint.

Miasma : California poppy.

Migraine : Basil, Calendula, California poppy, Eucalyptus, Marjoram, Mulberry, Papaya, Peppermint, Portulaca, Radish, Rose red, Sun Flower, Tuberose, Feverfew.

Mind : Peppermint, Radish, Tuberose, White rose, Harshringar.

Miscarriage : Asparagus, Bottle brush, Garlic, Ginger, Holly hock, Jasmine, Pomegranate, Radish, Walnut, Hibiscus.

Moistener : Basil.

Moles : Salvia.

Morning lethargy : Basil, Morning glory.

Morning sickness : Ginger, Lemon, Peppermint, Pomegranate, Curry leaf.

Mood swings : Geranium, Peach.

Mother : Basil, Bottle brush.

Mouth ulcer : Amaltas, Calendula, Canna, Drumstick, Geranium Harshringar, Hibiscus, Jasmine, Mulberry, Neem, Rose red, Water melon, Bottle brush, Holly hock, Lemon, Marjoram, Water melon, Mogra, Willow.

Mouth problems : Amaltas, Saunf.

Mouthwash : Ginger, Jasmine, Aloe vera, Banana, Bottle brush.

Mucus : Ginger, Onion, Pansy, Poppy red, Yarrow, Eucalyptus, Garlic, Jasmine.

Mucus colitis : Poppy red, Rose red.

Multiple Sclerosis : Ashoka, Bottle brush, I Rescue.

Muscles pain : Aloe vera, Bougainvillea, Calendula, Chamomile, Coriander, Eucalyptus, Ginger, Geranium, Him water, Mustard, Pear, Pine, Snapdragon, Sun flower, Walnut, Willow, Yarrow, Basil, Bottle brush, California poppy, French marigold, Oregano, Peppermint.

Muscle cystitis : Bottle brush.

Muscle stiffness : Mustard, Chamomile, Geranium, Lemon, Onion, Marjoram, Petunia.

Muscle pull : Calendula, California poppy. French marigold, Geranium, Mustard, Pine, Basil.

Muscular tissue deterioration : Bottle brush, Garlic, Pine, Aloe vera, Geranium.

Pricking sensations in the muscles followed by painful aching : **Eucalyptus.**

Nyth : Peepal.

Nail : Gooseberry, Radish, Lemon.

Narcotic : Ashwagandha, Lemon, Marjoram.

Nasal congestion : Jasmine, Peepal, Eucalyptus.

Nasal infection : Gooseberry.

Nasal passages : Eucalyptus.

Nausea : Basil, Calendula, Champa, Coriander, Ginger, Gooseberry, Jasmine, Marjoram, Mustard, Peppermint, Pomegranate, Curry leaf, Feverfew, Rose red.

Navel : Lemon **: shifting.**

Neck tension : Nasturtium, Periwinkle.

Nephritis : Banana.

Nervous : Banana, Champa, Coriander, Jasmine, Morning glory, Nasturtium, Onion, Peppermint, Periwinkle, Poppy red, Sunflower, Sweetpea, Celery, Grape fruit, Marjoram, Drumstick, Ox eye daisy.

Passion flower, Rose red, Ginger.

Neuralgia : Ashwagandha, Basil, California poppy, Eucalyptus, Fever few, Mustard, Onion, Passion flower, Tuberose.

Nicotine : Garlic.

Nightmares : Bottle brush, Chamomile, Corn, Fever few, Ox eye daisy, Pansy, Peepal.

Night blindness : Basil, Drumstick, Peepal.

Nodal : Bur.

Nose problem : Drum stick, Jasmine, Morning glory, Mogra, Neem, Peppermint, Rose red.

Nose bleeds : Banana, Calendula, Eucalyptus, Lemon, Nasturtium, Willow, Yarrow.

Nipples sore : Calendula.

Nourishing : Nasturtium.

Nutritious : Mulberry, Nasturtium.

Obesity : Calendula, Curry leaf, Gooseberry, Kachnar, Lemon, Neem, Onion, Peach, Radish, Walnut, Willow, Water melon.

Odour : Lemon, Mustard.

Old Age : Ashoka, Zinnia.

Operative post : Calendula.

Oesophagus : Snapdragon.

Ophthalmic : Banana, Periwinkle, Pomegranate.

Orchitis : see testicles.

Osteoporosis : Banana, Bottle brush, Champa, Garlic, Jasmine, Mustard, Tuberose.

Otorrhoea : Bur.

Ovaries : Aloe vera, Ashoka, Calendula, Sweetpea, Willow.

Oxygen : Ashwagandha, Eucalyptus, Peepal, Radish.

Pain : Ashoka, Amaltas, Balsam, Drumstick, Ginger, Jasmine, Onion, Passion flower, Peppermint, Poppy red, Portulaca, Yarrow, Ashwagandha, Banana, Periwinkle, Basil, Bottle brush, Bougainvillea, Calendula, Eucalyptus, California poppy, Canna, Champa, Curry leaf, Eucalyptus, Fever few, Garlic, Harshringar, Him water, Holly hock, Pine, Mustard, Lemon, Oregano, Petunia.

Palpitation : California poppy, Garlic, Peepal, Pansy, Peppermint, Rose red.

Pancreas : French marigold, Garlic, Nasturtium, Sweetpea, Drumstick.

Panic : Peepal.

Parasite : Garlic, Rangoon creeper.

Paralysis : Bottle brush, Bur, Drumstick, Ginger, Peepal, Poppy red, Amaltas.

Paranoia : [mental state] Bottle brush, Mulberry.

Parental problem : Zinnia.

Parkinson's : Bottlebrush, Basil, Jasmine, Passion flower.

Pelvic : Yarrow.

Pelvic and Bowel infection : Calendula, Yarrow.

Peptic Ulcer [see ulcer also] **:** Aloe vera, Calendula, California poppy, Chamomile, French marigold, Geranium, Marjoram, Mustard, Morning glory.

Peritonitis : Mustard.

Perspiration : Pine, Bougainvillea, Calendula, Fever few, Ginger, Lemon, Onion, Ox eye daisy, Peppermint, Yarrow.

Pharyngitis : Mulberry, Pomegranate.

Phlegm : Fever few, Gooseberry, Marjoram, Nasturtium, Basil, Eucalyptus, Ginger, Pansy, Rose red.

Physical : Mustard.

Physical pain : Balsam.

Physical weakness : Champa, Garlic.

Pigmentation : Aloe vera, Salvia, Radish, Yarrow.

Piles : Ashoka, Asparagus, Banana, Bottle brush, Bur, Canna, Curry leaf, Drumstick, Feverfew, Ginger, Hibiscus, Kachnar, Lemon, Loofah, Neem, Onion, Ox eye daisy, Periwinkle, Radish, Aloe vera, Chamomile, Geranium, Gooseberry, Pomegranate, Tamarind, Yarrow.

Pituitary glands : Aloe vera, California poppy, French marigold, Papaya.

Pimples : Bur, Calendula, Chamomile, Fever few, Lemon, Neem, Pansy, Peepal, Salvia, Ashoka, Radish.

Pineal gland : California poppy, Lotus.

Plague : Calendula, Lemon.

Pleurisy : Celery, Poppy red, White poppy.

Pneumonia : Eucalyptus, Jasmine, Mustard, Pine.

Poisoning : Ashoka, Ashwagandha, Asparagus, Garlic, Aloe vera, Champa, Basil, Kachnar, Walnut.

Polio : Sweetpea.

Pollution : Garlic.

Poly-urea : Bur, Hibiscus, Loofah.

Post operative : Poppy red.

Pregnancy problem : Bottle brush, Jasmine Chamomile, Ginger, Papaya, Watermelon, Yarrow.

Post natal : Jasmine, Rose red– **depression.**

Pre Menstrual Syndromes

Pain : Aloe vera, Ashoka, Banana, Basil, Chamomile, Champa, Geranium, Ginger, Jasmine, Mustard, Onion, Peppermint, Passion flower, Yarrow.

Irregular, excessive : Ashoka, Calendula. Peepal, Rose red, Feverfew, Hibiscus, Peepal Marjoram Periwinkle Pomegranate.

Heavy : Ashwagandha, Jasmine, Kachnar, Ox eye daisy, Willow, Rose red Yarrow.

Pneumonia : Eucalyptus, Mustard, Pine.

Post natal : Jasmine.

Pricking sensation : Eucalyptus.

Procrastination : Nasturtium.

Prostate glands : Jasmine, Peach, Peepal, Bottle brush, Corn, Water melon.

Psoriasis : Aloe vera, Oregano.

Puberty : walnut.

Pulmonary diseases : Sun flower, Water melon.

Punctures : Yarrows.

Purgative- Curry leaf.

Pyorrhoea : Amaltas, Harshringar, Kadam, Lemon, Neem, Periwinkle, Pomegranate, Tamarind.

Rashes : Bur, Calendula, California poppy, Chamomile, Coriander, Fever few, Ginger, Him water, Morning glory, Mulberry, Nasturtium, Peppermint, Petunia, Rose red, Salvia, Yarrow, I Rescue cream to apply : Aloe vera, Geranium, Periwinkle, Yarrow.

Rectum : Banana, Aloe vera, Kachnar.

Regenerates : Lotus.

Rehabilitation : Morning glory.

Rejuvenator : Aloe vera, Asparagus, Calendula, Nasturtium, Peepal.

Respiratory : Ashwagandha, Asparagus, Eucalyptus, Geranium, Holly hock, Oregano, Pansy, Passion flower, Sun flower, Celery, Ginger, Garlic, Jasmine, Mustard, Marjoram, Nasturtium.

Restlessness : Chamomile, Morning glory.

Retarded people : Mulberry.

Revitalization : Pine.

Rejuvenator : Ashwagandha.

Relaxing : Jasmine.

Rheumatism : Amaltas, Ashwagandha, Asparagus, Basil, Bougainvillea, Calendula, Champa, Garlic, Ginger, Harshringar, Loofah, Marjoram, Mustard, Oregano, Pansy, Pine, Sunflower, Walnut , Water melon, Drum stick, Lemon, Willow.

Rheumatoid : Ashwagandha.

Rhinitis : Garlic.

Rickets : Ashwagandha, Rangoon creeper.

Ring worm : Amaltas, Periwinkle, Aloe vera, Lotus.

Running nose : Rose red, Drumstick.

Sad- Geranium, Mustard, Pansy.

Salpingitis : Jasmine.

Scabies : Pansy, Pine.

Scalds and burns : Calendula, Gainda, Holly hock.

Scarbutic : Lemon.

Scarlet fever : Eucalyptus.

Scar tissue : Aloe vera, Lemon, Peepal, Petunia.

Schizophrenia : Corn, Morning glory, Portulaca.

Sciatica : Asparagus, California poppy, Chamomile, Feverfew, Harshringar, Mulberry, Mustard, Nasturtium, Peppermint, Periwinkle, Aloe vera, Ginger.

Sclerosis : Bur, California poppy.

Scorbutic : Lemon.

Scrofulous diseases : Kachnar, Walnut.

Scurvy : Banana, Lemon, Radish.

Sedative : Asparagus, Peach, Rose red, White poppy.

Sensitive : Mustard, Rose red.

Septic : Yarrow.

Sex vitality : Ashwagandha, Banana, Basil, Drumstick, Garlic, Jasmine, Onion, Pansy, Radish, Rose red.

Shaking : Bottle brush.

Shingles : Aloe vera.

Shock : Morning glory, Ox eye daisy, Peppermint.

Sinus : Basil, Bougainvillea, Chamomile, Eucalyptus, Feverfew, Garlic, Jasmine, Lemon, Marjoram, Mustard, Pine, Radish, Yarrow, Loofah, Peppermint, Petunia.

Skin disease : Basil, Coriander, Garlic, Hibiscus, Kachnar, Kadam, Ox eye daisy, Peach, Portulaca, Radish, Rangoon creeper, Salvia, Tuberose, Walnut, Water melon, White rose, Chamomile, Kachanar Jasmine Holly hock Loofah Onion Pansy Willow Bottle brush.

Spots : Geranium, Snapdragon, Willow.

Cream to apply : Aloe vera, Lemon, Lotus, Mustard, Neem, Pine, Rose red, Salvia, Yarrow.

Itching : Amaltas, Banana, Bur, Calendula, Curry leaf, Drumstick, Oregano, Grape fruit, Geranium, Peppermint, Periwinkle, Pomegranate.

Sleepiness : Poppy red, Morning glory, Yarrow.

Slipped disc : Peach.

Sluggish : Peppermint.

Small pox : Yarrow, Lotus.

Smell : Basil, Jasmine, Peepal.

Smoking diseases : Bur, Lemon.

Smoke inhalation : Eucalyptus.

Smoking quitting : Bottlebrush, Morning glory.

Snake bites : Aloe vera, Calendula, Ginger, Kadam, Kachnar, Peepal.

Sore : Pear, Walnut, Bottle brush, Geranium.

Sneezing : Bottle brush, Ginger, Peppermint.

Sour taste : Lemon, Onion.

Spasm : Aloe vera, Asparagus, Celery, Champa, Eucalyptus, Hibiscus, Ginger, Jasmine, Oregano, Ox eye daisy, Marjoram, Passion flower, Peppermint, Pine, Rose red, White poppy, Yarrow, Basil, Bougainvillea, Pear, California poppy, Portulaca.

Speech : Bottle brush, Snapdragon, Asparagus.

Sperm : Ashwagandha, Onion, Radish.

Spine : Banana, Bougainvillea, French marigold, Kadam, Pear, Sunflower.

Spleen : Aloe vera, Drumstick, Lemon, Loofah, Lotus, Onion, Papaya, Pomegranate.

Sprain : Banana, Calendula, Chamomile, Garlic, Holly hock, Marjoram, Onion, Periwinkle, Peach.

Stammering : Calendula, Harshringar, Lemon, Periwinkle, Radish.

Stiffness [see body stiffness] **:** Bougainvillea, Calendula, Harshringar, Periwinkle, Radish, Amaltas, Eucalyptus, Marjoram, Him water.

Stimulant : Harshringar, Ginger, Mustard, Peppermint, Calendula, Garlic, Geranium, Periwinkle.

Sting : Holly hock.

Stomach Pain : Ashwagandha, Basil, California poppy, Coriander, Kachnar, Kadam, Lemon, Loofah, Mulberry, Mustard, Papaya, Pomegranate, Portulaca, Amaltas, Balsam, Gainda, Peppermint, Calendula, Drumstick, Garlic, Ginger, Gooseberry, Rose red.

Stomach upsets : Aloe vera, Lotus, Chamomile, Curry leaf, Ginger.

Stool : Eucalyptus, Onion, Pomegranate.

Stones : Drumstick.

Stones and gravel : Nasturtium.

Strains : Holly hock, Marjoram.

Strangury : Portulaca.

Strength : California poppy, Eucalyptus, Ginger, Marjoram.

Streptococcal infections : Snapdragon.

Stress : Grape fruit, Lemon, Mustard.

Stroke : Garlic, Poppy red.

Stupor : Poppy red.

Stuttering : Balsam, Lemon, Petunia, Snapdragon.

Styptic : Ashoka, Bur.

Suffocation : Bottle brush, Eucalyptus, Peepal.

Sumac : Aloe vera.

Sun problem : Aloe vera, Calendula, Holly hock, Lemon, Lotus, Peach, Sunflower, Yarrow.

Sweating- Eucalyptus, Garlic, Mulberry, Pine, Chamomile, Ox eye daisy, Peepal, Peppermint, Salvia.

Swelling : Ashwagandha, Curry leaf, Chamomile, Drum stick, Peppermint, Pear, Bottlebrush, Calendula, Fever few, Jasmine, Ox eye daisy.

Syncope [faints] : Ashoka, Ashwagandha, Curry leaf, Him water, Pansy, Rose, Sun flower.

Synovitis : Bur.

Tapeworms : Pomegranate.

Tasteless : Peepal, Gooseberry, Peppermint.

Tear shedding : Pansy.

Tension- Garlic, Geranium, Petunia, Pear, Banana, Basil, Chamomile, Cosmos, Curry leaf, Zinnia, Grape fruit, Jasmine, Onion, Papaya, Peach, Water.

Hypertension : Aloe vera, California poppy, Canna, Champa, Cosmos, Fever few, Kachnar, Mulberry, Nasturtium, Onion, Periwinkle, Petunia, Rose red, Sun flower, Willow, Ashoka.

Terminal patients : Amaltas, Ashoka, Garlic, Geranium, Ginger, Hibiscus, Peepal Walnut.

Testicles : Ginger.

Tetanus : Snapdragon.

Thirst : Ashoka, Gooseberry, Lemon, Saunf, Rose red.

Thoracic : Bottle brush.

Throat sore : Bottle brush, Bougainvillea, Calendula, Chamomile, Cosmos, Drumstick, Eucalyptus, Garlic, Geranium, Ginger, Hollyhock, Jasmine, Kachnar, Marjoram, Mulberry, Mustard, Peppermint, Pine, Poppy red, Radish, Rose red, Snapdragon, Willow.

Thrombosis : Yarrow.

Thrush : Calendula, Garlic, Oregano.

Thymus : Eucalyptus.

Thyroid : Aloe vera, Canna, Cosmos.

Thyroid hyper active : Aloe vera, Balsam, Champa, Fever few, Gooseberry, Nasturtium, Periwinkle, Petunia, Sunflower.

Thyroid hypoactive : Ashwagandha, Basil, Jasmine, Poppy red.

Tiredness : Peppermint, Pine.

Tissue regeneration : Banana, Lotus.

TMJ (Temporomandibular joint) disorders : Banana, Snapdragon.

Tonic : Ashwagandha, Celery, Curry leaf, Gainda, Harshringar, Lemon, Mulberry, Mustard, Ox eye daisy, Rose red, Kadam, Oregano, Tuberose, corn Holly hock, Lotus, Nasturtium, Pine, Pomegranate, Basil, Champa, Garlic, Geranium.

Tonsillitis : Aloe vera, Ginger, Jasmine, Mustard, Onion, Poppy red, Sun flower, Calendula, Eucalyptus.

Tooth ache : Asparagus, Banana, Chamomile, Garlic, Marjoram, Oregano, Pine, Peppermint, Snapdragon, Yarrow, I Rescue, Bur Calendula California poppy, Mulberry, Radish, Nasturtium Lemon Mustard Snapdragon Holly hock Ginger.

Tooth enamel : Snapdragon, Lemon.

Toxaemia : Banana, Bottle brush, Garlic, Lotus, Nasturtium, Onion, Pansy Sunflower.

Toxins : Fever few, Garlic, Ginger, Morning glory, Nasturtium, Ox eye daisy, Pansy, Rose red, Calendula, Celery, Jasmine, Marjoram, Willow, Yarrow.

Tranquiliser : Celery.

Trauma : Ashoka, Fever few, Radish, Hibiscus.

Travel sickness : Calendula, Basil, Ginger, Peppermint.

Trembling : Bottle brush, Walnut, California poppy, Marjoram, Peepal.

Tremors : Chamomile.

Triglycerides : Aloe vera, Periwinkle, Nasturtium, Sunflower.

Tuberculosis : Ashwagandha, Amaltas, Celery, Curry leaf, Eucalyptus, Garlic, Ginger, Goose berry, Kachnar, Lemon, Onion, Neem, Peepal, Pine, Poppy red, Banana.

Tetanus : Snapdragon.

Tumour : Aloe vera, Ashoka, Calendula, Chamomile, Corn, Drumstick, Garlic, Loofah, Onion, Sweetpea, Jasmine, Periwinkle, Pomegranate.

Twitching eyelids : Aloe vera, Amaltas, Basil, Chamomile, Periwinkle, Feverfew.

Typhoid : Coriander, Eucalyptus, Garlic, Lemon, Poppy red.

Ulcer : Ashoka, Ashwagandha, Banana, California poppy, Canna, Garlic, Geranium, Harshringar, Kachnar, Mogra, Neem, Ox eye daisy, Radish, Sunflower, Walnut, Yarrow, Asparagus, Drumstick Balsam, Calendula, Chamomile, Curry leaf, Eucalyptus, Holly hock, Lemon, Willow, Loofah, Peppermint.

Urethra inflammation : Corn.

Uric acid : Morning glory, Sunflower.

Urinary problem : Basil, Bur, Calendula, Grape fruit, Oregano, Peepal, Pine, Radish, Tamarind Bottle brush, Saunf Corn and Holly hock, Coriander, Geranium, Nasturtium, Passion flower, Water melon.

Urine Scanty : Ashwagandha, Banana, Champa, Ginger Jasmine Marjoram.

Urine pain : California poppy, Celery, Chamomile, Lotus.

Urethritis : Eucalyptus, Pine.

Urticaria : Canna, Garlic, Periwinkle, Salvia, Tuberose, Yarrow.

Uterine infection : Ashoka, Ashwagandha, Grape fruit, Rose red, Saunf, Jasmine, Rose red, Willow.

Uterus : Aloe vera, Harsingar, Hibiscus, Mogra, Mustard, Rose red, Sweetpea, Ashwagandha, Calendula, Ginger, Gooseberry, Jasmine, Morning glory, Yarrow.

Vaginal infections : Drum stick, Garlic, Nasturtium, Yarrow, Aloe vera, Bur, Calendula, Chamomile, Jasmine, Sweetpea, Passion flower.

Varicose veins : Banana, Bottle brush, Canna, California poppy, Geranium, Ox eye daisy, Periwinkle Eucalyptus, Nasturtium Calendula, Chamomile.

Veins : Curry leaf, Mustard, Rose red, Yarrow.

Venereal diseases : Balsam, Banana, Drumstick.

Vermifuge : Mulberry.

Venomous bites : Peepal.

Vertigo : Ginger.

Vexation : Mulberry.

Viral : Champa, Garlic, Pansy, Zinnia, Oregano, Mustard.

Onion, Calendula, French marigold.

Vocal cord : Snapdragon.

Vomiting : Basil, Coriander, Curry leaf, Fever few, Ginger, Gooseberry, Mulberry, Lemon, Lotus, Oregano, Peppermint, Pomegranate, Willow.

Warts : Coriander, Garlic, Pansy, Peach, Salvia, Yarrow, Gainda.

Water bound diseases : Lemon.

Water retention [oedema] : Aloe vera, Chamomile.

Weakness general : California poppy, Coriander, Garlic, Drumstick, Pine, Pomegranate, White rose, Champa.

Weeping during sleep : Garlic.

Weight problem : Banana, Curry leaf, Neem, Onion, Gooseberry.

Wheezing : Fever few.

White discharge [see leukaemia] **:** Gooseberry.

White Patches : Bottle brush, Corn, Walnut.

Whooping Cough : Basil, Eucalyptus, Garlic, Mulberry, Onion, Ox eye daisy, Passion flower, Peach, Pine, Saunf, Sun flower, Ginger, Hibiscus.

Wind : Basil, Ginger, Marjoram, Peppermint, Chamomile, Coriander, Garlic, Eucalyptus.

Withdrawal : Morning glory.

Womb : Ashoka.

Worms : Banana, Bur, Champa, Curry leaf, Drumstick, Holly hock, Mulberry, Peach, Peepal, Radish, Walnut, Aloe vera, Amaltas, Basil, Papaya, Periwinkle, Pine, Ashoka, Ashwagandha, Garlic, Oregano, Calendula, Kachnar, Lotus, Neem, Onion, Pomegranate.

Wounds : Aloe vera, Ashoka, Banana, Chamomile, Champa, Garlic, Geranium, Kadam, Mogra, Mustard, Ox eye daisy, Peppermint, Rose red, Sunflower, Willow, Yarrow, Bur, Calendula, Harshringar, Hibiscus, Peepal.

Wrinkles : Aloe vera, Jasmine, Periwinkle, Rose red.

EMOTIONAL REPERTORY

How To Use The Repertory

This repertory does not alter the prescribing of any of the 63 remedies as described in 'Flowers That Heal'. It has been drawn up to help in any case of doubt. As an example: should a patient strongly indicate depression, look under the heading 'Depression' in the repertory. Decide whether the depression is due to doubt, or whether it descends on the sufferer like a black cloud, or from an unknown cause. Then read the full description of the remedies Holly hock and Mustard in the book 'Flowers That Heal' and decide which most closely describes the patient.

Only by reading the full description one can decide which remedy is required, then make that remedy. Give 4 drops 4 times a day to get satisfactory results.

EMOTIONAL REPERTORY

Abandonment : Hibiscus, Mulberry, Rose red, Sweetpea, Salvia, Water melon.

Absorption : Aloe vera, Canna, Morning glory, Neem, Poppy red, Salvia, Tamarind.

Abuse : Bougainvillea, Champa, Calendula, Ginger, Hibiscus, Pine, Snapdragon, Sunflower.

Abusive : Bougainvillea, Calendula, Fever few, Mulberry, Petunia, Periwinkle, Sunflower, Snapdragon, Willow.

Action : Aloe vera, Sunflower.

Active : Aloe vera.

Addictions : Basil, Bottle brush, California poppy, Chamomile, French marigold, Ginger, Morning glory, Peepal, Peppermint, Sunflower.

Adolescence : Basil, Bottle brush, California poppy, Chamomile, Corn, Mulberry, Mustard, Salvia, Sunflower, Sweetpea, Tamarind, Tuberose, Walnut, Willow.

Ageing : Aloe vera, Ashwagandha, Ashoka, Canna, Champa, Curry leaf, Harshringar, Hibiscus, Holly hock, Jasmine, Kachnar, Marjoram, Mulberry, Morning glory, Neem, Onion, Peepal, Peppermint, Poppy red, Rose red, Tamarind, Willow.

Aggressiveness : Calendula, Periwinkle, Snapdragon, Sunflower, Rose red.

Agitated : Calendula, Mulberry, Petunia, Zinnia.

Alone : Cosmos, Garlic, Marjoram, Periwinkle Rose red, Tamarind.

Alternating moods : Banana, Chamomile, Peppermint.

Anger : Aloe vera, Calendula, Champa, Chamomile, Cosmos, Fever few, Harshringar, Hibiscus, Him water, Mulberry, Onion, Periwinkle, Peppermint, Petunia, Rose red, Salvia, Sunflower, Tamarind, Willow, Zinnia.

Anticipation : Amaltas, Balsam, Bottle brush, Bougainvillea, Chamomile, Garlic, Geranium, Pine, Tuberose, Yarrow, Zinnia.

Anxiety : Amaltas, Balsam, Bottle brush, California poppy, Chamomile, Garlic, Geranium, Him water, Petunia, Peepal, Radish, Yarrow, Zinnia.

Apathy : Ashoka, Jasmine, Peppermint.

Apprehensive : Amaltas, Balsam, Bottle brush, Garlic, Geranium, Peepal, Rose red.

Argumentative : Aloe vera, Canna, Calendula, Harshringar, Kachnar, Rose red.

Arrogance : Onion, Rose red, Sunflower, Salvia, Tamarind.

Babies and kids : Aloe vera, Amaltas, Ashoka, Banana, Bottle brush, Canna, Calendula, California poppy, Chamomile, Champa, Fever Few, French marigold, Garlic, Ginger, Holly hock, Morning glory, Mulberry, Neem, Onion, Peepal, Periwinkle, Petunia, Poppy red, Rose red, Snapdragon, Sunflower, Tamarind, Walnut, White rose, I Rescue.

Behavioral problems : Aloe vera, Banana, Balsam, Calendula, California poppy, Champa, Chamomile, Eucalyptus, French marigold, Fever few, Garlic, Holly hock, Kachnar, Morning glory, Mulberry, Nasturtium, Onion, Periwinkle, Petunia, Peepal, Poppy red, Rose red, Salvia, Snapdragon, Sweetpea, Tamarind.

Bereavement : Radish, Ginger, Hibiscus.

Biting : Calendula, Mulberry, Petunia.

Bitterness : Amaltas, Bougainvillea, Calendula, Drumstick, Mulberry, Willow.

Blame : Bougainvillea, Calendula, Kachnar, Onion, Pine, Snapdragon, Willow.

Booster : Basil, California poppy, Lotus, Peppermint.

Bossy : Rose red, Sunflower.

Brain storm : Canna, Chamomile, Fever few, Lemon, Mulberry, Petunia, Peepal, Peppermint, Snapdragon.

Broad minded : Nasturtium.

Broken : Ashoka, Chamomile, Curry leaf, Heart, Holly hock, Jasmine Kachnar, Mulberry, Petunia, Hibiscus.

Calm : Balsam, Canna, California poppy, Cosmos, Chamomile, Garlic, Kachnar, Marjoram, Radish, Rose red, Tuberose.

Causes unknown : Amaltas, Jasmine, Mustard, Mulberry, Peepal.

Challenge : Basil, Bottle brush, Hibiscus, Jasmine, Radish, Zinnia.

Changeable : Banana, Peppermint, Yarrow.

Changing moods : Chamomile, Geranium, Peppermint.

Change : Corn, Walnut.

Children : Aloe vera, Ashoka, Ashwagandha, Amaltas, Basil, Bottle brush, Canna, California poppy, Chamomile, Champa, Cosmos, Coriander, Fever few, French marigold, Garlic, Ginger, Him water, Holly hock, Jasmine, Kachnar, Mulberry, Neem, Onion, Peepal, Periwinkle, Peppermint, Petunia, Poppy red, Radish, Rose red, Salvia, Sunflower, Tuberose, Yarrow, White rose.

Clarity : Canna, Geranium, Kachnar, Lemon, Ox eye daisy, Peppermint, Radish, Sweetpea.

Claustrophobia : Eucalyptus.

Coldness : Calendula, Ginger, Nasturtium.

Communication : Canna, Calendula, Cosmos, Hibiscus, Radish, Snapdragon, Tuberose.

Complaint : Calendula, Onion, Willow.

Competitiveness : Ashoka, Nasturtium, Periwinkle.

Concentration : Aloe vera, Basil, Canna, Cosmos, Lotus, Morning glory, Neem, Poppy red, Peppermint, Sweetpea, Yarrow.

Confidence : Aloe vera, Garlic, Gooseberry, Peppermint, Radish, Sunflower, Tuberose, Yarrow.

Conflict : Basil, California poppy, Calendula, Mulberry, Neem, Peppermint, Poppy red, Sunflower, Sweetpea.

Control loss of : Bottle brush, Calendula, Chamomile, Fever few, Mulberry, Petunia.

Convictions : Aloe vera, Banana, Harshringar, Him water, Onion, Peppermint, Radish, Snapdragon, Sunflower, Tuberose, Yarrow.

Coward : Champa.

Creativity : Aloe vera, Snapdragon, Tuberose.

Critical and Intolerant : Bougainvillea, Harshringar, Him water, Onion, Periwinkle, Pine, Sunflower, Willow.

Criticism : Aloe vera, Bougainvillea, Calendula, Drumstick, Him water, Onion, Periwinkle, Pine, Rose red, Snapdragon, Sunflower, Willow, Zinnia.

Cruelty : Calendula, Periwinkle, Rose red.

Darkness : Ashoka, Hibiscus, Mustard.

Day-Dreaming : Kachnar, Morning glory, Neem, Poppy red.

Death : Bottle brush, California poppy, Garlic, Neem, Poppy red.

Debility : Bougainvillea, Geranium, Ginger, Pine.

Decisiveness : Peppermint, Sweetpea, Yarrow.

Delusions : Peepal, Petunia.

Demanding : Rose red.

Depression : Aloe vera, Ashoka, Basil, Bougainvillea, Bottle brush, Canna, California poppy, Curry leaf, Fever few, Geranium, Holly hock, Hibiscus, Jasmine, Kadam, Marjoram, Morning glory, Mustard, Nasturtium, Petunia, Peppermint, Peach, Pine, Portulaca, Radish, Sunflower, Sweetpea, Tuberose, Water melon.

Desire : Basil, California poppy, Champa, Corn, Hibiscus, Him water, Peppermint, Snapdragon, Sweetpea, Walnut.

Despair : Ashoka, Bougainvillea, Ginger, Hibiscus, Mustard, Pine.

Desperation : Petunia.

Despondency : Basil, Bougainvillea, Hibiscus, Him water, Holly hock, Ginger, Jasmine, Nasturtium, Pine, Radish, Rose red, Salvia, Sunflower, Snapdragon, Tuberose, Zinnia.

Despondent : Ashwagandha.

Destructiveness : Calendula, Morning glory, Mulberry, Mustard, Onion, Petunia, Periwinkle, Salvia, Snapdragon.

Diplomatic : Rose red.

Direct others : Aloe vera, Rose red, Sunflower.

Discontent with self : Bougainvillea, Him water, Nasturtium, Pine.

Discontent with others : Calendula, Mulberry, Rose red, Willow.

Discouragement : Ashoka, Curry leaf, Holly hock, Mustard, Radish, Zinnia.

Disheartened : Curry leaf, Holly hock.

Disinterest : Ginger, Jasmine, Morning glory, Poppy red, Radish, Sweetpea, Tuberose, Yarrow, Zinnia.

Dislike : Mulberry, Onion, Salvia, Willow.

Disorganized : Basil, Morning glory.

Disorientation : Corn, Cosmos, Poppy red.

Dissatisfaction : Bougainvillea, Calendula, Corn, Him water, Mulberry, Nasturtium, Pine, Rose red, Walnut, Willow, Yarrow.

Disillusionment : Curry leaf.

Distress : Coriander, Ginger.

Distrust : Yarrow.

Doubt : Ashoka, Rangoon creeper, Tuberose, Yarrow.

Dominate : Rose red, Sunflower, Tamarind.

Dreading : Amaltas.

Dreamer : Basil, Cosmos, Marigold, Neem, Poppy red.

Dreams and Sleep : Basil, Morning glory, Poppy red.

Dry-nature : Aloe vera, Gooseberry, Nasturtium, Radish, Zinnia.

Dullness : Basil, Cosmos, Peppermint, Zinnia.

Dutifulness : Basil, Champa, Corn, Him water, Walnut, Zinnia.

Eater : California poppy, Corn, Fever few, Mulberry, Petunia, Walnut.

Eating Disorders : California poppy, Fever few, Him water, Jasmine, Morning glory, Peppermint, Petunia, Periwinkle, Salvia, Snapdragon, Walnut, Yarrow.

Egotism : Cosmos, Lotus, Mulberry, Nasturtium, Rose red, Sunflower, Tamarind.

Embittered : Calendula, Mulberry, Willow.

Emergency : Bottle brush, Ginger, Salvia, Yarrow.

Emotional : Aloe vera, Basil, Balsam, California poppy, Chamomile, Cosmos, Eucalyptus, Garlic, Ginger, Him water, Jasmine, Lemon, Lotus, Marjoram, Nasturtium, Periwinkle, Water melon, Yarrow.

Energy depleted : Basil, Jasmine, Morning glory, Nasturtium.

Environment : Corn, Onion, Salvia, Sweetpea, Yarrow.

Envy : Mulberry.

Erratic behavior : Morning glory, Peppermint, Periwinkle.

Escapism : Banana, Basil, California poppy, Corn, French marigold, Holly hock, Jasmine, Morning glory, Peppermint, Poppy red, Sweetpea, Walnut.

Exhaustion and Fatigue : Aloe vera, Ashwagandha, Basil, Bougainvillea, Canna, Coriander, Champa, Hibiscus, Jasmine, Morning glory, Nasturtium, Neem, Periwinkle, Peppermint, Pine, Poppy red, Yarrow, Zinnia.

Extrovert : Periwinkle.

Failure : Holly hock, Radish.

False Persona : California poppy, Sunflower.

Fanatic : Aloe vera, Fever few, Harshringar, Him water.

Fanaticism : Aloe vera, California poppy, Harshringar, Sunflower.

Fatigue and Weakness : Aloe vera, Ashwagandha, Basil, California, Champa, Coriander, Jasmine, Onion, Ox eye daisy, Pansy, Periwinkle, Radish, Salvia, Tuberose.

Fault-finding with others : Calendula, Mulberry, Onion, Periwinkle, Rose red, Willow.

Fault-finding with self : Bougainvillea, Him water, Pine, Snapdragon.

Fear : Amaltas, Balsam, Basil, Bougainvillea, Bottle brush, Canna, California poppy, Eucalyptus, Fever few, Garlic, Lemon, Lotus, Mulberry, Neem, Ox eye daisy, Peepal, Peppermint, Petunia, Poppy red, Rangoon creeper, Rose red, Sweetpea, Tamarind, Tuberose, Walnut.

Fidgety : Periwinkle.

Financial difficulties : Curry leaf, Petunia.

Foolish : Yarrow.

Flexibility : Calendula, Him water, Nasturtium, Sunflower, Willow.

Forgetful : French marigold, Loofah.

Fright Extreme : Amaltas, Bottle brush, Garlic.

Frustration : Aloe vera, Ashoka, Holly hock, Mulberry, Periwinkle, Sweetpea.

Fussy : Rose red.

Generosity : Pansy.

Gloom : Ashoka, Mustard.

Gloomy look : Mustard.

Good nature : Champa.

Goose flesh : Amaltas, Peepal.

Grace : Calendula, Lotus, White rose.

Greedy : Aloe vera, Harshringar, Him water, Rose red, Snapdragon, Sunflower, Tamarind, Yarrow.

Grief : Ashoka, Calendula, Eucalyptus, Ginger, Jasmine, Marjoram, Morning glory, Pansy, Rose red.

Grounded : Aloe vera, Jasmine, Hibiscus, Poppy red, Sweetpea, Wild Rose.

Guilt : Pine.

Harmful : Fever few, Mulberry, Petunia, Willow.

Harmony : Ashoka, Bur, California poppy, Chamomile, Garlic, Lotus, Mulberry, Nasturtium.

Harsh : Calendula, Harshringar, Him water, Lemon, Morning glory, Nasturtium, Onion, Pine, Snapdragon.

Hate : Bougainvillea, Calendula, Mulberry, Pine, Salvia, Snapdragon, Willow.

Hesitancy : Cosmos, Garlic, Peppermint, Periwinkle, Radish, Sunflower, Tuberose.

Helplessness : Ashoka, Bottle brush, Hibiscus, Mustard.

Hesitation : Garlic, Peppermint, Tuberose, Yarrow.

Hopelessness : Ashoka, Ginger, Hibiscus, Onion.

House-proud : Rose red, Salvia.

High standards : Him water, Snapdragon.

Humble over : Bougainvillea, Pine.

Humility : Balsam, Peach, Radish.

Humor : Lemon.

Hyper active : Aloe vera, Canna, Chamomile, Nasturtium, Petunia.

Hyper children : Aloe vera, Balsam, Chamomile, Fever few, Petunia.

Hysteria : Bottle brush, Chamomile, Fever few.

Icy Cold : Bottle brush.

Idealistic : Aloe vera, Harshringar, Him water, Nasturtium, Poppy red.

Ideas : Cosmos, Periwinkle.

Ignorance : Holly hock, Yarrow.

Imaginative : Peepal, Poppy red.

Imbalance : Ashwagandha, California poppy, Curry leaf, Fever few, French marigold.

Immobility : Morning glory, Bottle brush, Peppermint.

Impatience : Calendula, Cosmos, Chamomile, French marigold, Garlic, Gooseberry, Periwinkle.

Impulsiveness : Aloe vera, Amaltas, Calendula, Fever few, Periwinkle, Petunia.

Inability to complete : Ashwagandha, Ashoka, Basil, Champa, Garlic, Holly hock, Jasmine, Mustard, Peepal, Tuberose.

Inattentive : French marigold, Neem, Poppy red

Indecisive : Amaltas, Canna, Champa, Peppermint, Sweetpea, Yarrow.

Indifferent : French marigold, Poppy red.

Indiscipline : Morning glory, Onion.

Inferior : Ashoka, Bougainvillea, Drumstick, Kachnar, Pine, Radish, Water melon, White rose.

Inflexible : Harshringar, Him water, Pear, Sunflower, Willow.

Influence : Aloe vera, California poppy, Champa, Corn, Holly hock, Rangoon creeper, Sunflower, Walnut, Yarrow.

Inquisitive : Ashoka, Ashwagandha, Basil, Bottle brush, Coriander, Mustard, Rose red, Salvia, Yarrow.

Insanity : Petunia.

Insecure : Garlic, Peppermint, Salvia, Sweetpea, Yarrow, Zinnia.

Insecurity : Amaltas, Garlic, Gooseberry, Holly hock, Mulberry, Peepal, Pomegranate, Rose red, Sweetpea.

Insincere : Amaltas.

Insomnia : Balsam, Canna, Chamomile, Peepal.

Instability : California poppy, Periwinkle, Peppermint, Poppy red, Yarrow.

Intellectualism : Cosmos, Nasturtium, Zinnia.

Interference : Aloe vera, Canna, Kachnar, Mulberry, Periwinkle, Rose red, Sunflower, Tamarind, Yarrow.

Intolerance : Aloe vera, Balsam, Calendula, Jasmine, Onion, Periwinkle, White rose.

Introvert : Cosmos, Gooseberry, Pine.

Irrational : Gooseberry, Onion, Peepal, Petunia.

Irritability : Calendula, Chamomile, Mulberry, Mustard, Onion, Periwinkle, Rose red, Salvia, Snapdragon, White rose, Willow, Yarrow.

Isolation : Calendula, Cosmos, Ginger, Marjoram, Mustard, Willow.

Jealousy : Mulberry, Snapdragon.

Lack of focus : Neem, Poppy red.

Lack of motivation : Geranium.

Laziness : Basil, Harshringar, Peppermint, Radish.

Leadership : Aloe vera, Nasturtium, Sunflower, Zinnia.

Learning Difficulties : Chamomile, Cosmos, French marigold, Holly hock, Periwinkle.

Lethargy : Jasmine, Marjoram, Mustard, Peppermint, Poppy red, Yarrow.

Live in the past : French marigold, Kachnar, Morning glory.

Loneliness : California poppy, Cosmos, Eucalyptus, Garlic, Hibiscus, Jasmine, Marjoram, Morning glory, Mustard, Periwinkle, Rose red, Sweetpea, Tamarind.

Loss : Ginger, Holly hock, Morning glory, Walnut.

Manipulative : Rose red, Tamarind.

Martyrs : Aloe vera, Calendula, Champa, Him water, Rose red, Tamarind, Willow.

Masculine : Sunflower.

Materialism and money : Aloe vera, California poppy, Salvia, Sunflower, Zinnia.

Meditation : Canna, California poppy, Lotus, Periwinkle.

Melancholy : Ashoka, Holly hock, Mustard, Radish, Tuberose.

Mental clarity : Peppermint.

Mental gangrene : Petunia, Walnut.

Mental imbalance : Ashwagandha, Canna, Calendula, French marigold, Kachnar, Lemon, Mulberry, Mustard, Nasturtium, Onion, Petunia, Peppermint, Willow.

Mental sluggishness : Fever few, Jasmine.

Middle aged and old people

- ❖ Most old people need **: Champa, Marjoram.**
- ❖ Regret that one is getting old **: Marjoram.**
- ❖ On retirement **: Corn, Bottle brush.**
- ❖ On moving to an old people's home **: Corn, Bottle brush.**

❖ Male mid-life crisis : **Sweetpea, Bottle brush.**

❖ Passed mid life, realize that only a few hopes are fulfilled : **Calendula, Willow.**

❖ Soft gums and denture problems : **Snapdragon.**

❖ Infirmity of stomach : **Rose red.**

Mood swings : Peppermint.

Moodiness : Chamomile, Mulberry, Peach.

Narrow thinking : Morning glory.

Negativity : Calendula, Garlic, Holly hock, Morning glory, Mulberry, Onion, Pine, Snapdragon, Yarrow, Willow.

Nervousness : Aloe vera, Basil, Banana, Bottle brush, Bur, California poppy, Celery, Chamomile, Cosmos, Champa, Garlic, Geranium, Ginger, Morning glory, Nasturtium, Peppermint, Peepal, Petunia, Periwinkle, Poppy red, Rose red, Sunflower.

Non-attachment : Bottle brush, Calendula.

Nostalgia : Morning glory.

Observation : Canna, French marigold, Morning glory, Poppy red.

Obsession : Balsam, Canna, Champa, Harshringar, Him water, Kachnar, Lotus, Nasturtium, Petunia, Poppy red, Snapdragon, Salvia, Tamarind.

Obstinate : Aloe vera, Him water, Sunflower, Snapdragon.

Occultism : California poppy, Peepal.

Occupied : Aloe vera.

Old ties : Corn, Walnut.

Over-anxious : Balsam, Champa, Geranium, Him water, Neem, Petunia, Rose red, Salvia, Snapdragon, Tamarind, Yarrow.

Over-independence : Eucalyptus.

Over sensitive : California poppy, Champa, Corn, Feverfew, Garlic, Mulberry, Onion, Rose red, Walnut, Yarrow.

Overwhelm : Basil, Chamomile, Corn, Cosmos, Nasturtium, Petunia, Zinnia.

Panic : Amaltas, Bottle brush, Garlic, Hibiscus, Peepal.

Paranoia : Garlic, Mulberry, Peepal.

Past letting go : Calendula, Morning glory, Willow.

Peace : Bougainvillea, Bottle brush, California poppy, Pine.

People who are easily influenced : Champa, Chamomile, Corn, Holly hock, Morning glory, Peppermint, Rangoon creeper, Sweetpea, Yarrow.

People who need company : Aloe vera, California poppy, Tamarind.

Perfectionist : Aloe vera, Him water, Pine, Snapdragon, Zinnia.

Persistent unwanted thoughts : Canna, Kachnar.

Persuaded by others : Ashoka, California poppy, Champa, Chamomile, French marigold, Morning glory, Mulberry, Yarrow.

Petty angers : Onion.

Poise : Cosmos, White rose.

Possessiveness : Balsam, Rose red, Tamarind.

Poor concentration : Canna, Chamomile, Curry leaf, Kachnar, Neem, Peppermint, Poppy red.

Poor listener : Calendula, Salvia, Tamarind.

Power hunger : Sunflower.

Power less : Holly hock.

Pretender : California poppy.

Pride : Cosmos, Lotus, Sunflower, Tuberose.

Principle : Aloe vera, Him water.

Problems learning from life : French marigold.

Psychic : California poppy, Papaya.

Purification : Salvia.

Quick : Aloe vera, Periwinkle.

Quiet : Canna, Champa, Chamomile, Cosmos, Garlic, Kachnar, Peepal, Peppermint, Poppy red.

Religious : California poppy, Him water, Lotus, Peepal.

Relax : Hibiscus, Him water, Lotus, Peepal, Snapdragon.

Remorse : Ashwagandha, Bougainvillea, Drumstick, Geranium, Hibiscus, Jasmine, Pine.

Resentment : Calendula, Mulberry, Willow.

Reserved : Cosmos, Garlic.

Resigned : Ashoka, Ginger, Jasmine.

Responsibility : Calendula, Champa, Nasturtium, Willow, Zinnia.

Restless : Aloe vera, Balsam, Canna, California poppy, Chamomile, Marjoram, Morning glory, Peppermint, Periwinkle, Periwinkle, Rangoon creeper, Sweetpea.

Retarded : French marigold, Mulberry.

Retirement : Corn, Walnut.

Revenge : Bougainvillea, Calendula, Mulberry, Willow.

Rigidity : Aloe vera, Amaltas, Harshringar, Him water, Onion, Snapdragon, Sunflower.

Rude : Calendula, Chamomile.

Ruthless : Sunflower.

Sadness : Bougainvillea, Ginger, Holly hock, Mustard, Onion, Pine.

Self-abandonment : Bougainvillea, Him water, Pine, Snapdragon.

Self centered : Calendula, Rose red, Tamarind, Willow.

Self-concern : Garlic, Rose red, Tamarind.

Self confidence : Aloe vera, Calendula, Cosmos, Garlic, Gooseberry, Sunflower, Willow.

Self-criticism : Aloe vera, Bougainvillea, Pine, Tuberose.

Self-demand : Nasturtium.

Self-destruction : Calendula, Willow.

Self-disgust : Basil, Jasmine, Rose red.

Self-denial : Champa, Him water, Snapdragon, Sweetpea.

Self dislike : Nasturtium, Salvia.

Self distrust : Yarrow.

Self-esteem : Bougainvillea, Champa, Cosmos, Lotus, Sunflower, Snapdragon, Tamarind, Tuberose, Yarrow.

Selfish : Cosmos, Mulberry, Rose red, Salvia, Tamarind.

Self-isolation : Eucalyptus.

Self martyrdom : Champa, Him water, Rose red, Snapdragon.

Self pity : Calendula, California poppy, Nasturtium, Rose red, Tamarind, Willow.

Self-sacrifice : Champa.

Senses : Aloe vera, Ashoka, Bottle brush, California poppy, Canna, Champa, Nasturtium, Neem, Peepal, Poppy red, Periwinkle, Snapdragon.

Sexuality : Basil, Hibiscus, Salvia, Snapdragon.

Sexual debility : Rose red.

Sexual insecurity : Jasmine, Rose red.

Sexual/spiritual disjunction : Basil.

Shock : Bottle brush, Ginger, Hibiscus, Morning glory, Peepal, Peppermint, I Rescue.

Short sighted : Basil, Onion.

Shyness : Cosmos, Garlic, Radish.

Slow : French marigold, Poppy red, Peppermint.

Sluggishness : Basil, Morning glory, Peppermint.

Smoking : to quit – Bottle brush, California poppy, Drumstick, Eucalyptus, Lemon, Marigold.

Sorrow : Ginger.

Strain : Aloe vera, Basil, Him water, Periwinkle, Snapdragon.

Strength : Champa, Corn, Nasturtium, Snapdragon, Sunflower, Walnut, Yarrow.

Stress : Aloe vera, Ashoka, Basil, Bougainvillea, California poppy, Chamomile, Coriander, Corn, Ginger, Grape fruit, Hibiscus, Holly hock, Jasmine, Lemon, Lotus, Mustard, Morning glory, Petunia, Periwinkle, Pine, Portulaca, Rose red, Water melon, Yarrow, Zinnia.

Strict : Aloe vera, Rose red.

Strugglers : Nasturtium.

Stubborn : Aloe vera, Him water, Petunia.

Surrender : Bottle brush, Champa, Hibiscus, Jasmine, Nasturtium, Peepal.

Suspicion : Mulberry.

Sympathy : Onion, Rose, Sunflower, Tamarind.

Take advice : Yarrow.

Talkative : Aloe vera, Morning glory, Rose red, Tamarind, Yarrow.

Tears : Calendula, Onion.

Telepathy : California poppy, Lotus, Papaya.

Temperament : Aloe vera, Balsam, Petunia, Peppermint, Sunflower.

Tension : Aloe vera, Ashwagandha, Bottle brush, Chamomile, Curry leaf, California poppy, Garlic, Him water, Marjoram, Onion, Peepal, Periwinkle, Snapdragon, Petunia, Cosmos, Zinnia.

Terror : Bottle brush, Peepal.

Thinking : Balsam, Canna, Kachnar, Lemon, Nasturtium, Peppermint, Peepal.

Timid : Champa, Garlic.

Tiredness : Pansy, Pine, Radish.

Tolerance : Aloe vera, Calendula, Him water, Onion, Periwinkle, Sunflower, Willow.

Trauma : Ashoka, Bougainvillea, Ginger, Hibiscus, Onion.

True to Self : California poppy, Champa, Cosmos, Corn, Walnut.

Trust : Basil, Bottle brush, Champa, Geranium, Hibiscus, Jasmine, Petunia, Peepal, Yarrow.

Ugly : Salvia.

Uncertainty : Ashoka, Basil, Holly hock, Nasturtium, Peppermint, Rangoon creeper, Yarrow.

Unhappy : Ashoka, Bougainvillea, Calendula, Eucalyptus, Geranium, Ginger, Jasmine, Morning glory, Mulberry, Mustard, Pine, Willow, Zinnia.

Unknown causes : Mustard, Peepal.

Unreliable : Champa, Peppermint, Yarrow.

Unresolved emotions : California poppy, Corn, Walnut.

Violence : Mulberry, Onion, Petunia.

Vision : California poppy, Neem, Ox eye daisy, Papaya.

Vitality : Aloe vera, Amaltas, Ashwagandha, Champa, Garlic, Hibiscus, Jasmine, Morning glory, Mulberry, Nasturtium, Peppermint, Rose red, Tamarind, Yarrow.

Warmth : Calendula, Hibiscus, Nasturtium.

Weak : Amaltas, Champa, Garlic, Water melon.

Weak willed and tire easily : Basil, Bougainvillea, Champa, Chamomile, Peppermint, Rangoon creeper, Sweetpea, Tuberose, Yarrow, Zinnia.

Weakness : Ashwagandha, California poppy, Champa, Drumstick, Pine, Pomegranate.

Weaning : Balsam, Chamomile.

Will : Aloe vera, Bougainvillea, California poppy, Champa, Corn, Him water, Jasmine, Nasturtium, Onion, Rose red, Snapdragon, Walnut.

Workaholic : Aloe vera, Canna.

Work and exhaustion : Ashoka, Aloe vera, Nasturtium, Yarrow, Zinnia.

Worry : Aloe vera, Balsam, Basil, Canna, California poppy, Geranium, Rose red, Tamarind, Willow.

MEDICAL DICTIONARY

Abscess : A localized collection of pus anywhere in the body, surrounded and walled off by damaged and inflamed tissues.

Acidosis : Acidity.

Acne : A skin disorder, can be infected, cysts and scarring of the skin.

Adenoids : Mass of spongy tissue between back of nose and throat, often hindering inflation of lungs.

Adrenal glands : Two triangular endocrine glands, each of which covers the superior surface of the kidneys.

Adhesions : The force holding together the molecules of unlike substances in surface contact.

Acid : A sour substance.

Aldehyde : Colourless volatile fluid of suffocating smell, obtained by oxidation of alcohol.

Alkali : The name given to a substance that gives a solution in water with the pH of greater then seven. They may also be called a base.

Alkaloid : Probably the most important chemicals found in plants, as they usually have a medical action. They are organic substances, found in association with organic acids inmost plant groups, particularly the flowering plants.

Alterative : Medicine, treatments that alter the process of nutrition.

Amoebae : Microscopic animalcule perpetually changing shape.

Amenorrhoea : An absence of menstruation which is normal before puberty, during pregnancy and while breast-feeding is being carried out and following the menopause.

Anaemia : Excessive tiredness and fatigue, breathlessness on exertion and poor resistance.

Anaesthesia : Loss of feeling or sensation in part or all of the body.

Anodyne : A drug that eases and soothes pain.

Anorexia : Loss of appetite.

Anthelmintic : A substance that causes the death or expulsion of parasitic worms.

Anthraquinones : Glycoside compounds present in some plants and that are used to prepare dyes and purgative drugs.

Antiperiodic : A drug that prevents the return of recurring diseases, e.g. malaria.

Antiscorbutic : A substance that prevents the scurvy and contains necessary vitamins, e.g. vitamin C.

Antiseptic : A substance that prevents the growth of disease-causing micro-organisms, e.g. bacteria, without causing damage to living tissue. It is applied to wounds to cleanse them and prevent infection.

Antispasmodic : A drug that diminishes muscles spasms.

Aperient : A medicine that produces a natural movement of the bowel.

Aphrodisiac : A compound that excites the sexual organs.

Apnea : Temporary cessation of breathing from any cause.

Aromatic : A substance that has an aroma.

Arteriosclerosis : Any of several conditions affecting arteries or arteries ageing process.

Arthritis : Inflammation of the joint or spine, the symptoms of which are pain and swelling, restriction of movement, redness and warmth of the skin.

Asthenia : Loss of strength.

Asthma : A condition characterized by breathing difficulties caused by narrowing of the airways (bronchi) of the lungs.

Astringent : Is used in lotions to bind and protect the skin, and to reduce bleeding from minor abrasions.

Atheroma : A degenerative condition of the arteries.

Atrophy : Wasting of a body part due to lack of use, malnutrition or as result of aging.

Balsamic : A substance that contains resins and benzoic acid and is used to alleviate colds and abrasions.

Bell's Palsy : Paralysis of the facial nerve, causing weakness of the muscles of one side of the face an inability to close the eye.

Bilious : Containing bile.

Bites venomous : Bites of poisonous snakes, scorpions etc.

Bitter : A drug that is bitter-tasting and is used to stimulate the appetite.

Bitters : The name given to herbs that have a bitter taste.

Boil (or furuncle) : A skin infection in a hair follicle or gland that produces inflammation and pus.

Bone marrow : The tissue contained within the internal cavities of the bone.

Bronchitis : Inflammation of the air passage, which is caused by virus.

Bruises : Injuries of, and leakage of blood into, the subcutaneous tissues, but without an open wound.

Bursitis : Inflammation of the 'bursa' resulting from injury, infection or rheumatoid synovitis.

Burns : Burns and scalds show similar symptoms and require similar treatment, the former being caused by dry heat, the latter moist heat.

Calculus : Stones formed within the body, particularly in the urinary tract (gravel) or gall bladder (see gallstones).

Cancer : Malignant tumour.

Candidiasis : Infection with yeast like fungus of the genus 'candida". It occurs in moist arcas of the body : like skin folds, mouth, respiratory tract and vagina.

Carbohydrates : These compounds are formed in plants as a result of photosynthesis. They include sugars, starches and cellulose which all have an important nutritional value.

Carbuncle : A collection of boils with multiple drainage channels.

Carcinogen : Any substance that when exposed to living tissue may cause cancer.

Cardiac : Compounds that have some effect on the heart.

Cardio vascular system : Circulatory system.

Carminative : A preparation to relieve flatulence and any resultant griping.

Catarrh : Excessive secretion of thick phlegm or mucous by the mucus membrane of the nose, sinuses or air passages.

Cathartic : A compound that produces an evacuation of the bowels.

Cellulitis : Inflammation of the connective tissue between adjacent tissues and organs.

Cervical : Relating to the neck.

Chicken pox : A mild highly infectious disease caused by a herpes virus that is transmitted by airborne droplets.

Chilblain : A round, itchy inflammation of the skin that usually occurs on the toes or fingers during cold weather, and is caused by a localized deficiency in the circulation.

Cholagogue : The name given to a substance that produces a flow of bile from the gall bladder.

Cholera : An acute infection of the small intestine, which causes severe vomiting and diarrhea leading to dehydration.

Chorea : A disorder of the nervous system characterized by the involuntary, jerky movements of the muscles mainly of thecae, shoulders and hips.

Cirrhosis : A disease of the liver in which fibrous tissue resembling scar tissue is produced as a result of damage and death to cells.

Cold (common cold) : Widespread and mild infection of the upper respiratory tract caused by a virus.

Colitis : Inflammation of the colon. The usual symptoms are diarrhoea, sometimes with mucous and blood and lower abdominal pain.

Coma : A state of unconsciousness.

Congestion : An accumulation of blood or mucous within an organ.

Conjunctivitis : An inflammation of the conjunctiva in the eye causing redness and swelling.

Constipation : The condition in which the bowels are opened too infrequently and the faeces become dry, hard and difficult and painful to pass.

Convulsions : Also known as fits, these are involuntary, alternate, rapid, muscular contractions and relaxations throwing the body and limbs into contortions.

Cooling : A substance that reduces the temperature and cools the skin.

Coumarins : Glycoside compounds widely distributed in plants. They provide the distinctive smell of many grass species.

Cramp : A prolonged and painful spasmodic muscular contraction that often occurs in the limbs but can affect certain internal organs.

Croup : A group of diseases characterized by a swelling, partial obstruction and inflammation of the entrance to the larynx, occurring in young children.

Cystitis : Inflammation of the urinary bladder often caused by infection.

Degeneration : The deterioration and loss of specialized functions of cells of a tissue or organ.

Delirium tremens : uncontrollably wild excitement resulting chiefly from excessive drinking.

Demulcent : A substance that soothes and protects the alimentary canal.

Deobstruent : A compound that is said to clear obstructions and open the natural passages of the body.

Depression : A mental state of extreme sadness dominated by pessimism and in which normal behavior patterns (sleep, appetite, etc.) are disturbed.

Dermatitis : Inflammation of the skin caused by outside factors.

Detergent : a substance that has a cleansing action, either internally or on the skin.

Diaphoretic : A drug that causes an increase in sweating which stimulates the sweat glands directly.

Diarrhea : Increased frequency and looseness of bowel movement, involving the passage of unusually soft faeces.

Diphtheria : A serious infectious disease generally affecting the throat.

Diuretic : A substance that stimulates the kidneys and increases urine and solute production.

Douche : A forceful jet of water used for cleaning any part of the body, usually the vagina.

Dropsy : Old-fashioned name for oedema.

Dysentery : An infection and ulceration of the lower part of the bowels that causes severe diarrhea with the passage of mucus and blood.

Dyslexia : A learning disability where an individual experiences difficulty with written symbols.

Dysmenorrhoea : painful menstruation. There are two main types, primary and secondary. Primary or spasmodic dysmenorrhoea is extremely common, but is normally mild and short-lived in duration.

Dysentery : An infection of the intestinal tract causing severe diarrhoea with blood and mucous.

Dyspepsia : Indigestion, usually applied to pain or discomfort in the lower chest or upper abdomen after eating and sometimes accompanied by nausea or vomiting.

Eczema : an inflammation of the skin that causes itching, a red rash and often small blisters that weep and become encrusted. This may be followed by the skin thickening and then peeling off in scales.

There are several types of eczema, atopic being one of the most common. (Atopic is the hereditary tendency to form allergic reactions due to an antibody in the skin.) A form of atopic eczema is infantile eczema that starts at three or four months and it is often the case that eczema, hay fever and asthma is found in the family history.

Elimination : The entire process of excretion of metabolic waste products from the body by the kidneys and urinary tract

Emetic : A drug that induces vomiting.

Emmenagogue : A compound that is able to excite the menstrual discharge.

Emollient : A substance that softens or soothes the skin.

Enteritis : Inflammation of the small intestine usually causing diarrhea.

Epstein Barr virus : The virus thought to be the causative agent of "glandular fever"

Epilepsy : Any one of a group of disorders of brain function, characterized by recurrent attacks that have a sudden onset.

Erysipelas : Acute skin infection causing purplish patches.

Esophagus : The gullet – a muscular tube that extends from the pharynx to the stomach.

Ester : Organic compounds produced when an acid and an alcohol react.

Estrogen : Any of several female sex hormones.

Expectorant : A group of drugs that are taken to help in the removal of secretions from the lungs, bronchi and trachea.

Fatty acid : An organic compound made up of a hydrocarbon chain and a terminal carboxyl group (—COOH).

Febrifuge : A substance that reduces fever.

Fever glandular : An infectious disease caused by Epstein Barr Virus that affects the lymph nodes in the neck, armpits and groin.

Flavonoid glycosides : Compound made up of glycoside sugars and a flavones compound.

Fibroids in ovary : A benign tumour of fibrous and muscular tissue.

Fistula : An abnormal opening between two hollow organs or between such an organ or gland and the exterior.

Galactogogue : An agent that stimulates the production of breast milk or increases milk flow.

Gallstones : Stones of varying composition, that form in the gall bladder.

Glands swollen : Swelling of the glands : an organ or a group of cells that are specialized for synthesizing and secreting certain fluids.

Gleet : Discharge due to chronic gonorrhoea.

Glucoside : Molecules made up of two sections, a sugar and another chemical group.

Gonorrhea : A venereal disease caused by bacteria that affects the genital mucous membranes of either sex.

Gooseflesh : The reaction of the skin to cold or fear when the hair 'stands up.'

Gout : A disease in which a defect in uric acid metabolism causes an excess of the acid and its salts to accumulate in the bloodstream and joints.

Gravel : This name refers to small stones formed in the urinary tract.

Gut : The part of the alimentary canal that extends from the stomach to the anus.

Gynaecological problems : Problems relating to women and their reproductive organs.

Haemorrhoids : Enlarged veins in the wall of the anus, usually a consequence of prolonged constipation or diarrhoea; Piles.

Haemostatic : a drug used to control bleeding.

Hepatic : a substance that acts upon the liver.

Hepatitis : Inflammation of the liver due to a virus infection or diseases like amoebic dysentery.

Herpes : Inflammation of the skin caused by viruses and characterized by collections of small blisters.

Hydrocarbons : Compounds made up of carbon and hydrogen alone.

Hydrogogue : A substance that has the property of removing accumulations of water or serum.

Hypnotic : A drug or substance that induces sleep.

Hypoglycaemia : A deficiency of glucose in the blood stream causing weakness : it generally occurs in diabetic patients.

Hysteria : A type of neurosis that is difficult to define and in which a range of symptoms may occur. These include paralysis, seizures and spasms of limbs, swelling of joints, mental disorders and amnesia.

Hysterectomy : The surgical removal of the womb, either through an incision in the abdominal wall or through the vagina.

Incontinence : The inappropriate involuntary passing of urine resulting in wetting.

Influenza : A highly infectious disease caused by a virus that affects the respiratory tract.

Insecticide : A substance that kills insects.

Irritant : A general term encompassing any agent that causes irritation of a tissue.

Isomer : Compounds can have the same chemical composition and molecular weight but differ in their physical structure and hence are termed isomers.

Jaundice : A yellowing of the skin and whites of the eyes indicating excess bilirubin in the blood.

Knee cartilage : A dense connective tissue made up of a matrix produced by cells, which become embedded in the matrix. It is capable of withstanding considerable pressure.

Laceration : A tear in the flesh producing a wound with irregular edges.

Laryngitis : Inflammation of the larynx and vocal chords due to infection by bacteria or virus.

Laxative : A substance that is taken to evacuate the bowel or soften stools.

Leucorrhoea : White or yellow discharge from the vagina.

Leukaemia : Any malignant disease in which the bone marrow and other blood forming organs produce increased numbers of certain types of white blood cells, which suppress the production of normal white cells, red cells and platelets – causing cancer.

Liver : The largest gland of the body. It synthesizes 'bile', carbohydrates, proteins and fat. It regulates the amount of blood sugar, converting excess glucose to glycogen.

Liver cirrhosis : A condition in which the liver responds to injury or death of some of its cells by producing interlacing strands of fibrous tissue between which are nodules of regenerating cells.

Loss of libido: No sex desire left.

Lumbar pain : Pain in the region of the back and side of the body between the lowest rib and pelvis.

Lymphatic congestion : Accumulation of blood or fluid in the network of vessels that convey electrolytes, water, proteins etc. from the tissue fluids to the bloodstream.

Malaria : An infectious disease caused by the presence of minute parasitic organisms of the genus Plasmodium in the blood.

Malaise : General feeling of being unwell.

Measles : Highly infectious virus disease mainly in children.

Meningitis : An inflammation of the connective tissue membranes that line the skull and vertebral canal and enclose the brain due to infection by viruses or bacteria of pneumonia, syphilis or tuberculosis.

Menopause : Irregular intervals of menstruation. Can occur at any age between late thirties and mid-fifties.

Migraine : Recurrent throbbing headaches that usually affect one side of the head.

Mouth ulcer : A break in the skin of the mouth that fails to heal and is often inflamed.

Mucilage : A gum-like substance found in the cell walls or seed coats of plants.

Multiple sclerosis : A chronic disease of the nervous system which affects different parts of the brain and spinal cord.

Mydriatic : A compound that causes dilation of the pupil.

Narcotic : A drug that leads to stupor and complete loss of awareness.

Nervine : A name given to drugs that are used to restore the nerves to their natural state.

Nephritic : A drug that has an action on the kidneys.

Nephritis : Inflammation of the kidney that may be due to one of several causes.

Neuralgia : strictly, pain in some part or the whole of a nerve (with out any physical change in the nerve) but used more widely to encompass pain following the course of a nerve or its branches whatever the cause.

Neurasthenia : A set of psychological and physical symptoms including fatigue, irritability, anxiety and intolerance of noise.

Nutrient : Substance for energy.

Nutritive : A compound that is nourishing to the body.

Oedema : Excessive accumulation of fluid in the body tissues causing swelling.

Ovaries : The main female reproductive organ, which produces ova or egg cells and steroid hormones in a regular menstrual cycle.

Palsy : The term used formerly for paralysis and retained for the names of some conditions.

Pancreas : A compound gland lying behind the stomach, containing enzymes, which aid digestion.

Paranoia : A mental disorder characterized by delusions organized in the system without hallucinations or other symptoms of mental illness.

Parasite : Any living thing that lives in or on another living organism

Parasiticide : A substance that destroys parasites internally and externally.

Parkinson's : A disorder characterized by tremor, rigidity and a poverty of spontaneous movements.

Pectoral : A term applied to drugs that are remedies in treating chest and lung complaints.

Peptic ulcers : A breach in the lining of the digestive tract produced by digestion of the mucous by pepsin and acid.

Phenol : A strong disinfectant.

Piles : see Haemorrhoids

Pineal gland : cone shaped gland of unknown function behind the third ventricle of the brain.

Pituitary gland : The master endocrine gland of pea size situated beneath the hypothalamus at the base of the skull, which secretes thyroid-stimulating hormone.

Pleurisy : Inflammation of the pleura (covering of the lungs) usually due to pneumonia in the underlying lung.

Pneumonia : Inflammation of the lung caused by bacteria in which the air sacs fill up with pus so that air is excluded and the lung becomes solid.

Prolapse : A moving down of an organ or tissue from its normal position due to the supporting tissues weakening.

Prostate : A male accessory sex gland that opens into the urethra just below the bladder.

Psoriasis : A chronic skin disease in which itchy scaly red patches form on the elbows, forearms, knees, legs, scalp and other parts of the body.

Puberty : The time at which the onset of sexual maturity occurs and the reproductive organs become functional.

Purgative : The name given to drugs or other measures that produce evacuation of the bowels. They normally have more severe effect than aperients of laxatives.

Refrigerant : A substance that relieves thirst and produces a feeling of coolness.

Resin : Naturally-produced acidic polymer obtained from trees.

Resolvent : A substance that is applied to swellings to reduce them in size.

Rheumatism : Any disorder in which aches and pains affect muscles.

Rickets : A disease affecting children that involves a deficiency of vitamin D. Vitamin D can be manufactured in the skin in the presence of sunlight but dietary sources are important, especially where sunlight is lacking.

Ringworm : A fungus infection on the surface of the skin, particularly the scalp and feet and occasionally the nails.

Rubefacient : A compound that causes the skin to redden and peel off. It causes blisters and inflammation.

Sacrum : A curved triangular element of the backbone consisting of five fused vertebrae.

Saponins : Glycosides that form lather when shaken with water.

Scalds : To burn with hot liquid.

Sciatica : Pain felt down the back and outer side of the thigh. Leg and foot.

Scorbutic : Affected by scurvy.

Sclerosis : An abnormal hardening of body tissues esp. of the nervous system or the walls of arteries.

Scarlet fever : An infectious disease, mainly of childhood, caused by the bacterium Streptococcus.

Scurvy : A deficiency disease caused by a lack of vitamin C (ascorbic acid) due to a dietary lack of fruit and vegetable.

Sedative : A drug that lessens tension, anxiety and soothes overexcitement of the nervous system.

Sedentary habits: Done sitting down, little exercise.

Shingles : Inflammation of the skin, usually starts with pain along the distribution of a nerve (often in the face, chest or abdomen), followed by the development of vesicles.

Sinews: Tough fibrous tissue joining muscle to bone.

Sinus : An air cavity within the bones of the face or skull.

Sinusitis : Inflammation of one or more of the mucous lined air spaces in the facial bones that communicate with the nose.

Smallpox : A highly infectious viral disease that has nonetheless been eradicated.

Spondylosis : Degeneration of the inter vertebral disks in the cervical, thoracic or lumbar regions of the backbone.

Stimulant : A drug or other agent that increases the activity of an organ or system within the body.

Stone : Another name for calculus.

Strangury : The desire to pass urine, which can only be done in a few drops and with accompanying pain.

Syphilis : An infectious, sexually-transmitted disease, caused by the bacterium Treponema palladium that shows symptoms in three stages.

Styptic : Applications that check bleeding by blood vessel contraction or by causing rapid blood clotting.

Stuttering or stammering : Halting articulation with interruptions to the normal flow of speech and repetition of the initial consonants of words and syllables.

Sudorific : A drug or agent that produces copious perspiration.

Sugars : A group of water-soluble carbohydrates with a sweet taste.

Syncope : Fainting.

Temporomandibular joint : Hinge joint, like knee and elbow.

Tetanus : An acute infectious disease affecting the nervous system caused by bacteria.

Thoracic region : The region of the chest.

Throat cancer : A malignant tumour in the throat area.

Thrombosis : A condition in which the blood changes from a liquid to a solid state and produces blood clots.

Thymus : A bilobed organ in the root of the neck above and in front of the heart.

Thyroid : Endocrine glands situated in the base of the neck. It is concerned with regulation of the metabolic rate by the secretions of thyroid hormone.

Tonic : Substances that are traditionally thought to give strength and vigour to the body and that are said to produce a feeling of well being.

Torpor : A state of physical and mental sluggishness that accompanies various mental disorders, some kinds of poisoning and may be present in elderly people with arterial disease.

Toxaemia : Blood poisoning that is caused by toxins formed by bacteria growing in the local site of infection.

Tuberculosis : A group of infections caused by the bacillus (bacterium) mycobacterium tuberculosis of which pulmonary tuberculosis of the lungs (consumption or phthisis) is the best known form.

Tumours : Any abnormal swelling in or any part of the body, an abnormal growth of tissue, which can be benign or malignant.

Ulcers : A break in the skin or in the mucous membrane lining the alimentary tract that fails to heal and is often accompanied by inflammation.

Urethritis : Inflammation of the urethra.

Uric acid : Nitrogen containing organic acid that is the end product of nucleic acid metabolism and is a component of the urine.

Urticaria (hives, nettle rash) : An acute or chronic allergic reaction in which red round wheals develop on the skin, ranging from small spots to several inches across.

Varicose veins : Veins that are distended, lengthened and tortuous. Cause may be obstruction to blood flow.

Venereal disease : An infectious disease transmitted by sexual intercourse.

Venous haemorrhage : haemorrhage in the veins.

Verruca (wart) : Small benign growth in the skin caused by virus.

Volatile oil : These compounds are formed from alcohol and a hydrocarbon.

Whooping cough (pertussis) : An infectious disease. The mucous membranes lining the air passages are affected and after a one to two week incubation period, fever, catarrh and cough develop.

AT A GLANCE FLOWERS THAT HEAL

1. **Aloe Vera** – Workaholic.
2. **Amaltas** – Dreading of terror and anger.
3. **Ashoka** – Trauma, failure, depression.
4. **Ashwagandha** – Faint feeling.
5. **Balsam** – Deep emotions.
6. **Basil** – Nervous system.
7. **Bottle Brush** – Anxiety.
8. **Bougainvillea** – Inferiority complex.
9. **Calendula** – Harsh words.
10. **California poppy** – All that glitter is gold /Miracles to happen.
11. **Canna** – Over active mind.
12. **Chamomile** – Moody.
13. **Champa** – Subservient.
14. **Corn** – Love with nature.

15. **Cosmos** – Intellectual but introvert.
16. **Curry leaf** – Tension.
17. **Drumstick** – Negative thinking.
18. **Eucalyptus** – Low oxygen level.
19. **Fever few** – Hysteria.
20. **French Marigold** – Slow learner.
21. **Garlic** – Fear.
22. **Geranium** – Unhappy in life.
23. **Ginger** – Shock.
24. **Goose berry** – No confidence.
25. **Harshringar** – Inflexible.
26. **Hibiscus** – Extreme anguish.
27. **Him water** – Too rigid.
28. **Holly Hock** – Lack of trust.
29. **Jasmine** – No complains from life.
30. **Kachnar** – Inflamed thought.
31. **Lemon** – Mental block.
32. **Lotus** – Meditation.
33. **Marjoram** – Feel lonely.
34. **Morning glory** – Addiction.
35. **Mulberry** – Envy.
36. **Mustard** – Unknown sadness.
37. **Nasturtium** – Dry intellect.
38. **Neem** – Difficulty in concentration in exams.
39. **Onion** – Domestic disturbances.
40. **Ox eye daisy** – Vision in life.

41. **Pansy** – Fear of viral.
42. **Peepal** – Anticipatory fear.
43. **Peppermint**– Swing between two things.
44. **Periwinkle** – Impatience.
45. **Petunia** – Mischievous.
46. **Pine** – Guilt feeling.
47. **Pomegranate** – Insecure women.
48. **Poppy Red** – Day dreamer.
49. **Radish** – Unable to cope with circumstances.
50. **Rangoon Creeper** – Loner, wanderer.
51. **Rose Red** – Demands love.
52. **Salvia** – Feels unclean.
53. **Snapdragon** – Misdirected libido energy.
54. **Sunflower** – Egoism.
55. **Sweet pea** – Find difficult to settle down.
56. **Tamarind** – Selfish nature.
57. **Tube Rose** – Tired due to multifarious activities.
58. **Walnut** – Linker breaker.
59. **Water Melon** – women for fertility.
60. **White Rose** – Social illiteracy or socially not refined.
61. **Willow** – Self pity.
62. **Yarrow** – Disturbed by life forces.
63. **Zinnia** – Too serious.

'I Rescue'– Any emergency.

REFERENCES

1. *The Complete Floral Healer.* By Mc Intyre.
2. *The Illustrated Encyclopedia of Healing Remedies.* By C. Norman Shealy (M.D., P.H.D.).
3. *Readers Digest Food those Harm and that Heal.*
4. *The Garden of life.* By Naveen Patniaк.
5. *The Encyclopedia of Flower Remedies.*
6. *Flower Essence Repertory.*
7. *DK Pocket Encyclopedia Herbs.*
8. *The Nature Doctor.* By Dr. H.C.A. Vogel.
9. *Magic and Medicine of Plants Readers Digest.*
10. *Gardening in India.* By late S. Percy Lancaster.
11. *The New Illustrated Gardening Encyclopaedia.* By Richard Sude.l.
12. *Flower Essences and Vibrational Healing.* By Gurudas.

13. *Chamomile and its cultivation in India*. By central institute of Medicinal and Aromatic Plants.

14. *The Nature Doctor*. By Dr H.C.A. Vogel.

15. *Kalyan Arogyaank*. Geeta Press.

16. *Flowers – Their Spiritual Significance*. By The Mother.

17. *Green Remedies*. By Dr. S. Suresh Babu.

18. *Ayurved ka prana*. Van Aushdhi Vigyan.

19. *Ayurvedic Pharmacy and Therapeutic Uses of Medicinal Plants*. By Vaidya V.M. Gogte.

NOTES

NOTES

NOTES